TO CHELSEY, Almost a Year Later

Seduced by our impassioned vision of healing we moved ahead
 of the medicine
Already anticipating celebrations of reawakened immune systems
And parents' tearful joy on hearing: "Mommy, Daddy, I love you"
 for the first time.

In fact, the journey grows longer than expected—and steeper—
 and perplexing
How many times have you, now almost nine, sent us back to our
 lovers' laboratory
Dark with dashed expectations, challenging us to let go and try
 again?

We fear losing ground to your hormonal budding, burgeoning
 strength
And a will that shouts "Wake up! You still haven't seen clearly who
 I am behind the
Veils of seeming indifference, wild destructiveness and insatiable
 orality."

"I take no prisoners; nothing short of complete surrender—
 of who you think you are
What your life is about, and all that you know about healing and
 love—will do.
Nothing less than a heart completely devoted to *seeing* me will
 open mine."

There is no alternative…The past has been shaken up, uprooting
 patterns of a life
Devoted to getting ready to take the leap, always preparing, always
 on the brink
Of learning the secret to turning just one child's life around.

(continued)

"Don't you see? There is no one child to heal, no secret curriculum
    for healing
No great knowledge to acquire, no success or end to the dance
Just show up a little more every day without expectations, and be
    with me."

"Touch me softly, treat me roughly; Gramma, don't hold back the
    grief and frustration
Wooing is too one sided to entice me into a world wild with fear
And whipped into insanity by leaders falsely claiming fearlessness."

"Maybe I will woo you instead, away from the advancing darkness
Mirroring what I see until you all feel the great cry of danger from
    the world's shared
Immunity now rapidly reaching a state of irreversible pollution."

"Listen! It is not too late. Come be with me, Grampa—no drama,
    just day-to-day
Fulfill your assignment, stop stalling with that which you have
    already accomplished
Just look out the windows of your heart and write and swim and
    play with me"

"I assure you every seduction will meet its match as I fulfill my
    mission—
Not exactly chosen—birthed in me by the mystery that you two
    will also encounter
When love finally disappears you and there is no one left
    to write about it."

Jack Zimmerman
January 2003

(Other poems by Jack Zimmerman can be found on pages 214 and 285-286)

CHILDREN *with* STARVING BRAINS

A MEDICAL TREATMENT GUIDE for AUTISM SPECTRUM DISORDER

2nd Edition

JAQUELYN McCANDLESS, MD

With Contributions by
Teresa Binstock and
Jack Zimmerman, PhD

BRAMBLE❖BOOKS
A DIVISION OF THE BRAMBLE COMPANY

For information please contact:
Bramble Books
E-mail address: info@bramblebooks.com

Library of Congress Cataloging-in-Publication Data

McCandless, Jaquelyn.
    Children with starving brains : a medical treatment guide for autism
spectrum disorder / Jaquelyn McCandless ; with contributions by Teresa
Binstock, and Jack Zimmerman.—2nd ed.
    p. ; cm.
Includes bibliographical references and index.
    ISBN 188364710X (alk. paper)
    1. Autism in children. 2. Autistic children—Rehabilitation. 3. Parent and child.
    [DNLM: 1. Autistic Disorder—therapy—Child—Popular Works. 2. Autistic Disorder—
etiology—Child—Popular Works. 3. Complementary Therapies—Child—Popular Works. 4. Diet
Therapy—Child—Popular Works. WM 203.5 M4775c 2003] I. Binstock, Teresa. II. Zimmerman,
Jack, PhD. III. Title.

RJ506.A9M425 2003
618.92'898206—dc21

                          2003000311

Cover art: Ken Bennett

First Printing 2002, First Printing 2nd Edition 2003

3 5 7 9 10 8 6 4
04 06 08 00 09 07 05

Printed in United States of America

The paper used in this publication meets the minimum requirements of
American National Standard for Information Sciences—
Permanence of Paper for Printed Library Materials, ANSI Z39.48-1984

CONTENTS

FIVE
Gastrointestinal Healing 87

SIX
Feeding the Starving Brain 115

PART III

NINE

with Teresa Binstock,
Researcher in Developmental and Behavioral Neuroanatomy

**It is recommended that you check
the Autism-Rx Guide Book Web site
frequently for updates and new developments.**

www.autism-rxguidebook.com

ABOUT THE AUTHOR

 **Jaquelyn McCandless** received her Doctorate in Medicine at the University of Illinois College of Medicine and is certified as a Diplomate of the American Board of Psychiatry and Neurology. Doctor McCandless has been in private practice in Southern California since 1966. Since the early 1990's, her interest in women's issues and sexuality led to an alternative medicine practice with a focus on anti-aging, brain nutrition and natural hormone therapy. In 1996 after her granddaughter was diagnosed with autism, she returned even more to basic medicine and began working with biomedical aspects of developmentally delayed children. She now utilizes the knowledge she gained searching for treatments for her grandchild to help other ASD children.

PREFACE
AND ACKNOWLEDGMENTS

In 1996, my beloved granddaughter Chelsey was diagnosed as having Autism Spectrum Disorder (ASD) at two years, nine months of age. Her diagnosis and unusually compelling nature inspired a reorientation of my professional life from the practice of psychiatry with a focus on alternative and anti-aging medicine to an immersion into the biomedical aspects of autism. Despite decades as a practicing physician, my embarrassing lack of knowledge about autism necessitated my going back into the basics of medicine. The heart of my journey which led to the writing of this book is actually a love story. Coming from a very large and loving family, having five biological children and three step-children plus thirteen grand-children certainly had already created a crucible of great love, wonder, and support for me. Yet something about Chelsey opened a part of my heart unbeknownst to me before. I discovered that all the children with this diagnosis touch that same place in me.

In my passion to understand the causes and therefore possible treatments for Chelsey, my medical brain became activated and information I didn't remember I had ever learned started becoming available to me in a new way I did not understand. The complexity of autism required me to put together a lot of medical information I hadn't connected before and led me into an entirely new approach to the practice of medicine which continues unabated today. For me, this transition has become a continuing and passionate adventure of mind-heart expansion, during which I have had enormous help. The ASD epidemic too well known now to families, teachers, and health care workers throughout this nation is opening up new paradigms in education and medicine, and I am excited to be a part of this movement. As my journey in these new directions continues, I want to recognize—in chronological order—individuals who have been particularly instrumental in helping me better understand and work with these children.

Dr. Bernard Rimland's ARI (Autism Research Institute) website and his studies about the treatment efficacy of vitamin B6 first started me on the path to seeing autism as a biochemical disorder. The B6 effect on Chelsey's hyperactivity was immediately noticeable. When the vitamin was skipped once for a few days, she managed to knock out her front teeth. Needless to say, we have never missed her daily dose since then. I consider Dr. Rimland the "grand god-father" of the movement for understanding biomedical treatment of autism. The organization DAN! (Defeat Autism Now!) that he co-founded is made up of the most generous, helpful, hopeful group of physicians, researchers, and parents as one could ever encounter. Many, including "Bernie" and myself, are parents or grandparents of a child with an autism-spectrum disorder. The DAN! group's willingness to share information about autism's biological nature and ways to help our children affected by autism merits respect and appreciation.

Though I have never had the privilege of personally meeting him, I saw a film portraying Dr. Ivar Lovaas at work with severely autistic children when Chelsey was three. His passionate dedication and effectiveness convinced me that many of these children are teachable, if you can get their attention, and inspired us to get Chelsey started on an intensive ABA program that has helped her immensely.

Karl Reichelt, MD, PhD, is an esteemed and caring researcher who helped me persuade Elizabeth, Chelsey's mother-of-four young children, to add the challenge of attempting a gluten-free, casein-free diet for Chelsey into her already very busy life. Dr. Reichelt patiently and generously e-mailed me from his research laboratory in Norway extensive and convincing information for implementing a dietary regime which in those days sounded like an impossible task. Within a week of starting this diet, Chelsey had her first formed bowel movement, leading not only to improvement in her health but finally to successful toilet training. That in itself was a more than adequate reward for the effort involved in enacting the diet.

Autism internet discussion boards have been and continue to be a resource not only for giving and sharing information but a way of being part of a passionate community of persons focused on autism as I am. Anytime of the day or night one can ask for and get help and encouragement from other parents and professionals all over the world. From the moment I ventured an e-post in 1998 to what was then the Secretin list (now called abmd) my professional life began changing course. The e-list groups have contributed greatly to my information base and strong desire to share what I've learned with as many parents and professionals as possible.

My friend and colleague Teresa Binstock told me she was formally diagnosed with Asperger's Syndrome in graduate school in 1997; she calls herself "aspergerian." Teresa's research and writings—both published and informal—first introduced me to the importance of investigating immune dysregulations, chronic viral infections, and other pathogenic aspects of subgroups within autism. She has assisted me in some of my most troubling cases and has "proof-read" and advised me on scientific aspects of this book, all of which has helped me immeasurably. She has tirelessly procured references and research papers for me to read during this writing project, especially for Chapter Eight on Immunity and Viruses. She envisions future directions of diagnostics and treatments in Appendix C, and generally is a fierce champion of the need for a change in the medical paradigm for autism. One of Teresa's manuscripts in preparation— Autism Spectrum Malnutrition—helped finally clarify for me that the end-point for most autism-spectrum children is a malnourished brain that can result from a variety of etiologies. This concept— along with DAN! publications and conferences, published studies, internet explorations and discussions, and especially my own clinical experience—has led to my operational dictum, "Heal the gut, feed the starving brain, treat for pathogens, remove the toxins, and help the immune system in every way possible," of course, all at the same time!! As a clinician, effective treatment is always my bottom line, and I and others (both parents and doctors) count on Teresa to lead us to the latest research, clarification of diagnosis, and optimal directions for healing.

I have Amy Holmes, MD to thank for inspiring me to work twice as hard as I ever have while making half the income. Prompted by Edelson et al, Bernard et al, and by the disciplined clinical protocols of Stephanie Cave, MD, Doctor Holmes became the beloved and respected "god-mother" of heavy-metal chelation for children with autism. She fully deserves the gratitude and love of the many hundreds of families she has helped. As an inspired mother of an ASD child herself, she insisted that I should not even consider retiring now. She believed that doctors with children or grandchildren on the spectrum can be on the forefront of critically important changes in the prevailing medical model for diagnostic evaluation and treatment of these children. Needless to say, biomedical approaches to autism are not easy, and Amy and I can both testify that the field is primarily for doctors who thrive on a sustained devotion to constant learning and lots of hard work.

I want to give a special acknowledgement to the person who helped me start writing this book. Just when I despaired of ever finding time to write because my autism patient waiting list was getting longer and longer, Dr. Maury Breecher contacted me and asked, "Do you want help in writing your book?" Maury is a medical writer and author with academic degrees in Mass Communications and Public Health. He told me that my passion for helping autistic kids attracted him to me. He shared my urgency about the importance of getting this material out to parents as quickly as possible. Maury helped me get started by a very productive series of interviews that got me in touch with how much I still needed to learn about autism. Those comprehensive, in-depth interviews and his early editorial guidance helped me get started on the task of organizing complex material into a comprehensible format that I hope will be helpful to the parents and their doctors who have been entrusted with the care of these special children.

Ironically, I must also credit the pediatricians and other doctors who dismiss autism spectrum children as having psychological problems, being products of bad parenting, or as hopeless genetic cases

—and who make these judgments without biomedical testing while refusing to think "out of the box." My frustration with such physicians and their obsolete models has helped create a strong desire in me to provide information to parents so they can understand what their doctors may not yet realize: that *whatever else it is, I believe most if not all children with autism have a complex medical illness and merit biomedical diagnostics and medical treatment.* Although the current epidemic of autism-spectrum disorders is forcing more doctors to contemplate this model, the field is so complex that evaluation and treatment must be specific to each individual child. Practitioners need to consider immune impairments, chronic infections, low-level accumulations of heavy-metals, special diets, and child-specific nutrient supplementation. Much of this new biochemistry of autism was not learned in their medical training.

It surely goes without saying that none of the experiences and explorations leading to this book would have happened for me if it had not been for Chelsey and all the other children with autism whose parents have entrusted me to help them in their efforts to heal their children. I especially want to thank my daughter Elizabeth for doing all the 24/7 hard work of all the biomedical treatments I've come up with in the seven years Chelsey has been teaching us about autism. Liz has become a magnificent, wise, incredibly loving and understanding mother in this process, as is true for so many of the mothers (and fathers!). These special children are calling all of us to wake up; they are the messengers for what is happening in our toxic world and of what needs to happen in our institutions of medicine, education, and family life.

Last, first, and always: my husband of 28 years, Dr. Jack Zimmerman has helped me expand the love of our eight children and thirteen grandchildren to encompass all children. A PhD mathematician turned visionary educator, author, and director of the Center for Council Training (an extension of the Ojai Foundation in Ojai CA), he has helped to develop a network of council facilitators that brings this process of authentic communication to tens of thousands of children in schools not only in Southern California but all over the country, with recently launched programs in Europe, Israel, and Hawaii. He is currently exploring with other concerned educators ways to introduce council to groups of special needs children in both private and public schools. His unstinting love and support in our healing work with Chelsey and his constant encouragement have helped me see the larger message that these hundreds of thousands of autism-spectrum children are bringing to the world. His role as editor has helped offset some of my limitations as a writer; our collaboration has deepened our love even more. His writing in Chapter Ten will give you the opportunity to experience his visionary mind and wonderful heart. Jack is a blessing and ever deepening source of strength and inspiration to me and to everyone who knows him.

Jaquelyn McCandless, MD

PREFACE TO THE 2ND EDITION, 2003, AND UPDATE, MARCH 2004

When I started writing the first edition of this book in January of 2002, my intention was to simply describe how I had come to my current views about autism and detail the sequence of treatments I advise and use in my practice. With the help of my support team, notably Teresa Binstock and Jack Zimmerman, I ended up saying much more, and the book has received a very positive response.

The second edition is actually an "improved" reprinting of the first, with minor changes and corrections being made throughout the book as well as the addition of an index. I took the opportunity to create an additional appendix on some important treatments that were added to my protocol since the publication of the first edition, and have added more to this appendix for the 2004 update. This Appendix D contains information on the use of transdermal TTFD (allithiamine) as a welcome addition to our armamentarium for heavy metals detoxification. I also discuss our increasing awareness of the importance of Vitamin B12 in the form of methylcobalamin, and describe a child/parent-friendly way to administer it most effectively. A third new treatment I describe is the use of Intravenous Immunoglobulin (IVIG) in an oral formulation, representing another attempt to address the gut/autoimmune issues besetting our children.

Various other treatments have been updated throughout this 2004 printing, especially more information added to Appendix D. This includes new material on our increasing interest in methylation, with new scientific evidence now becoming available on the methylation disorders we find to be an important part of ASD. New treatments are suggested by the science, as well as an understanding of why some older treatments have been benefiting our children.

On the frontice page of the 2nd Edition, Dr. Jack Zimmerman (Grampa) has given us his poetic version of our continuing journey with our beloved Chelsey, and in this 2004 update his latest poem appears on p 284-285.

INTRODUCTION

CHILDREN WITH REAL MEDICAL ILLNESSES

A Message of Hope

*C*hildren with Starving Brains is a message of hope to parents of children diagnosed with autism or any of the disorders associated with autistic spectrum disorder (ASD). This message is especially important if your child has recently been diagnosed and you are just embarking on the complicated journey of trying to find proper medical care. The book is also intended for parents who believe something is wrong with their child but do not know how to find qualified and knowledgeable medical help for diagnosis and treatment. If you do not already know, you will learn in Chapter One that we are in the midst of an epidemic of ASD. Many cases are as yet undiagnosed. Traditional treatment modalities encompass sensory integration, visual and auditory training, and behavioral modification; these are all important and are already well described in the current literature about autism. This book rather focuses on recently developed bio-medical treatments that are showing great promise in improving the health and neurologic function of many children on the autism spectrum.

Autism is a condition often characterized by a failure to bond, lack of social interaction, avoidance of eye-to-eye contact, difficulties in language development, and repetitive behaviors known as "stimming" (self-stimulation). There are associated milder forms

1

of this condition such as Asperger's Syndrome, PDD (Pervasive Developmental Disorders) and ADD/ADHD, or Attention Deficit/ Hyperactivity Disorder. These are all known collectively as Autism Spectrum Disorder(s), or ASDs.

My main thesis in this book is that ASD is a complex syndrome based on physiological and bio-chemical disorders that have as a common end-point the cognitive and emotional impairment we associate with autism. In other words, these are medically ill children who can be greatly helped medically, behaviorally, and cognitively by proper diagnosis and treatment of their underlying medical conditions. This is a vital breakthrough in understanding and one that many old-line practitioners have had a hard time grasping. In the past, autism and other conditions in the autism spectrum were considered "psychiatric" or behavioral disorders, with only psychiatric or behavioral approaches considered as appropriate treatments. As we grow in our understanding that these are medical rather than mental disorders, we are exploring and learning new ways to use medical treatments tailored to meet each child's individual needs.

As a physician who is the grandparent of a child diagnosed with autism in 1996, I have come to realize that the traditional means of diagnosis and treatments for ASD leave much to be desired. By and large, the prevailing or mainstream treatment protocols are driven by the old-fashioned belief that ASDs are simply behavioral conditions caused by incurable genetic defects. For many years, the genetic-model represented progress, for at least it replaced the long-held psychoanalytic belief that autism was caused by "refrigerator mothers" who were unable to bond with and love their children properly. However, the current belief that autism is primarily or only genetic means that until very recently prevailing treatment protocols rarely advise anything other than behavior modification or educational therapy sometimes aided by mood-controlling drugs such as SSRI's (Prozac, Zoloft etc), stimulants (Ritalin, amphetamines etc), or behavior-controlling drugs such as Risperidone (Risperdal).

Since many mainstream physicians have been trained to accept that the basis for ASD is genetic, they routinely screen for genetic disorders such as Down syndrome or Fragile X and do not order appropriate laboratory tests for the gastrointestinal, immunological, and infection-related issues that beset ASD children. Often, parents are told there are no known treatments other than what behavior modification offers; some parents have even been informed emphatically that there is no evidence that vitamins or dietary changes would be of any benefit to their children. I intensely disagree with these judgments based on solid clinical experience. Increasingly, the old diagnostic and treatment models for ASD are being augmented by the biomedical approach. This significant paradigm shift is in part the result of the current epidemic of ASD, since now there are many health professionals who have a child, grandchild, nephew, niece, or someone close to them recently diagnosed with autism. Many of these physicians with "autism in the family" are contributing to the realization that the syndrome is actually a biomedical illness needing and responding to biomedical treatments.

After a long career in general psychiatry, my own practice has shifted primarily to specializing in the treatment of developmentally delayed children, most of them on the ASD spectrum. Since I consider attention deficit disorder (ADD) and attention deficit hyperactivity disorder (ADHD) to be milder versions of the same problem, I also evaluate children with these disorders whose parents prefer to explore improvement through dietary, nutrient, and sometimes detoxification protocols before turning to stimulants or other prescription drugs. In trying to learn everything possible to help my granddaughter and the other children that have come into my practice, I have scoured the medical literature, attended medical conferences, participated in research-oriented internet groups, and surveyed alternative treatments being pioneered by an increasing number of physicians.

Defeat Autism Now! (DAN!)

It was a relief to learn that I was not alone in my search. I have been influenced by pioneering researchers including Bernard Rimland, PhD, William Shaw, PhD, and Karl Reichelt, MD, PhD, as well as such pioneering physicians as Sidney Baker, Michael Goldberg, Woody McGinnis, Amy Holmes, Stephanie Cave, and Jeff Bradstreet. Significant contributions to my clinical practice have come from independent researchers Teresa Binstock and Susan Owens, as well as parent-researchers such as Victoria Beck, Sallie Bernard, Allison Plant, and Jim Adams among many others.

These individuals and countless others I have met along my learning path have helped me realize that, when considered as a group, children on the autism spectrum have a multi-faceted disorder that may affect any and sometimes all of the major systems of the body. Inter-individual variation is the most consistent characteristic. In other words, each child is unique. The notion "one treatment size fits all" does not pertain to these children. Some of the factors that need to be considered in evaluating ASD children include:

- Were they autistic "from birth" or had they "regressed" after a period of normalcy?

- Are they low, medium, or high-functioning behaviorally and cognitively, including level of receptive and expressive speech and ability to learn?

- How are their biochemical profiles revealed by lab-tests correlated with symptoms?

- What is the familial history of autoimmune disorders, allergies, etc.?

- What is the child's personal developmental and medical history?

These categories help target diagnostic and treatment protocols. Most of the researchers and physicians just named, among many others, have joined together in a movement called Defeat Autism Now! (DAN!) that was started by Bernard Rimland, PhD, director of the Autism Research Institute in San Diego. I am proud to be associated with this movement. Members of DAN! are bonded by their belief that autism and associated ASD's are primarily medical disorders with behavioral and cognitive impairments that are by-products of the physical illnesses these children suffer. In other words, aside from rare genetic cases such as an autism derived from fragile X syndrome, these are physically ill children with real medical disorders. Since they are physically ill, they need bio-medical intervention to maximize their healing potential.

My clinical experience, when combined with the recent research and experience of dozens of DAN! practitioners, has led me to develop biomedical protocols for diagnostic evaluations and subsequent treatments. I think of this as a broad-spectrum approach. My patients and their parents have been my greatest teachers; some treatments that have become a mainstay of my practice were brought to me originally by parents seeking a doctor with an open mind to new tests and treatments they had heard about before I did. Nearly every child I have worked with has had immune irregularities, nutritional deficiencies, and gastrointestinal problems. Nevertheless, I have found each child to be remarkably different from each of his or her ASD "peers," not only in regard to biomedical profiles (as indicated by laboratory results) but also in response to various treatments. In an era when autism's primary model is changing, it is not surprising that parents also vary in their openness to a new medical model, in their willingness to do the indicated testing (assuming the financial means), and in their ability to follow through on the recommended treatments. The bottom line is that the protocol must be individualized for each child in the context of the family and circumstances in which he or she lives.

What Can a Parent Expect From Bio-Medical Interventions?

From my experience and that of many DAN! physicians and caregivers, the behavioral and cognitive symptoms of many ASD children can be noticeably improved with proper bio-medical treatments. Sometimes the improvement is dramatic enough for a child to lose his or her ASD diagnosis. That is a startling statement, so let me be clear so as not to raise false hopes. I am not promising that every child will get complete recovery. Nor am I promising that every child will show major improvement. My message of hope is that, if you try the treatments described in this book, your child is very likely to get better at least to some degree and, for some ASD children, perhaps even improve remarkably.

More specifically:

- A parent won't know how much his or her child will improve unless the various diagnostic methods and treatment protocols are tried.

- Not every child will enjoy profound improvements. Some, however, will. Most parents will see some improvement. Some parents may see no improvement or such improvements as occur will take much longer.

- Occasionally a child may get worse before he/she gets better. Lately, we're finding that many if not most of the regressions we see during treatment are being caused by gastrointestinal pathologies that we are learning more about as new research comes in. As these pathologies are identified and treated, improvement often resumes.

- Neutraceutical companies are working to find new immune enhancers, better enzymes, and better forms and mixtures of other vital nutrients to help in the various treatments.

- The earlier the evaluation is made and treatment started, the likelier it is that the child will improve.

Unfortunately, many pediatricians and other physicians are not experienced in diagnosing autism or any of the related ASD's. Some physicians may fear making the diagnosis because they were trained to believe that the autistic form of ASD is incurable. Also, although many of these children are actually quite ill, I sometimes hear a parent tell me, "But my child with autism never gets sick like my other kids do!" I have noticed that, although many children I see have a history of recurrent ear infections in their first year of life, this early pattern may be followed by a period of seemingly strong immunity. This may be because of a hyper-immune status in response to low-grade chronic infection. It also has been amazing to see an apparently healthy ASD child who has, nevertheless, had chronic diarrhea for years and has self-selected a daily diet limited to a few usually non-nutritious foods such as French fries, apple juice or Pepsi Cola, and corn chips. Consequently, busy doctors after a quick physical may say the child looks fine, and parents may be told that their child's continuous loose stools are just "toddler diarrhea, a condition that will eventually be outgrown." In a neurotypical child, such pronouncements sometimes may be true. However, for an ASD child, intestinal treatment or change of diet may not only be warranted but essential for them to improve. Similarly, a pediatrician may counsel that a child who does not talk by 1-1/2 or 2 years of age is just a "late talker." In some instances this may also be true, but my advice is that any child who is not trying to talk by age 1-1/2 or at least by 2 ought to be evaluated for ASD, particularly if there are any other behavioral, gastrointestinal, or cognitive symptoms, however subtle they may seem.

This level of diagnostic sensitivity is important because effective treatment has a golden window of opportunity that unfortunately diminishes as the child gets older. This is true for both educational and bio-medical interventions. If your child has chronic diarrhea, frequently wakes up at night, self-selects a very restricted diet, has suffered repeated ear or other infections in the first year or at the cessation of breast feeding, isn't trying to say words by around 18 months, has a history of bad reactions to vaccinations, doesn't seem interested in other kids, and doesn't show the kind of curiosity and relatedness that most other kids do, find a physician to screen for ASD as soon as possible.

My personal experience and that of other DAN! physicians leads to an important principle: Don't accept your doctor's advice if he or she counsels a "wait-and-see" attitude or promises that your child will "catch up." Especially hurry to seek help if your child had a period of normal development and then regressed. If your child has exhibited any of the traits described or has already been diagnosed with autism or ASD, this book will give you some guidelines for seeking interventions that may be of considerable help. Some of these interventions can be instituted by parents. However, diagnostics and treatments that include laboratory testing or prescription medications must, of course, be done with the cooperation of a health care professional.

My Personal and Professional Involvement in the Bio-Medicine of Autism

My granddaughter Chelsey was diagnosed with autism in 1996 at 33 months of age. I had been working for many years in private practice in California as a physician certified by the American Board of Psychiatry and Neurology. I made it a point to keep abreast of all the new studies and medications pertaining to biological psychiatry as well as the psychotherapeutic approaches to emotional/mental illnesses. In the early nineties, I had begun an exploration of alternative medicine to learn how to use natural hormones, vitamins and other nutrients to help aging brains and bodies stay youthful and healthy. This research has helped me personally and in my current work with ASD children.

However, at the time Chelsey received her diagnosis, I knew almost nothing about autism. In 30 years of clinical practice I had seen but a few people with this diagnosis and had mainly been consulted for drug-based behavior control for these mysteriously impaired people. In retrospect, I realize I was woefully ignorant about autism. In my initial search to find help for Chelsey in 1996, I discovered to my dismay that my medical colleagues who practiced pediatric medicine knew little more than I. The prognosis they offered Chelsey was grim. As I regretfully look back on Chelsey's parents' as well as my own denial of the diagnosis and at the apparent scarcity of bio-medical information available about autism, I now realize that we wasted precious time getting effective treatments started.

In fact, the importance of time is a prime reason for this book. It is designed to help parents get their children started on effective treatments faster. If you are a parent, this book will help you understand the rationale for the new treatments that are available now. If you are a physician, the book may help guide you through the process of deciding which testing and treatments to start first and in what order to initiate the others. This book should also provide information on where to go for additional knowledge about complicated, ASD-related conditions that are beyond the scope of the present discussion.

Another prime reason for documenting my broad-spectrum approach is that I and every autism specialist I know has a waiting list of anxious families who have heard about the new treatments and are having a hard time finding out how to get help for their children. I am hoping that this book will empower parents to put pressure on their doctors and their insurance companies to investigate the information becoming available that offers new hope for ASD children.

At the time we received Chelsey's diagnosis, it was thought—and unfortunately, in some quarters it is still believed—that autism is incurable and that it was caused by cold mothers who lacked nurturing and other parental skills.

I have never accepted that my granddaughter and other ASD children are incurable. I also know without doubt that Chelsey's mother wasn't a *refrigerator mother.* Elizabeth has three other happy, thriving, normal children and is a dedicated loving parent to all of her children. Over the past few years I have met hundreds of parents of ASD children and have been impressed by how the challenges of raising such a child often brings out the best in them. Their willingness and persistence to do everything possible to help their offspring proves that the parents of these developmentally challenged kids are among the most loving and capable of all caregivers.

Over the years we have tried many different forms of therapy for Chelsey, some which seemed to help and many which did not. My beloved grandchild, the inspiration for this book, remains my first and most challenging case. At the time of her diagnosis, we only knew about various types of behavioral therapy, which we immediately instituted and continued full time for several years. Though early educational intervention and applied behavioral analysis did help her to focus and learn verbal skills, she remained quite impaired relationally, and suffered from chronic diarrhea and a severely restricted diet. I know now that chronic diarrhea is very common in these children and a sure tip-off that their biochemistry is abnormal. When she was almost five years old, we finally instituted a diet that removed certain common foods that we now know were toxic to her, even though the usual allergy testing did not reveal this. The results were dramatic; for the first time she started having normal bowel function. This lesson taught me the importance of food hypersensitivity awareness and testing for food allergies early in treatment.

Because many of the biomedical aspects of my current treatment protocol weren't developed until Chelsey was over five years of age, she didn't benefit from the *early* bio-medical and detoxification therapies that are responsible for improvements, some quite dramatic, in my current crop of young patients. Unfortunately, biomedical improvement seems to take longer and may not be as complete with older children since biochemical abnormalities and toxic conditions have already become a part of their cellular functioning and are therefore harder to change. Though her recovery progresses at a slower pace than some of my younger patients, I will continue to remain open to new discoveries sure to come in this rapidly evolving field, while loving her with all my heart however she grows.

The "golden window" of opportunity I mentioned earlier is usually between 18 months to 5 years of age. Remember, however, that although that age range is an optimum period to begin treatment, it does not mean older children cannot improve. Older children and even adults can be helped, some remarkably so. It is never too late to provide every ASD person the benefits of the new diagnostics and therapies now available.

I and most other DAN! doctors have come to believe that early (even in utero or neonatal) injury to the immature immune systems of these children by toxins or pathogens starts a series of bio-chemical events that culminates eventually in neurocognitive deficits and behavioral challenges. Though there may be a genetic vulnerability in many autism spectrum children, increasing evidence suggests that a toxic mercury-based preservative long used in vaccinations may have been the "trigger" for a susceptible subset of children, particularly since 1991 when Hepatitis B vaccinations were mandated for every newborn. I join many autism experts and parents who believe that the current epidemic of regressive autism began with this mandate. Statistics show a progressive rise in incidence beginning in 1988 when the MMR vaccination was mandated (although itself does not contain any mercury), and I will be discussing the recent findings about MMR in other places in the book. However, the incredibly steep rise in incidence started in 1991, coinciding with the requirement for newborns to receive the HepB often within hours of birth. We believe that early injury by toxins—likely preceded by genetic predisposition and augmented by allergies, illnesses, and repeated antibiotic use—are among the factors that can initiate a cascade of problems starting with a weakened immune system and inflamed intestinal tract. A weakened immune system opens the door to bacterial and viral infections, overuse of antibiotics, intestinal yeast overgrowth, gut inflammation, and impaired nutritional status. The frequently noted "leaky gut" syndrome and its various effects enable toxins to spread throughout the body including the brain. Furthermore, in a transiently or chronically vulnerable child, immunizations with live viruses such as the MMR pose another challenge. In this complex scenario of possibilities, vaccine-associated mercury, viruses, or other toxins as well as the child's own overactive immune components (autoimmunity) can attack neurons and thereby interfere with synaptic development and nerve signaling. With much variation from child to child, these factors can combine to create brain malnutrition and the cognitive impairment characteristic of ASD children.

Description of the Book

I will explain more about ASD causation models in Chapter One to help parents understand the rationale behind the various treatments. Chapter Two discusses nutritional deficiency as a common denominator in almost all ASD children and emphasizes the importance of the gastrointestinal tract and its relationship with the immune system. Accumulation of toxins, especially heavy metals and the "autism/vaccination" controversy are discussed at length in Chapter Three on Impaired Detoxification, Toxic Accumulations, and Politics. Chapter Four is dedicated to diagnostic evaluations, including a description of laboratory tests that help guide treatment and monitor its progress.

Chapters Five to Eight delineate the Biomedical Treatments for ASD that I use in my practice. These include Gastrointestinal Healing, Feeding the Starving Brain, and Chelation Therapy (Removing the Toxins)—based on the DAN! Protocol—and Immunity, Autoimmunity and Viruses.

In Chapter Nine I have asked my colleague Teresa Binstock to join with me in envisioning where diagnostics and treatments may be heading in this new and burgeoning field. This chapter also includes a brief summary of the diagnostic and treatment approach emphasized in this book. In Chapter Ten, I have invited Jack Zimmerman, PhD, mathematician, author, and visionary educator (and my husband) to touch on the cultural significance of such large numbers of these special children coming into the world at this time. He looks at what the epidemic of ASD may say about family dynamics and medicine and the importance of hearing the message they bring as we learn ways to heal them and ourselves.

Appendix A is a continuation of Jack Zimmerman's discussion of the cultural significance of the ASD epidemic in relation to education and the environment.

Appendix B presents an alternative version of the now famous "autism/mercury paper" written by Sallie Bernard, Albert Enayati, Heidi Roger, Lyn Redwood, and Teresa Binstock, with an introduction by Teresa Binstock. This was the paper that led to the removal of thimerosal from the Hepatits B newborn vaccinations by late 2001, reproduced here by permission.

Appendix C is an article by Teresa Binstock on future directions in autism.

Appendix D is new in the 2nd Edition, and contains "Recent Treatment Developments" that have been implemented in my work since the publication of the 1st Edition. I describe my use of a new "gentle" transdermal detoxification agent, allithiamine (TTFD) and my increasing awareness of the importance of Vitamin B12 and its use through a concentrated injectable form of methylcobalamin. I also describe the use of an oral form of IVIG (intravenous immunoglobulin) as more ammunition in our fight to heal the autoimmune disorders that beset most of our children.*

Appendix E is an open letter to doctors: "A Call to Pediatricians and Family Doctors," a request for physicians to open themselves to learning about hopeful new therapies for a condition previously thought to be incurable. I am hoping parents will take or send a copy to their doctors.

---

* In the 2004 reprinting, I have discussed our new interest in methylation disorders and treatments.

In summary, *Children With Starving Brains* will:

- **Help** parents understand why their child may have become chronically ill and how biomedical intervention may help

- **Identify** important diagnostic tools that can provide crucial information to help parents and physicians select the best treatment sequence

- **Explain** those therapies and identify safe and effective treatment options that can be started by parents or caregivers even before laboratory tests are ordered. This is important for parents having trouble finding a physician trained in treating children with ASD. Bio-medical intervention for autism is new.

Many physicians have not heard of or learned how to use these treatments as yet. However, a growing number are starting to take the time to learn these modalities because of the sheer numbers of children being diagnosed with ASD who need treatment now. Growing awareness in parents accelerates this process.

- **Encourage and inspire** parents to be their children's advocates in obtaining proper medical care (as they are doing in the field of education), and fight for insurance reform that will help them obtain the care they need. Joining support groups both locally and through the internet will provide a comforting and highly informative companionship with other parents who understand as no one else can what it means to love and care for a special needs child.

PART ONE

The Foundation for a Broad Spectrum Bio-Medical Approach to Autism Spectrum Disorder

ONE

CAUSATION MODELS

The Worldwide Autism Spectrum Disorder (ASD) Epidemic

C ould changes in diet calm your child and help him or her return to the world, pay attention. and behave better? Could the addition of certain nutrients help your child make giant leaps in developing vocabulary? Could the removal of mercury and heavy metals from his or her body set the stage for outgrowing the Autism Spectrum Disorder (ASD) diagnosis?

Yes. These treatments, sometimes individually but most often in combination with one another, have enabled some children to actually lose the diagnosis of autism or ASD. Many others, while remaining in the autistic spectrum, have made notable advancements in cognition, behavior, and physical health.

This message of hope is needed now more than ever before. We are in the midst of a worldwide ASD epidemic.[1] In one year alone (from 1998 to 1999), there was a 26.01% increase in the numbers

---

[1] There is no general rule about the number of cases that must exist for an outbreak to be considered an epidemic. The classic definition of the term was stated by an epidemiologist by the name of Benenson in 1980. He defined an epidemic as "The occurrence in a community or region of a group of illnesses ... of similar nature, clearly in excess of normal expectancy." In other words, an epidemic exists whenever the number of cases exceeds what is expected based on past experience for a given population.

of school age children classified as autistic, according to the U.S. Department of Education.[2] In California, the number of school age children diagnosed as autistic rose 210% in an 11-year period.[3] There has been a sevenfold increase in ASD in the past decade.[4] Similar increases in the incidence of autism and ASD have been reported on the European continent. Included in the spectrum of autistic disorders are Attention Deficit Disorder (ADD) and Attention Deficit Hyperactivity Disorder (ADHD). Six million children in the U.S. suffer from ADD or ADHD. Over two million children currently take Ritalin for either ADD or ADHD.

Definition of ASD and Incidence of Classic vs. Regressive Autism

The diagnostic criteria for autism agreed upon by most authorities are: severe abnormality of reciprocal social relatedness; severe abnormality of communication development (including language); restricted, repetitive behavior and patterns of behavior, interests, activities and imagination; and early onset (before age 3 to 5 years). Many authors would consider another criterion to be that of abnormal responses to sensory stimuli.[5]

Autistic Spectrum Disorder (ASD) is a group of developmental disorders ranging from full-fledged autism as described above to Attention Deficit Disorder (ADD), Attention Deficit Hyperactivity Disorder (ADHD) and Pervasive Developmental Disorder, (PDD). PDD is a catch-all diagnosis that children get when they do not meet developmental milestones and exhibit autistic symptoms, yet still retain at least some ability to speak and communicate. A child diagnosed with ADD has trouble maintaining focus. A hyperactive

---

[2] 22nd Annual Report to Congress on the Implementation of the Individuals with Disabilities Education Act, Table AA11, "Number and Change in Number of Children Ages, pp. 6-21, Served Under IDEA, Part B."

[3] *U.S. News & World Report,* June 19, 2000, p. 47

[4] Testimony on April 25, 2001 before the U.S. House of Representatives Committee on Governmental Reform by James J. Bradstreet, M.D., director of research for the International Autism Research Center.

[5] Gillberg, C and Coleman, Mary, "The Biology of the Autistic Syndromes," 3rd Edition, 2000 Mac Keith Press, Chapter, Clinical Diagnosis

child with ADD is labeled ADHD. Both are considered milder forms of ASD. Typically, parents do not seek help for children with any of these conditions until they become aware that their child is not talking or developing as rapidly as other toddlers.

At the top end of the autistic spectrum is Asperger's Syndrome. It is the term used to describe an autistic child who functions at a high level. These children are often extremely intelligent. They use and understand a large vocabulary, but they have very narrow interests and exhibit many social deficits. An Asperger's Syndrome child may become the world's expert on washing machines, but washing machines may be the only thing he or she wants to talk about.

There are two basic types of autism: autism from birth (classic autism once known as Kanner's Syndrome) and regressive autism which generally occurs between 12 and 24 months of age after a period of normal development and behavior. The incidence of autism from birth remains an infrequent event—one or two out of 10,000 births. It is the incidence of regressive autism and associated autistic spectrum disorders that has soared, striking as many as one out of 250 children, according to dozens of studies.

Some studies peg that estimate even higher. A recent one indicates that as many as one out of 150 California children may have regressive ASD.[6] A similar figure was reported by the Center for Disease Control (CDC) in a study of a township on the East Coast. That study identified 6.87 cases of ASD per 1,000 children, which is approximately one out of 150.[7] As far as the total number of ASD children, Dr. Jeff J. Bradstreet told a congressional committee that, "The government's own data indicate that there are as many as two million children in the U.S.A. with a significant developmental delay that can be categorized as ASD." *U.S. News & World Report* put it this way: "One out of every six children in America suffers from problems such as autism, aggression, dyslexia, and attention deficit hyperactivity disorder."[8]

---

[6] *Report on Autism to the California Legislature,* 1999.

[7] Centers for Disease Control (CDC), April, 2000. "Prevalence of Autism in Brick Township, New Jersey, 1998: Community Report" available on the CDC website, http://www.cdc.gov/nceh/programs/cddh/dd/report.htm.

[8] Shelia Kaplan and Jim Morris, "Kids At Risk," *U.S. News & world Report,* June 19, 2000, p. 47.

It is considered by most of those now working with large numbers of ASD children that ADD, ADHD, PDD, and Asperger's Syndrome are the result of a milder version of the same pattern of genetic predisposition coupled with environmental triggers which we believe causes ASD. The environmental insults that trigger the damage can occur before birth while the fetus is still developing, during infancy, or while the child is a toddler. Whatever the timing, those environmental insults overburden undeveloped or just developing immune systems, often causing the children's immune systems to turn against their own bodies. When the immune system starts damaging its own body the process is called an autoimmune disease. Allergies, arthritis, and diabetes are other examples of autoimmune diseases. Many autistic/ASD children have families with histories of autoimmune diseases.

What Causes Autism and Other ASDs?

No one claims to understand everything about the causes of this epidemic, but there are theories that parents (and doctors) should be acquainted with because they are the basis for the treatments that will be described in later chapters. There is growing agreement that most cases of autism and ASD derive from a combination of genetic and environmental factors. Genetic factors may set the stage for ASD, yet in many individual cases, environmental factors appear to be the necessary trigger whereby genes then cause the disorder to be expressed.

There are many theories regarding the exact identity and mechanism of the environmental insults that trigger the cascade of physical, mental, and emotional dysfunctions which result in the starvation of a child's brain. No study, however, has definitively pinpointed a specific environmental toxin or contaminant as the one "smoking gun" behind autism, nor is it likely that just one toxin will be identified as the culprit. Instead, there is strong evidence incriminating not one, but several toxins and mechanisms of entry as primary villains behind the damage suffered by many of our children.

SIMPLY GENETIC?

Scientists have long thought that autism is a genetic disease. Yet gene research has been unable to identify a specific chromosome or location on a gene that is the site of a primary autism defect. These children rarely present facial and bodily dysmorphic features characteristic of the children with chromosomal defects that occur in very early gestation such as Down, Williams', and Fragile X children. Although a specific understanding of how genetics contributes to autism is still lacking, it is clear that there is likely to be a genetic "predisposition" or vulnerability in many ASD children. We know this from studies by Reed P. Warren and also because autism tends to show up more in twins than in the normal population. Furthermore, autism is nearly four times more prevalent in boys than in girls. These several findings suggest an association between autism and various genetic factors but do not mandate a clear role for genetics in every case of autism. In any one child, a clustering of environmental triggers may have been etiologically crucial for the onset of ASD. In many such children—with or without genetic predispositions—one or several of the environmental triggers may remain as a treatable pathology, such as a subclinical viral infection or heavy metal toxicity.

Aside from a few purely genetic syndromes that can induce autism, gene researchers have discovered an assortment of genetic markers common to many, but not all, autistic children. One of the genes that control the function and regulation of the immune system, the C4B gene, is involved in eliminating pathogens such as viruses and bacteria from the body. A deficient form of the C4B gene has been shown to have an increased frequency in autism, ADHD, and dyslexia.[9]

We talk about children with ASD as having "genetic susceptibility."—even as we realize that a "genetic susceptibility" may actually not exist in individual cases. At this time, however, acquired and genetic types of susceptibility are just beginning to be elucidated. Not surprisingly, studies about immune-related genes already appear in the autism literature.[10]

[9] Warren, R.P., et al. (1996) 'Immunogenetic studies in autism and related disorders.' Molecular and Chemical Neuropathology, 28, pp. 77-81
[10] Ibid

THE TOXIC CHEMICAL MODEL

It is shocking to realize that mothers-to-be may be drinking contaminated water, breathing air inside the home that is more dangerous than the air downwind of an industrial city, and absorbing toxic-chemicals from foods that may be acting as a time bomb within their bodies and those of their unborn children.

A recent report by a group of physicians in Boston states that millions of U.S. children exhibit learning disabilities, reduced IQ, and destructive, aggressive behavior because of exposure to toxic chemicals.[11] The report links pre- and post-natal toxic exposures to lifelong disabilities. In addition, a report from the National Academies of Science states that a combination of neurotoxicants and genetic factors may account for nearly 25% of developmental problems.[12] That includes Autism Spectrum Disorder. An important class of toxic chemicals are the polychlorinated biphenyls (PCBs) and organophosphate pesticides. The NAS report showed that babies who had significant amounts of PCBs performed poorer than unexposed babies in visual face recognition tests, ability to shut out distractions, and overall intelligence. The report went on to say that pesticides such as Dursban and Diazinon can cause brain damage. It was only in 2000 that the Environmental Protection Agency (EPA) banned Dursban from household use. It had been marketed to consumers in popular indoor roach and ant killers since 1956.

THE HEAVY METAL CONTAMINATION MODEL

It is even more shocking to learn that the immune systems of genetically susceptible infants may have been attacked by heavy metals such as lead and mercury.

- **Lead:** The Boston Physicians' report referred to in the previous section states that one million American children currently have levels of lead in their bloodstreams above the threshold recognized by the (EPA) as adversely affecting behavior and cognition. Where does the lead come from? Many houses and apartments built before 1978 have paint that contains lead.

---

[11] IN HARM'S WAY: TOXIC THREATS TO CHILD DEVELOPMENT published in 2001 by the Greater Boston Physicians for Social Responsibility organization.

[12] National Academies of Science Report, 2000.

Although the ban on lead paint has been in existence since the late 1970's, the presence of lead in older housing poses a serious hazard, especially to young children. Opening or closing a painted frame window can create small paint chips or lead dust that can be inhaled or which settles to the floor. Infants and very young crawling children often put their hands in their mouths and eat the dust and paint chips because they taste sweet. The CDC and the U.S. Public Health Service in a joint statement say: "Lead poisoning remains the most commonly and societally devastating environmental disease of young children." We now know that large numbers of children may suffer adverse health effects at blood levels that were once considered safe. Long-term exposure to low levels of lead may cause a buildup in the brain and other tissues resulting in neurological damage to children even before they are born, according to the EPA booklet that homesellers and landlords are required to give buyers or renters of dwellings that may still contain lead paint.[13] Consequently children's exposure to lead can retard and impair mental and physical development. "Lead exposure has already cut in half the number of U.S. children who might have had superior I.Q.'s (125 or higher)—some two million kids," says Herbert Needleman, MD, a professor of Psychiatry and Pediatrics at the University of Pittsburgh.[14] In a study released in June 2000, Dr. Needleman found that juvenile delinquents had significantly higher levels of lead in their bones than nondelinquent youths.[15]

- **Mercury:** Mercury, the substance found in old-fashioned thermometers, is ubiquitous in the environment. Fish are known to contain high levels of mercury. According to *U.S. News & World Report*, a toxicologist by the name of David Brown helped prepare a study of the mercury levels in the lakes of eight Northeastern states and three Canadian provinces. He found much higher levels of mercury in fish from

---

[13] "Protect Your Family from Lead in Your Home," EPA and United States Consumer Product Safety Commission pamphlet, 747-K-94-001, May, 1995.

[14] Maury M. Breecher, PhD, M.P.H., *Healthy Homes in a Toxic World,* John Wiley & Sons, Inc.

[15] *U.S. News & World Report,* June 19, 2000, p. 48.

supposedly pristine lakes than had been expected. Brown concluded that a "pregnant woman who ate a single fish from one of those lakes could, in theory, consume enough mercury to harm her unborn child."[16]

Another source of prenatal exposure might be the mercury contained in the amalgam dental fillings of their pregnant mothers. No one realized the potential danger at the time, but Elizabeth, my own daughter, had dental repairs including fillings containing mercury when she was four months pregnant with Chelsey. Other countries such as Sweden and Canada have more stringent limits on amalgams for women of child-bearing age. Because of what we have learned about mercury, we now believe it is possible that those amalgams may have been a trigger for Chelsey's autism. No matter what the route or the combination of routes, it is my belief that a large portion of the current epidemic of regressive autism and ASD generally is a direct result of the mercury or other heavy metals that have entered the bodies of our kids. An important part of my practice at the present time is focused on evaluating and treating for toxic heavy metals in these children, as I describe in Chapter Seven.

VACCINATIONS

In infants and toddlers with increased susceptibility, vaccination with live viruses may have contributed to the child's autistic regression. Another contributor to the problem preceding the live virus injection was almost certainly the ethylmercury (in the form of thimerosal) which until recently was used as a preservative in multi-dose vials of some vaccines mandated for newborns. The correspondence between autistic traits and those that occur from mercury poisoning is highly significant and includes varying degrees of autoimmunity. In fact, all traits that define or are associated with autism have been described previously in mercury-poisoning literature (see Appendices B and C).

---

[16] Shelia Kaplan and Jim Morris, "Kids at Risk: Chemicals in the Environment Come Under Scrutiny as the Number of Childhood Learning Problems Soars, " *U.S. News & World Report,* June 19, 2000, p. 51.

Mercury was for years used as an anti-fungal in paint but, due to toxicity, was taken out of indoor paint in 1991. Similarly, FDA hearings led, in 1982, to merthiolate's discontinuance because it contained ethyl-mercury. Unfortunately, no one thought to remove ethylmercury from the many vaccines mandated to protect our children from childhood illnesses. The mercury in those vaccines is a component of Thimerosal,™ which is 49.6% ethylmercury by weight and which was used as a preservative to retard spoilage of vaccines in multi-use vials. Vaccinal ethylmercury may have "spoiled" the lives of thousands upon thousands of children and their families.

Indeed, the current cohort of kids being diagnosed with ASD has had more exposure to mercury from vaccines than the EPA thinks is safe for adults. That's because kids today have more total vaccinations (22 before two years of age) and have them closer together and earlier in life than ever before in history.

Prior to 1991, babies just learning to crawl were exposed to mercury fumes from commercial indoor paint. As we have just mentioned, in that year the FDA pressured paint manufacturers to remove mercury from their indoor house paint. The paint manufacturers complied. It is tragically ironic that in the same year the federal government, for public health reasons, mandated the unprecedented practice of inoculating newborn infants with the Hepatitis B vaccination on the very day of birth. Until 2001, that vaccine contained Thimerosal. So, while one part of the government was mandating that mercury be taken out of indoor paints, another was mandating that newborn infants be injected with the mercury-containing Hepatitis B vaccine. According to the CDC recommended immunization schedule, infants who get all their shots were exposed to 12.5 micrograms of mercury at birth, 62.4 micrograms at two months, 50 micrograms at four months, 62.5 micrograms at six months, and 50 micrograms at approximately 18 months. It is my belief that the mercury-containing Hep B vaccination given at birth when the immune system and liver are immature acted as a "trigger" that set into motion the cascade of events that have resulted in the gastrointestinal and neurological deficits we see in the current epidemic of autism. While a causal link between thimerosal and the current epidemic of autism has not yet been definitively proven, epidemiologic data support the connection. More recently the Institute of Medicine's staff has concluded that, indeed, the hypothesis is plausible. I feel it is only a matter of time before thimerosal's adverse effects are acknowledged; I might even use the term "admitted."

When British physician Andrew Wakefield first suggested the possible link between the MMR vaccine, acquired gut pathology, and autism, his work was belittled in a flurry of hastily assembled rebuttals. Nonetheless, special studies of inflamed intestinal tissue in a subgroup of ASD children demonstrated that measles virus (MV) was present in their biopsied intestinal tissue and that the measles virus found there was indeed the vaccine strain.[17] Other research has linked ASD with measles virus gut infestation. Recently, Harvard gastroenterologist Timothy Buie, MD described a cohort of nearly 400 children and reported that a subgroup indeed had the ileal-lymphoid hyperplasia first described by Wakefield and colleagues.[18] Importantly, independent Japanese researchers Kawashima et al reported that the vaccine-strain of MV was also present in the peripheral blood mononuclear cells in an ASD subgroup,[19] which may contribute to blood-brain-barrier inflammation and to low levels of viral infiltration into the central nervous system (CNS).

Most vaccinated children have been injected with a weakened form of the measles virus. The measles virus infects 40 million people and kills one million per year by suppressing the immune system and affecting the CNS. Most individuals who become seriously affected by wild-type measles virus live in under-developed nations. Overall, the measles vaccine has saved millions of lives. However, the measles vaccine is now given in a combination three-in-one shot that also contains mumps and rubella vaccines. The combined vaccine is called the MMR. The MMR is described as continuing to save millions of lives, but—given the intestinal-pathology data linked to vaccine strains of measles virus—the MMR may also have induced or contributed to regressive autism in thousands of children. That is the belief of Dr. Andrew Wakefield, who until recently

---

[17] Wakefield, A.J. et al., "Ileal-lymphoid-nodular hyperplasia, non-specific colitis, and pervasive developmental disorder in children", Lancet 1998 Feb. 28;351(9103): 637-41

[18] www.feat.org/FEATnews: Report of Oasis 2001 Conference for Autism in Portland OR "Harvard Clinic Scientist Finds Gut/Autism Link, Like Wakefield Findings"

[19] Kawashima H. et al., "Detection and sequencing of measles virus from peripheral mononuclear cells from patients with inflammatory bowel disease." Dig. Dis. Sci. 2000 Apr;45(4): 723-9

worked as a gastroenterologist/researcher at the Royal Free Hospital in London, England.

This highly regarded clinician-researcher discovered a possible connection between autism and the specific measles viral strain associated with the MMR vaccination. As mentioned earlier, Dr. Wakefield found vaccine-derived viral genomes within intestinal tissue and peripheral blood mononuclear cells of a subgroup of autistic children. Those findings prompted an autism model in which the MMR can trigger the body's autoimmune reactions against the myelin basic protein (MBP) for a certain group of susceptible children. This model is consistent with data reported by long-time autism researcher VK Singh, whose articles describe that a high percentage of ASD children have elevated titers for antibodies against MBP and that these titers often co-occur with elevated titers against measles virus or human herpesvirus 6 (HHV-6).

Many experts including Bernard Rimland believe Dr. Wakefield's findings shed light on etiologically significant processes for a subgroup of ASD children. Despite medical officials' protests to the contrary, many parents, physicians, and researchers believe (a) that the MMR vaccine may be a real cause contributing to the rising incidence of autism, and (b) that adverse consequences may be more likely if the vaccinations occur as additional multiples (e.g., the MMR plus the DPT, all on the same day), and if the infant or toddler has increased susceptibility—whether acquired and/or genetic—at the time of vaccination.

THE AUTO-IMMUNITY/ALLERGY MODEL

As biomedical profiling increases, it is becoming clear that autism-spectrum children break down into defined "subgroups." For instance, a good number of autism spectrum children have elevated titers against various brain proteins. Similarly, many also have familial autoimmune or allergic diseases; many autistic children themselves have signs or symptoms of autoimmunity or allergy.[20]

An allergy results when the body's immune system overreacts to what it perceives to be a foreign invader. When a substance causes

---

[20] Comi, A.M. et al., "Familial clustering of autoimmune disorders and evaluation of medical risk factors in autism," Jour. Child. Neurol. 1999 Jun;14(6): 338-94

the body's immune system to respond, the substance is referred to as an "allergen." When an allergen such as dust or a plant pollen is inhaled, it is soon identified by the immune system as an intruder. The immune system then creates an antibody (a defender) to combat the perceived intruder. For example, in response to a plant pollen such as ragweed, an antibody called "immunoglobulin E," or simply IgE, is formed. The IgE antibodies attach themselves to tissue cells called mast cells and to other cells in the bloodstream called basophils. The mast cells and basophils (generally white blood cells) target the allergen and cruise through the blood stream, transporting the IgE to its target. When the allergen is reached, the IgE attaches to it and the mast cells and basophils release histamine. That chemical causes swelling in the lining of the nose and causes extra mucus to form. The afflicted person suffers congestion, sneezing, inflamed and irritated itching eyes and perhaps itching on skin areas exposed to the allergen. We take anti-histamines to combat those symptoms, but it is those symptoms that cause trapped allergens to be expelled along with the mucus.

Many autism spectrum children at least initially appear to have an immune dysregulation, in some ways overactive, in other ways suboptimal. Some researchers and physicians have theorized that when a particularly susceptible child suffers an environmental insult such as exposure to mercury or even to the weakened viruses in vaccines, the child's immune system responds by attacking not only the actual antigens but also look-alike antigens that are actually molecular structures within the child's brain.

A tip-off that an autoimmune process is at work is that the blood tests on many autistic children have been found to contain autoantibodies to a central nervous system protein known as myelin basic protein (MBP).[21] In a controlled study[22] that compared 33 autistic children with 18 normal children, 20 mentally retarded children, and 12 children with Down syndrome, anti-MBP antibodies were found in 19 of 33 (58%) of the autistic children, but in only in 8 of 88 (9%) of all the other subjects. This is an intriguing finding

---

[21] Singh VK, Lin SX, Yang VC. Serological association of measles virus and human herpesvirus-6 with brain autoantibodies in autism. Clin Immunol Immunopathol 1998 Oct; 89 (1): pp. 105-8

[22] Brain, Behavior, and Immunity (Volume 7, pp. 97-103, 1993).

because myelination is an essential part of human brain development. Nerves can only conduct pulses of energy efficiently when properly sheathed with myelin. Like insulation on an electric wire, the fatty coating of myelin helps keep the electrical pulses confined, thus maintaining the integrity of the nerve's electrical signal. When the insulation on a wire is damaged or destroyed, the flow of electrical current may be interrupted and short-circuits occur. When the immune system attacks the body's own myelin, "short-circuits" can occur within the brain. Nerve axons cease to function properly.

The autoimmune findings in autism provide support for other subgroups and their causal models. As mentioned earlier, vaccinations that included ethylmercury or that contained live viruses may have affected children with dysregulated immunity, impaired nutritional status, and increased susceptibility.[23] In addition, a growing amount of clinical data suggest that some autistic children have chronic, *seemingly* subclinical infections which are etiologically significant to the child's negative traits.

THE VIRAL MODEL

The etiological significance of viral infections in ASD is well established by clinical data. Sidney Baker, MD, and Michael Goldberg, MD are physicians directing two major autism clinics. Both Baker and Goldberg have reported that approximately 30% of their autistic patients respond favorably to acyclovir or Valtrex (an acyclovir variant). Efficacy studies have shown that, with descending usefulness, acyclovir is effective against herpes simplex virus, varicella, Epstein-Barr virus, and human herpesvirus 6 (HSV, VZV, EBV, HHV-6). My own clinical experience, though limited, parallels what Baker and Goldberg report. When I first started seeing autistic patients I prescribed acyclovir or Valtrex for any of them that had elevated viral titers and found a positive response in about one-third of those treated. I was just learning, and may not have given a high enough dose for a long enough time for some of the children. This was my main treatment approach after diet, nutrients, and gut healing prior to starting to remove the heavy metals through chelation.

---

[23] Kawashima, H., et al., "Detection and sequencing of measles virus from peripheral mononuclear cells from patients with inflammatory bowel disease and autism." Dept. of Pediatrics, Tokyo Medical Univ., Japan, Dig. Dis. Sci. 2000 Apr;45(4): 723-9

As we will see in Chapter Eight, these clinical findings have profound implications for the treatment of ASD children. First of all,
acyclovir is benign for most children and adults. Thus a trial with
acyclovir is easily enacted. Secondly, various herpes viruses are associated with verbal impairment, seizures, demyelination, and other
autism-spectrum traits. All of this must be seen in the context of a
child's overall medical portrait. Gut pathology must be minimized,
nutritional status maximized, and heavy metals removed by physician-supervised chelation. A net effect of these treatments is that
the child's immune status may improve to the point that his or her
subclinical infection can be more successfully immunosuppressed.
Generally, with notable exceptions based on a particular child's
medical picture and lab findings, I will always heal the gut and start
optimizing the nutrient intake first, chelate if there is evidence of
heavy metal toxicity, and treat the viruses later in the treatment plan.
However, my clinical experience has taught me that some children
need a pharmaceutical antiviral like acyclovir or the plant alternative
anti-virals right away along with or even preceding the chelation
process. There is no doubt in my mind that viruses are a big player in
many of our children's clinical pictures and further evidence of the
immune dysregulation they endure. Since these infections are difficult to treat, I prefer to get the toxic load down and get the child's
body into optimum health hoping their own immune system can
start doing its job of viral immunosuppression.

THE GLUTEN/CASEIN, ENZYME DEFICIENCY, AND YEAST OVERGROWTH MODEL

Many autistic children have an inability to digest gluten and/or
casein. Gluten refers to a mixture of proteins contained in wheat
and found in numerous other products. Casein is a milk protein.
Alan Friedman, PhD, and fellow researchers theorize that an enzyme
vital for the digestion of those substances ("DPP-IV") is missing
(probably for genetic reasons) or is inactivated, possibly due to an
autoimmune mechanism. Friedman's model posits that the absence
or inactivation of the missing DPP-IV enzyme allows the accumulation in the body of opioid or morphine-like substances known as
dermorphins. The buildup and accumulation of those substances

may be one reason that autistic children frequently appear "spaced out." A common characteristic of autism is that the children generally ignore other people and seem to be living in their own inner worlds. Regardless of Friedman's hypothesis, many autistic spectrum children have one or several food hypersensitivities as determined by food-allergy tests and by elimination diets. Most ASD children studied have been shown to have inflamed gastrointestinal tracts, and it is believed that certain foods that the child is sensitive to such as gluten and casein irritate their intestines. Studies have shown that antibiotics also irritate the gut lining as well as impair the immune system. An initial and primary treatment for the inability to digest gluten and casein is a Gluten Free/Casein Free (GF/CF) diet. Chapter Five describes how to start and maintain your child on such a diet.

Children with impaired immune systems and inflamed intestines are particularly vulnerable to invasions by fungi, especially yeast of the Candida species. Fecal cultures and other lab-tests often identify overgrowths with *Candida albicans*. Indeed, some research indicates that Candida species and other fungi may be a significant cause of many of the untoward behaviors and health problems we see in autistic patients. Many of the children's medical histories document numerous episodes of ear infections and repeated use of antibiotics. As a result, the beneficial or "probiotic" flora in such children are likely to have been destroyed, thereby setting the stage for adverse fungal as well as bacterial colonizations. Similarly, organic mercury compounds can adversely affect intestinal flora. Thus vaccinal ethylmercury—which exits the body primarily via the intestinal tract—may also injure intestinal flora. When vaccinal ethylmercury poisoning is accompanied by antibiotic overuse, probiotic flora may decrease, resulting in an adverse intestinal colonization and the flourishing of intestinal yeast.

As these species of yeast multiply they excrete toxins. William Shaw, PhD, who has been conducting groundbreaking research on yeast and its effects on autistic children, points out that these toxins are capable of impairing the central nervous and immune systems.[24]

---

[24] Shaw, William, Chapter 3, Biological Treatments for Autism and PDD, revised 2002 edition. Lenexa KS 66214

An additional possible adverse connection with mercury is that it and other heavy metals destroy leukocytes and neutrophils, the specialized white blood cells that normally protect against fungi and bacteria.

Some of the health problems known to be caused by *Candida* overgrowth include diarrhea, stomachache, gas pains, constipation, headache, fatigue, and depression. Behavior problems include concentration difficulties, hyperactivity, short attention span, irritability, and aggression.

There are many safe ways to treat yeast overgrowth. These include taking "probiotics" (nutritional supplements which repopulate the intestinal tract with "good" microbes) and the use of anti-fungal nutraceuticals or mild prescription drugs to combat stubborn *Candida*. Some children need to be put on special diets, low in sugar and other foods that cause yeasts to thrive. After treating their yeast infections, I have seen improvements in afflicted patients ranging from decreased hyperactivity and "stimming" to increased eye contact, better concentration, and increased speech.

THE METALLOTHIONEIN THEORY

This section discusses the work of William Walsh, PhD, a noted biochemist who works at the Pfeiffer Treatment Center in Naperville, IL. Based upon findings in thousands of individuals and nearly a thousand autism spectrum children, Dr. Walsh theorizes that a small peptide called metallothionein is the "missing link" in this disorder. Metallothionein (MT) is a protein with many roles in the body.[25] It is involved in the:

- Regulation of zinc and copper levels in the blood

- Detoxification of mercury and other toxic metals

- Development and functioning of the immune system and brain neurons

- Production of enzymes that break down casein and gluten

- Response to intestinal inflammation

---

[25] Booklet, "Metallothionein and Autism." Pfeiffer Treatment Center, Naperville IL Oct 2001

MT also participates in the hippocampus region of the brain that modulates behavior control, emotional memory, and socialization. MT is such a vital substance that Dr. Walsh concludes that dysregulations of MT may be the primary cause of autism. He theorizes that autism results from the combination of a genetic defect involving marginal or defective MT functioning and an environmental insult during early development which disables MT.

In chemical profiles of 503 ASD patients Walsh and fellow researchers at the Pfeiffer Treatment Center, Naperville, IL discovered that 99% of those patients exhibited abnormal metal metabolism and showed evidence of MT dysfunction. He stated at the October 2001 DAN! conference in San Diego that environmental insults during gestation, infancy or early childhood may disable the metallothionein protein system, resulting in halted neuronal development and provoking the onset of autism.

In recent years, research studies and clinical lab-data have revealed that children with ASD have abnormal copper and zinc levels in their blood. Since MT has an important role in regulating the balance of copper and zinc in healthy individuals, the fact that 99% of the patients in the Pfeiffer Treatment Center study had copper/zinc inbalances supports MT dysfunction as an important part of ASD pathology. Walsh's MT findings and supportive clinical lab-data have important treatment implications. Dr. Walsh and colleagues point out that MT functioning can be greatly improved through a two-step process that involves the removal of excess copper and other toxic metals in conjunction with nutrient therapies using zinc and other supplements known to encourage MT production and effectiveness. Walsh also believes that chelation techniques may enable removal of toxic metal accumulations. The Pfeiffer Center continues to actively research alternatives for autism prevention and treatment.

How Models of Causation
Lead to Treatments That Work

The experts agree that autism spectrum disorder is a multi-factorial disorder. That means, for example, that no one believes mercury is the sole environmental insult or trigger for this disorder. Indeed, while many children get better when mercury and other heavy metals are removed from their bodies and brains, not all do. That fact alone implicates other causes in various subgroups and necessitates that we remain aware of other causation models in autism. In medical schools and universities, professors often tell their students, "There is nothing so practical as a good theory." That is because a theory is an attempt to explain a group of facts or phenomena. Once we have a model about what might be causing a disease, diagnostics and treatments can be designed in ways that address patterns of biomedical pathology.

Historically, valid medical theories often took decades before acceptance was commonplace. For instance, in the 19th century, Hungarian physician Ignaz Philipp Semmelweiss theorized that Childbirth Fever, that was killing huge numbers of women who had just given birth, somehow was transmitted by the hands of their doctors. In that era, doctors did not wash their hands very often and the germ theory of disease had not yet been accepted. Many doctors at that time actually performed autopsies on deceased childbirth fever victims and then assisted in live births without washing their hands! Semmelweiss was ridiculed by other physicians for his beliefs. It took years and the deaths of thousands of women before his theory was accepted. Now, thanks to the work of researchers such as Louis Pasteur, the germ theory of disease is accepted.

In my work I have come to believe that many autism spectrum children do not need drugs such as Ritalin or anti-psychotic medications. If possible, I want to correct the root of the problem and not just control behavior or other symptoms. In my opinion, the common denominator underlying the developmental disorders of almost all of these children regardless of the etiology is that proper nourishment does not reach their brain cells. I and many other clinicians are finding that almost all children begin improving when we (1) heal their inflamed digestive systems, (2) strengthen their immune systems by providing needed supplemental vitamins, minerals, and other nutrients; and (3) remove the toxins from their diets and the heavy metals from their bodies.

It was Dr. Bernard Rimland's pioneering work on the importance of Vitamin B6 for proper brain functioning and his publicizing of the benefits of DMG (dimethylglycine) for a certain subset of autistic children that started me on my search for information on the biochemical imbalances that underlie autism spectrum disorder. Because so many of these children self-restrict their diets to only a few, usually non-nutritious foods, it is easy to see that they need those nutrients as well as the replacement of other vitamins and minerals. It was clear to me that immune impairment was also a factor as shown by the history of high numbers of infections and antibiotic treatments in these children as well as immune deficiencies revealed by lab tests. I was avidly pursuing what role viruses might be playing in this disorder when I started hearing about the dangers of mercury toxicity from amalgams, mercury-laden fish, and vaccines. From e-mail communication with Amy Holmes, MD, of Baton Rouge, LA, the picture started getting clearer for me in a new way. Hearing about the use and benefit of oral chelation to reduce the heavy metal loads carried by these children, I began learning all I could about the harm mercury can inflict in a subset of susceptible children.

The presence of opportunistic viruses as shown by the high viral titers exhibited by many of these children went along with the mercury toxin idea, since mercury is a likely trigger to start this whole cascade of illness. Impaired immunity, gut inflammation, higher infection rate, increased use of antibiotics, impaired nutritional status, maldigestion/malabsorption, and decreased ability to handle toxins in the form of heavy metals or pathogens—including viruses—is a sequence that fits most ASD children. I began to understand also that toxins in the brain, whether they are heavy metals, viruses or other pathogens, set up conditions that prevent nutrients from gaining entry into the brain cells even if the gut problems allow some nourishment to reach the brain. Autism spectrum disorder children's brain cells are starving for nutrients. An important part of my healing program is built around restoring healthful nutrition to their *starving brains.* One has to heal the gut, build up the child's immune system through a non-harmful diet and tailored supplementation, and block the intake of new toxins while lowering the load of those that have already accumulated. Only then is the brain enabled to take up needed nutrients.

Before parents and physicians can agree on the best treatment decisions, a good diagnosis is critical. Many treatment options are available and I have found that most of these children need many kinds of therapy, some applied simultaneously and some sequentially, to optimize the outcome. The different models of causation I have discussed in this chapter help me place children into subgroups so I can sequence the treatment optimally, starting with the most likely problem and working toward more esoteric treatments which are sometimes more expensive and require more invasive testing when the child is not making the improvement we had hoped for. The GF/CF diet is a good example. Since I can say from direct experience and that of many others that almost all children benefit from removing casein and gluten from their diet, I do not have to advise an endoscopy and gut biopsy to prove the inflammation before suggesting this diet be adopted. Fortunately, dedicated researchers have already done the work for us.

History, family background, symptoms, and testing help me organize my treatment protocols based on which of the causation models are most likely operating. Like other DAN! doctors I use lab testing to biomedically profile and specifically treat autism spectrum children. Patterns in these laboratory results and in treatment efficacy are prompting models of causation that may become the foundation for future autism protocols in mainstream medicine.

TWO

GASTROINTESTINAL PATHOLOGY

Nutritional Deficiencies

Nutritional Deficiency as a Common Denominator

In this chapter, I will explain how medical researchers and DAN! clinicians are clarifying and solving pieces of the autism spectrum puzzle. Our discussion will broaden and deepen the understanding of some of the biomedical topics just touched on in Chapter One. The reader more interested in the treatment of autism than its biomedical origins can use this chapter as reference material for what comes later. Our recent progress in treatment is reflected in ever better understanding of the use of diagnostic testing and thus more effective treatments for individual children within subgroups of the underlying disease processes of this complex disorder. The shared symptom that integrates these seemingly disparate subgroups is the clinically substantiated fact that most autism-spectrum children have what I've come to call *starving brains*. Abnormalities shown in studies on these children compared to controls with neurotypical children reveal higher incidences of:

- Higher serum copper
- Zinc deficiency
- Magnesium deficiency
- Iron deficiency
- Higher copper/zinc ratios
- B12 deficiency
- Below normal glutamine
- Lower plasma sulphate
- Lower Vitamin B6
- Lower amino acids tyrosine, carnosine, lysine, hydroxylysine
- Lower methionine levels
- Higher glutamate
- Fatty acid deficiencies
- Calcium deficiency
- Inadequate levels of Vitamin D, E, and A

I cannot emphasize enough that the brain does not function in isolation. It is a team player; it needs vital nutrients as well as informational input. To fill these needs the brain depends heavily on complex interactions between the immune, endocrine, and gastrointestinal systems.

The early medical histories of many autism spectrum children indicate gastrointestinal challenges and/or recurrent otitis media (ear infections). When these findings are integrated with food-elimination results and studies of immune shifts and weaknesses, our attention is called to the significant interplay of gastrointestinal health, nutritional status, and immune competence. This cluster of interrelationships has relevance to diagnostics and treatments of ASD children, with many showing evidence of impaired immune systems and nutritionally deprived brains.

As the autistic child grows, parents, other physicians, and I are finding that the key to best outcome for many children is early bio-medical diagnostics followed by treatments which strengthen the immune system, heal the gut, and restore a healthful nutritional status. The proper combination of these treatments often succeeds in helping the brain receive the nourishment and neuronal input it needs to function properly. I call this series of treatments a "broad-spectrum approach;" most DAN! doctors simply refer to it as the DAN! protocol.

This philosophy is based on years of laboratory experiments and trial-and-error clinical treatments involving thousands of patients. After sharing knowledge about several thousand cases, many DAN! doctors began to realize that, with much inter-individual variation, their autistic patients suffered from an interplay of immune dys-regulations and gastrointestinal challenges with neurological ramifications. A primary clue toward developing a biomedical model of how to help ASD children was the oft-repeated observation that a great number of them have intractable diarrhea or constipation, abdominal pain, gaseousness and bloating, and—in many cases—foul smelling, light colored stools. In the historical context of a refrigerator-mother model that yielded to a "must be genetic" model, many pediatricians failed to connect these symptoms to the disease. In contrast, I and most, if not all DAN! practitioners believe we must treat the gastrointestinal problems to put these children on the road to recovery.

A second piece of the puzzle is that many children with autism, to the despair of their parents, have trouble sleeping through the night. In many cases, the first and second pieces of the puzzle are connected. Intestinal discomfort can impair sleep. Among DAN! doctors who recently participated in a well-attended physician training conference on autism in San Diego (October 2001), many agreed with Dr. Karl Reichelt's statement that many autistic children who awaken wailing and crying during the night suffer from reflux esophagitis.[1] That is, poor sleep habits occur because, during the night, stomach acid rises and burns the esophagus, the muscular membranous tube through which food passes to the stomach. No wonder these children wake up crying, often unable to tell us what is hurting them!

---

[1] Karl Reichelt, MD, PhD, at the DAN Fall, 2001 conference, Oct. 5-7, San Diego, CA.

Causes of Gastrointestinal Problems in ASD Children

There can be many causes of gastrointestinal problems in children with autism. Multiple studies have shown malabsorption, maldigestion, gut pathogen overgrowth (fungal, bacterial and viral), and abnormal intestinal permeability in many ASD children. Many parents do not realize at first that there is a connection between their child's autism and their gastrointestinal abnormalities. Unfortunately, many doctors also have not yet learned about that connection. Constipation and diarrhea, and sometimes both at alternate times, are frequently reported by parents, as well as abnormal amounts of gas, belching, and foul smelling stools. Clinical biopsies reveal that many autistic children have an autism-specific ileal hyperplasia.[2][3][4] Many DAN! doctors and medical researchers believe that a primary factor in the children's chronic gastrointestinal disturbances is immune system impairment. However, since these two systems are so interrelated, it is often impossible to know whether the immune dysregulation or the gastrointestinal pathology came first. As we have already indicated in Chapter One, a history of food intolerances or allergies, inability to digest gluten and casein, and chronic fungal (yeast) infections are tip-offs that an immune impairment—whether acquired and/or genetic—contributes to the gastrointestinal pathology. An increasing amount of evidence supports the triggering role of external influences in starting the immune and gastrointestinal problems, such as vaccinations containing heavy metals and repeated antibiotics—environmental factors whose effects are magnified in children with increased susceptibility, be it transient or chronic, acquired or genetic.

The interplay of these complex domains—gastrointestinal, immune, infectious, and nutritional—makes it important to gather extensive information not only about the child's medical and vac-

---

[2] Wakefield A.J. et al., "Enterocolitis in children with developmental disorders." Amer Jour Gastroenterology 2000 Sep;95(9): 2285-95

[3] Furlano R.I. et al., "Colonic CD8 and gamma delta T-cell infiltration with epithelial damage in children with autism." Jour Pediatrics 2001 Mar;138(3): 366-72

[4] Buie, Tim, Pediatric Gastroenterologist, Mass Gen Hosp, Harvard Med School, Presentation Oasis II Conference 14 Oct 2001

cination history and symptoms, but also the family's medical history. In particular, we need to ascertain whether there is a family history of autoimmune, allergic, or infectious disease. I will provide more information about my philosophy of testing, the usefulness and costs of tests, and the sequence of testing I usually recommend in Chapter Four.

How the Immune and GI Systems Interact

To understand why we need to take a broad spectrum approach to treating ASD children, it may be helpful to understand some basics about how the immune and gastrointestinal systems interact. The immune system is our body's chief defense against pathogenic bacteria, fungi, and viruses. It distinguishes between self and foreign molecules inside the body and mobilizes armies of defensive cells and antibodies against those foreign molecules. However, it is supposed to kick into action only if something is wrong. Many and possibly most children with autism have some form of immune system malfunction. Often, such malfunction involves misidentifying cells as foreign that are actually part of *self.* In this type of immune dysfunction, the immune system is attacking its host's body. This is one type of process among others that can cause inflammation of the gastrointestinal tract. Examples include viral persistence within intestinal tissues[5] as well as adverse colonizations by fungal or bacterial pathogens. As we have indicated, gastrointestinal inflammation and its underlying causes contribute to a cascade of other difficulties that constitute a major part of the disease process in many autism spectrum children.

Because the intestinal tract represents an important barrier between external pathogens and our internal organs, nature has incorporated a number of immune mechanisms into the epithelium, the gut lining whose job it is to block outside pathogens from doing any damage. When the specialized immune cells lining the intestinal tract detect unknown or possibly harmful antigens, signals are

[5] Wakefield A.J. et al., "Detection of herpesvirus DNA in the large intestine of patients with ulcerative colitis and Crohn's disease using nested polymerase chain reaction Jour. Med. Virology 1992 Nov;38(3): 183-90

generated and immune reinforcements are sent. Eventually, this response can include an "army" of cells to fight the invading antigens.
This "army" has several types of specialized "soldiers." For instance,
researchers have indentified Natural Killer cells (NK), cytotoxic T
cells, helper T-cells, and B-cells. Some T-cells construct special molecules that aid in identifying and eliminating pathogens, while other
cells produce and release antibodies that help only in the elimination
process. A further distinction is that many T-cells can be categorized in accord with their primary role, with Thymus 1(Th1) cells
participating in cell-mediated immunity and Th2 cells helping with
antibody-mediated defenses. Recent studies demonstrate that an immune profile tending to have more Th2 cells is conducive to chronic
fungal infections.[6] Autism-research studies have documented that
many autistic children have immune-cell counts that demonstrate a
Th2-like profile.[7] Not surprisingly, fecal-culture evaluations of many
autistic children reveal intestinal colonization by Candida species.

Long-time autism-researcher Sudhir Gupta, MD, PhD
—a professor of neurology, pathology, microbiology, and
molecular genetics at the University of California, Irvine—
has documented immune abnormalities in autism-spectrum
children.[8] He found that a large group of autistic patients
had relatively more Th2 cells than Th1 cells compared to
neurotypical children. Dr. Gupta believes the decrease in
Th1 cells may explain the susceptibility of autistic children
to viral and fungal infections. In addition, the increase in
their Th2 cells may also explain their increased autoimmune
responses against brain tissue as indicated by Dr. Singh's
findings of antibodies to the myelin basic protein (MBP)
mentioned in Chapter One.

Dr. Gupta also points out that the immune system controls the
release of various inflammatory mediators including Interleukin 1,
Interleukin 8, and tumor necrosis factor (TNF)—all of which cause
marked degrees of inflammation in the gut. His data and observa-

---

[6] Gupta, Sudhir, MD, PhD, Professor of microbiology and molecular genetics at Univ CA
    at Irvine, Presentation at DAN! Conference, Oct 5, 2001, San Diego
[7] Ibid
[8] Ibid

tions are helping identify at least a few of the immune dysfunctions and inflammatory bowel pathologies that cause so many autistic children to suffer. Furthermore, Dr. Gupta went on to say that the autopsied brains of autistic patients reveal alterations in neurotransmitters and neuropeptides, possibly even a loss of myelination (the protective covering) on nerve fibers similar to findings in the autopsied brains of multiple sclerosis patients. The brains of many autistic patients also showed increased levels of TNF, which creates inflammatory effects along the blood-brain barrier. Dr. Gupta stated that TNF increase causes inflammation leading to decreased blood flow and mitochondrial injury within the cells, decreased intracellular glutathione, and abnormal conduction or even cell death. Clearly, ischemic (oxygen deficient) brain cells would not be able to take in a full set of nutrients, even if provided by the diet.

HOW YEAST OVERGROWTH CAN INJURE THE GASTROINTESTINAL SYSTEM

It is well known that a weakened immune system—whether through genetic predisposition or acquired as a result of intestinal problems—leaves children open to chronic infections. Therefore, it is not surprising that Canadian researchers found a strong relationship between the incidence of autism and the prevalence of ear infections. In fact, they found that the increased incidence of ear infections correlated with the most severe form of autism.[9] Similar studies of other symptoms that make up the autism spectrum follow a similar pattern. For example, studies on children with ADHD show that high rates of ear infections in a child's early years correlate with greater amounts of hyperactivity.[10]

Although in most affected individuals the infections are probably not the primary cause of autism or ADHD, they may be a first step because otitis media is generally presumed to have an infectious, bacterial origin and because bacterial infections are generally treated with antibiotics. Ironically, large, PCR-based (polymerase chain reaction) studies by Tasnee Chonmaitree and colleagues have dem-

---

[9] M. Kontstantareas and S. Homatidis, "Ear Infections in Autistic and Normal Children, *Journal of Autism and Developmental Diseases, Vol. 17*, p. 585, 1987.

[10] R. Hagerman and A. Falkenstein, "An Association Between Recurrent Otitis Media in Infancy and Later Hyperactivity," *Clinical Pediatrics, Vol. 26*, pp. 253-257, 1987.

onstrated that approximately 35% of ear inflammations are not bacterial in origin. Furthermore, while antibiotics have saved millions of lives since World War II, many studies indicate that most medical doctors prescribe antibiotics far too often. One consequence of antibiotic overuse is that numerous bacteria are becoming resistant to antibiotics. Another ramification is that these "wonder drugs" kill protective (probiotic) bacteria in the gut as well as the pathogens. The destruction of beneficial gut-bacteria merits major concern. The process opens the door to overgrowth by fungi and bacteria. In many individual cases, the child's chronic diarrhea or constipation may be a symptom of yeast overgrowth.

How important are adverse intestinal colonizations by pathogenic fungi and/or bacteria? A noted researcher and clinical lab director—William Shaw, PhD—has written: "Abnormal byproducts of yeast and drug-resistant bacteria absorbed into the body from the intestine following the excessive use of antibiotics is the cause of these epidemics."[11] While I subscribe to the view that there are many factors and various causes for the current epidemic of autism, I certainly agree that, in many autistic children, bacterial and fungal overgrowths are etiologically significant in the cascade of events that result in autism or one of the other autism spectrum disorders.

When we are healthy, Candida lives in an uneasy balance or truce with our mixtures of beneficial and potentially harmful bacteria. Furthermore, as can some species of bacteria such as Clostridia, Candida can survive without oxygen and does so by changing into an anaerobic (without oxygen) fungal form. Most antibiotics kill only oxygen-breathing bacteria. Candida survives antibiotics and can spread like wildfire following the sudden die-off of intestinal bacteria. If for any reason, an infant or toddler already has a weakened immune system, the resulting colonizations—whether fungal and/or bacterial—can be unhealthy for the intestine.

"LEAKY GUT", INCREASED PERMEABILITY OF THE INTESTINAL MUCOSA AND MALABSORPTION

Many yeast species excrete toxic by-products which cause a variety of digestive illnesses including irritable bowel syndrome,

---

[11] William Shaw, *Biological Treatments for Autism and PDD,* self-published, 1998.

chronic constipation, or diarrhea. One of these toxic byproducts is an enzyme that allows the yeast to burrow into the intestinal wall which can contribute to what is termed the "leaky gut" syndrome. The yeast-generated toxins literally drill holes through the intestinal wall and seep into the child's bloodstream.[12] Ultimately, the toxic substances may inflame or cross the blood/brain barrier and, by interfering with the flow of nutrients to the brain, impair consciousness, cognition, speech, or behavior.

Another mechanism that may cause these children to have *starving brains* involves inadequate or inappropriate absorption of protein nutrients by the intestine. A healthy digestive system is able to take complex foods and break them down to forms that the cells of the body can absorb and metabolize into energy. As we have pointed out earlier, many children with autism have trouble digesting casein or gluten. Casein is a milk protein, and gluten is a plant protein found in wheat and related grains. Proteins are made of building blocks called amino acids; short strings or chains of amino acids are called peptides. During digestion, many proteins are broken down into single amino acids; others are transported as slightly larger chains. When ingested proteins are only partially digested, what remains are longer chain peptides. Some autism researchers have published articles in the scientific literature about malabsorption, maldigestion, and the related findings of unusual proteins and peptides in the urine of people with autism.[13] In many autistic children, those indigestible proteins and peptides come from casein and gluten; soy and corn can also be problematic.

Many peptide chains are flushed out in the urine. However, because many autistic children have leaky guts, an unacceptable amount of those substances can enter the bloodstream. The researchers we have already mentioned in Chapter One who found

---

[12] D'Eufemia P. et al. "Abnormal intestinal permeability in children with autism." Acta Paediatr 1996 Sep;85(9): 1076-9.

[13] *Malabsorption*
   B. Walsh, "85% of 500 autistic patients meet criteria for malabsorption," *J. Autism/Childhood Schizo*, 1971 1(1): 48-62;
   Maldigestion—elevated urinary peptides
   P Shattock, *Brain Dysfunct* 1990; 3: 338-45 and 1991; 4: 323-4)
   K. L. Reicheldt (*Develop Brain Dys* 1994; 7: 71-85, and others)
   Z. Sun and R. Cade (*Autism* 1999; 3: pp. 85-96 and 1999; 3: 67-83)

the unusual proteins and peptides in the urine of autistic patients discovered that those substances, when carried to the brain, have an opioid-like effect with a potency several times that of morphine, and named those unusual peptides *opioids*.

Paul Shattock, PhD, of the Autism Research Unit at the United Kingdom's University of Sunderland School of Health Sciences, says his studies indicate that there is "a rough correlation between the amount of opioids in the bodies of autistic children and the degree of severity of their impairments."[14] These natural morphine-like substances seem to drug the children and interfere with motivation, emotions, perception, response, and the normal development of their brains. Dr. Shattock says opioid peptides overstimulate nerve synapses and block normal signal transmissions to the brain.

In some children, the failure of the gut to properly digest the gluten and casein may, in part, be due to a low level of digestive enzymes. Such impairments can be acquired and, in some children, may be genetic. For children with impaired digestion, one treatment is to supplement their diet with certain digestive enzymes. However, a recent study found that although digestive enzymes helped, they were only half as effective as simply eliminating gluten and wheat from the diet. Furthermore, Dr. Shattock informs us that a two-year study found that many children with autism improve on the GF/CF diet, but that some regress if they return to eating wheat and milk products.

In my own practice, I have seen dramatic improvements in patients whose parents encourage or, let's be honest, require them to adhere to healthier diets. Even two-year-old ASD children are usually picky eaters. Regardless of age, it is often difficult, at least at the beginning of a new treatment plan, to encourage the child to discontinue sweet drinks and Chicken McNuggets. However, the potential benefits are worth it. As I will keep repeating, at present I strongly recommend that every parent of an autistic child totally eliminate gluten and casein from their children's diets for at least a four to six-month trial. In Chapter Five, I will tell you how to accomplish this.

---

[14] DAN Fall, 2001 conference, Oct. 5-7, San Diego, CA

FURTHER NOTES ON
THE MERCURY/VACCINE CONNECTION

Many extensively researched papers and books have been written describing the toxic effects of mercury. Dr. Sudhir Gupta at the Fall 2001 DAN! Conference said, "Genes load the gun, environment pulls the trigger." He explained that sulfhydryl groups are present in cellular mitochondria, that mercury binds these groups, necrotizing DNA, altering cell membrane permeability, and affecting calcium transport. Mercury causes a shift from Th1 to Th2 immunity, dysregulates signaling mechanism, and induces autoimmunity. The noted researcher stated, "Thimerosal is a mitochondrial poison and autism is a disorder of mitochondria." This poison disturbs the ratio between death and rebirth of cells. Gupta produced a graph from his studies showing an increase in cell death rising in direct proportion to the amount of thimerosal present. Evidence is accruing that vaccinal mercury could have been a likely trigger for an entire generation of kids who, due to individual susceptibility, may have succumbed to this unanticipated form of mercury poisoning. I will be discussing the issue of impaired detoxification mechanisms and mercury more extensively in Chapter Three.

Putting the Puzzle Pieces Together

Which comes first, the "chicken" or the "egg?" This riddle can serve as an analogy for the controversy about which are the primary causative agents behind autism and other autism spectrum disorders. One can start from the proposition that abnormally large spaces present between the cell walls of the gut (possibly caused by genetics or by adverse pathogen colonizations) allow opioids and other toxic materials to enter the bloodstream. Since they are "out of place," the immune system recognizes these substances as foreign and makes antibodies against them. I didn't mention earlier that the immune system also has a "memory." When it sees what it perceives as an invader for the second, third, or subsequent time, it mobilizes even larger armies of antibodies to strike back. In our gastrointestinal tracts, the antibodies made to protect against those abnormal proteins and peptides get aimed at the foods that originated them. This appears to be one route by which food allergies and sensitivities arise.

Of course, those antibodies trigger inflammatory reactions in the gastrointestinal tract when the offending foods are consumed. Thus chronic inflammation, perhaps originally caused by yeast or perhaps by other invading microorganisms, keeps renewing itself. The constant inflammation weakens the protective coatings of another type of antibody (immunoglobulin A or IgA) that is normally present in healthy intestines. IgA is made in bone marrow and lymphoid tissue and protects us against bacterial and viral infections by facilitating phagocytosis (the absorption and destruction of pathogenic cells by the immune cells). IgA also inhibits the inflammatory effects of tumor necrosis factor, and is an important defense mechanism to prevent colonization of yeast and Clostridia. Patients with gastrointestinal pathology often have reduced levels of IgA. A child so affected would be less resistant to viruses, bacteria, parasites, and yeast.

Although some intestinal pathogens continue to pass through the permeable intestine into the bloodstream, they generally are destroyed by the immune reaction. Yet their cell-wall fragments can induce inflammation and, to some extent, may be transported to locations throughout the body including the liver, blood brain barrier, and the brain itself. In large enough amounts, those toxic substances can impair or even overwhelm the liver's ability to detoxify them. I believe that the buildup of this pathogenic debris can result in symptoms including brain fog, memory loss, and confusion. So you see, where we start the analytic process doesn't matter; autistic children's underlying pathologies are complex and remarkably interlinked. Nonetheless, of primary importance is what these various processes tell us about how we might intervene with healing treatments.

Clinical lab data from children with intestinal pathology, food hypersensitivities, or "leaky gut" often reveal a long list of vitamin and mineral deficiencies. In fact, I and many DAN! physicians believe that gastrointestinal pathology is why the majority of autistic children have abnormal nutritional profiles. Various tests and studies have documented deficiencies in many important vitamins and minerals including calcium, copper, magnesium, and zinc. Similarly, other studies have shown that ADHD children are deficient in vitamins B6 and B12; some have fatty acid deficiencies. All these deficiencies are physical manifestations of medical problems that can be treated. We will be discussing tests to diagnose these deficiencies in Chapter Four and nutrient-replacement treatments in Chapter Six.

Like the classic "chicken and egg" puzzler, what is cause and what is effect in the etiology or development of ASD in many individual cases may remain an unanswerable question. However, it is important that we are unraveling and understanding more and more about those complex processes. We don't need perfect understanding to begin effective treatments. Since research study data and clinical lab data increasingly point in similar directions, we now have sufficient evidence to try several common-sense treatment approaches.

In the present environment of increasingly hopeful understanding, the concept *subgroups* is vitally important. We know that some children respond to certain treatments and others respond to different ones. The variability of response may have to do with the initial trigger, the intensity of the injury, the length of time the condition has existed, and the amount of damage that has been done to the immune and gastrointestinal systems as well as to various body organs before treatment was initiated.

We cannot lose sight of the bottom line: even with variable responses to various treatments, most children improve with biomedical treatment. That is why several different treatment approaches have to be taken and possibly continued even if some of the treatments overlap. The earlier parents begin treatment, the greater the chances that the child will get better. Often, a synergistic effect occurs between treatments. That means a composite treatment approach may be more effective than implementing one treatment protocol at a time.

You, as a parent or a physician, may be thinking, "Which treatments come first?" We will talk about that question in Chapters Five to Eight. However, in the next chapter, I want to help you understand why I and many other DAN! physicians believe that removing mercury and other heavy metals from the bodies of these children is essential when testing reveals impaired detoxification or a problematic presence of toxic metals. Basically, our current understanding is that treatments often helpful to the ASD child will take longer to be effective if they work at all, *as long as the children remain toxic*. We cannot afford to waste precious time during their early developing years.

THREE

IMPAIRED DETOXIFICATION, TOXIC ACCUMULATIONS, AND POLITICS

Toxic Threats to Child Development

An increasing body of clinical data indicates that many children with autism spectrum disorder cannot efficiently dispose of toxic substances that enter their bodies. For example, as metals accumulate, these children become ill with various forms of heavy metal poisoning. Laboratory tests documenting chelation induced metal outflow reveal that many ASD children have accumulated lead, tin, mercury, and/or some other heavy metals. Many of these children treated with physician supervised chelation preceded by gut-healing and nutritional support are showing major alleviation of autism-spectrum traits. Some children on this protocol have outgrown their diagnosis of autism.[1]

The reasons why natural detoxification is impaired for many ASD children remain to be determined. However, medical histories

---

[1] Amy Holmes, MD, Jane El-Dahr, MD, Stephanie Cave, MD, DAN! Conference Panel Presentation, San Diego CA, Oct. 2001

and medical literature are providing strong clues. The recent report by Greater Boston Physicians for Social Responsibility entitled *In Harm's Way: Toxic Threats to Child Development*[2] referred to in Chapter One links lifelong disabilities to toxic exposures of lead, mercury, other heavy metals, and pesticides prevalent in our environment during early childhood or even before birth. The Boston physicians' report states that "learning and behavioral disorders are increasing in frequency." They cite research that indicates toxic substances such as mercury, lead, and pesticides contribute to many neurobehavioral and cognitive disorders. The report further states: "Unlike an adult, the developing child exposed to neurotoxic chemicals during critical developmental windows of vulnerability may suffer from lifelong impacts on brain function."

Findings and news releases from the FDA and EPA have stressed that pregnant women should minimize fish consumption so as to reduce the intake of dietary mercury that can affect fetal development. In this context, it is not surprising that distinguished immunologist Hugh Fudenberg, MD, PhD, has long recommended the removal of metals for autistic children. In addition, Stephen Edelson, MD[3] and colleagues have published peer-reviewed studies wherein autism spectrum traits were significantly eliminated in response to chelation and related therapies. More recently, a revolutionary paper, first drafted by parents of autistic children and then published in 2000, called attention to the similarities between autism-spectrum traits and those induced by mercury poisoning.[4] That paper also drew upon FDA data regarding the presence of ethylmercury in some childhood vaccines and suggested that, at least in infants and toddlers with increased susceptibility, the ethylmercury injected during vaccinations may have induced intestinal and neurologic damage.

This seminal paper was pivotal in prompting an expanded interest in removing toxic metals from ASD children, which has led to

---

[2] Greater Boston Physicians for Social Responsibility, May 2000, "In Harm's Way: Adverse Toxic Chemical Influences on Developmental Disabilities," 11 Garden St, Cambridge MA 02138, phone 617-497-7440

[3] Edelson, S.B., Cantor, D.S. "Autism: xenobiotic influences." Toxicol Ind Health 1998;14: 553-563

[4] Bernard, S., Enayati A., Redwood L., Roger H., Binstock T., "Autism: A Novel Form of Mercury Poisoning , Med Hypotheses 2001 Apr;56(4): 462-71. Original long version, online at http://www.autism.com/ari/mercury.html

encouraging clinical results thus far. In fact, pursuant to a vaccinal ethylmercury hearing on July 16, 2001, the Institute of Medicine (a division of the National Academy of Sciences) found the mercury/ autism hypothesis to be plausible and subsequently funded two on-going clinical studies wherein autism spectrum children are receiving chelation therapy in the context of gut healing and nutritional support. To say the least, all these developments are exciting and profoundly important to the treatment of ASD. To understand the impaired detoxification process more deeply, some background information about heavy metals will be helpful.

Heavy metals enter our bodies as a result of eating and breathing. Yes, food and air contain tiny quantities of toxic metals. They can even be absorbed through our skin. Furthermore, heavy metals are "bio-accumulative." That is, they can chemically bond to molecules within mammalian bodies, be difficult to excrete, and be passed up the food chain to humans. This is the reason we are warned of the dangers of mercury accumulation in fish, especially tuna and the large predator fish such as shark and swordfish. When heavy metals enter and accumulate in body tissues faster than the body can excrete them, a state of toxicity can develop that injures tissue and nerve cells. As we have stressed in previous chapters, a growing number of physicians, researchers, and parents now believe that impaired detoxification and excessive accumulation of toxic metals are primary etiological factors in many cases of autism and other autism spectrum disorders.

A recent study by James Adams, PhD, backs up that belief. In research financed by Arizona State University, he explored the question of whether "Mercury and other heavy metals contribute to the causes and/or symptoms of autism."[5] Dr. Adams and his colleagues studied 55 ASD children ages three to 24 and compared them to a control group of 30 "typical" children. Parents of both groups of children filled out a questionnaire designed to rate their known exposure to heavy metals. All the children also had hair analyses, dental exams, and underwent psychological testing including the Gilliam Autism Rating Scale, a commonly used test instrument to determine the severity of autism. The autistic children were found

---

[5] Interview with Dr. Adams, 01-18-2002. Copy of handout about the study is available at http://eas.asu.edu/~autism/

to have ten times the number of ear infections during the first three years of life compared to the normal children. Eighteen percent of the autism spectrum children also had experienced severe reactions to vaccines compared to zero percent of the "typical" children. The ASD children also had lower levels of mercury and lead in their hair than the "typical" children, indicating that excretion was not taking place as it did in the control group children. Dr. Adams points out that antibiotics which are often used to treat children's earaches, "greatly reduce mercury excretion." He stated that ASD children excrete "five times as much mercury" as typical children when given DMSA, an oral chelating agent used to remove heavy metals from the body.

"Together, our study suggests ASD children have inhibited ability to excrete heavy metals," Dr. Adams told scientists gathered at an international autism meeting in San Diego, CA in November of 2001. "Overall, mercury appears to be a major risk factor for ASD," he and his team of researchers concluded.[6]

Animal studies of lead and mercury have revealed that scientists previously had underestimated the levels of human exposure to these metals.[7] According to EPA guidelines, many neonates, infants, and toddlers have been injected with unsafe levels of ethylmercury through vaccinations. In retrospect, some of these children were certain to have become more susceptible to developing adverse effects as a consequence.[8] In short, our nation's children have experienced unprecedented exposure to heavy metals. This fact may be reflected in various epidemics whose increase cannot be due merely to "genetics." Our children's minds are at risk. The epidemics of autism, autism-spectrum disorders, and even Alzheimer's and other diseases may well be reflections of increased exposure to heavy metals.

---

[6] Ibid
[7] Greater Boston Physicians for Social Responsibility, May 2000, *In Harm's Way: Toxic Threats to Child Development*, p. 7.
[8] Hattis D. et al. "Distributions of individual susceptibility among humans for toxic effects. How much protection does the traditional tenfold factor provide for what fraction of which kinds of chemicals and effects?" Ann NY Acad Sci 1999;104:s2: 381-90

The Mechanism of Heavy Metal Toxicity

As we have emphasized, mercury and other heavy metals can adversely affect the gastrointestinal, immune, nervous, and endocrine systems. Heavy metals alter cellular function and numerous metabolic processes in the body, including those related to the central and peripheral nervous systems.[9] Much of the damage produced by heavy metals comes from the proliferation of oxidative free radicals. A free radical is an energetically unbalanced molecule, composed of an unpaired electron that "steals" an electron from another molecule. Free radicals occur naturally when cell molecules react with oxygen (oxidize). However, excessive free-radical production occurs when a person is exposed to heavy metals or when an adult or child has genetic or acquired antioxidant deficiencies. Unchecked, the free radicals can cause tissue damage throughout the body including the brain. Fortunately, laboratory and clinical studies have shown that antioxidants such as vitamins A, C, and E, can protect against and, to some extent, repair free-radical damage.[10] Another substance important to proper detoxification is glutathione, which is considered elsewhere in this book.

Specific Heavy Metals: Lead and Mercury

LEAD

Lead is known as a neurotoxin—in plain English, a killer of brain cells. Excessive lead levels in children's blood have been linked to learning disabilities, to attention deficit disorder (ADD) and hyperactivity syndromes, and to reduced intelligence and school achievement scores. The greatest risk for harm, even with only minute or short-term exposure, occurs among infants, young children, and pregnant women and their fetuses. After a century of intensive study, the harm from lead "can now be characterized with fair certainty.[11]

---

[9] Klassen C.D., editor. Casaret & Doull's Toxicology: the Basic Science of Poisons, 5th ed; McGraw-Hill, 1996

[10] James W. Anderson, MD and Maury M. Breecher, PhD, MPH, *Dr. Anderson's Antioxidant, Antiaging Health Program*, 1996, Carroll & Graf, Inc., NYC, p. 6

[11] Ibid, p. 119

Since childhood lead exposure has been ongoing since lead paint was first introduced in the 1890's, five generations of children have been injured while science has slowly advanced to where it is now capable of appreciating the magnitude of the problem. This same pattern of "after-the-fact" recognition of harm has been repeated for mercury.

In 1984, a federal study conducted by the Center for Disease Control (CDC) estimated that three to four million American children have unacceptably high levels of lead in their blood. This is an even higher figure than in the Boston Physicians' Report mentioned earlier. Dr. Suzanne Binder, a CDC official, stated, "Many people believed that when lead paint was banned from housing [in 1978], and lead was cut from gasoline [in the late 1970s], lead-poisoning problems disappeared, but they're wrong. We know that throughout the country children of all races, ethnic backgrounds, and income levels are being affected by lead already in the environment."[12]

In 1989, the U.S. Environmental Protection Agency (EPA) reported that more than one million elementary schools, high schools, and colleges are still using lead-lined water storage tanks or lead-containing components in their drinking fountains. The EPA estimates that drinking water accounts for approximately 20% of young children's lead exposure.[13] Other common sources are lead paint residue in older buildings (common in inner cities) and living in proximity to industrial areas or other sources of toxic chemical exposure, such as commercial agricultural land.

MERCURY

It is not as if the dangers of mercury had not already been understood by the chemical and pharmaceutical industries. No less a historic personality than Isaac Newton is said to have been affected by mercury poisoning. Historians note that Newton's personality changed dramatically at age 35, and again at age 51, after he conducted experiments involving heated mercury. In modern times, scientists who analyzed a lock of Newton's hair found unusually

---

[12] Breecher, M., Linde, S., 1992, *Healthy Homes in a Toxic World,* John Wiley and Sons, Inc.
[13] Ibid

high levels of mercury probably from inhalation of the dangerous fumes.[14] Even 19th Century author Lewis Carroll knew that mercury is one of the most toxic substances on earth. Indeed, he indirectly referred to its dangers through the "Mad Hatter," his *Alice in Wonderland* character. When Lewis Carroll wrote that book, hat makers used mercury in the process of making hats. One of their occupational hazards was a type of mercury induced insanity called "Mad Hatter's" disease. Modern day manufacturers also have recognized the dangers of mercury.

As we have stated previously, concern about mercury stems from its effects on the brain, nervous system, and gastrointestinal system. Mercury poisoning induces cognitive and social deficits, including loss of speech or failure to develop it, memory impairment, poor concentration, word comprehension difficulties, and an assortment of autism-like behaviors including sleep difficulties, self-injurious behavior (e.g. head banging and self-biting,) agitation, unprovoked crying, and staring spells.[15]

Sources of mercury exposure include air and water pollution, amalgam dental fillings,[16] batteries, cosmetics, shampoos, mouthwashes, toothpaste, soaps, mercurial diuretics, electrical devices and relays, explosives, residues in foods (especially grains), fungicides, fluorescent lights, freshwater fish such as bass, pike, and trout, insecticides, pesticides, paints, petroleum products, saltwater fish such as halibut, shrimp, snapper, swordfish, shark, tuna, and shellfish. According to EPA estimates, about 1.16 million women in the U.S. of childbearing years eat sufficient amounts of mercury-contaminated fish to risk damaging the brain development of their children.[17]

Dental fillings are an important source of mercury contamination. Amalgam fillings release microscopic particles and vapors of mercury. This shedding of mercury is increased by chewing and

---

[14] Maury M. Breecher, PhD, MPH and Shirley Linde, PhD, 1992, *Healthy Homes in a Toxic World,* John Wiley and Sons, Inc., p. 141.

[15] Bernard, S. et al., "Autism: a Novel Form of Mercury Poisoning," Med. Hypotheses 2001 Apr;56(4): pp. 462-71. Original long version, Jun 2000, http://www.autism.com/ari/mercury.html

[16] Eggleston, D. et al., "Correlation of dental amalgams with mercury in brain tissue," J. Pros. Dent. 58: 704-7, 1987

[17] Greater Boston Physicians for Social Responsibility, May 2000, *In Harm's Way: Toxic Threats to Child Development,* p. 4.

by drinking hot liquids. Those vapors are absorbed by tooth roots, mucous membranes of the mouth and gums, and are inhaled and swallowed, thereby reaching the esophagus, stomach, and intestines. University of Calgary researchers report 10% of amalgam mercury eventually accumulates in body organs.[18]

Years after amalgam removal, some of my adult clients have shown high mercury urine output with a chelation challenge, with subsequent improvement in health after chelation.

Ingested mercury can be passed to the fetus in wombs of pregnant mothers from the mother's amalgams when she chews, and particularly when she has either placement or removal dental work involving amalgams. In March 2002 the parents of a five-year-old child brought suit against the American Dental Association, alleging mercury in the mother's nine dental fillings caused her son's autism. Also named as defendants were the California Dental Association and more than 20 corporations that deal in materials used to produce amalgam fillings, which are about 50% mercury by weight. The lawsuit accused them of fraud, negligence and illegal and deceptive business practices. Many lawsuits have been filed against drug companies alleging links between autism and vaccines containing mercury, but attorneys and scientists familiar with such litigation say this is believed to be the first to allege a connection between autism and amalgam fillings.

"I don't know that it's proven, but it's credible, very credible," said Dr. Boyd Haley, chairman of the chemistry department at the University of Kentucky and an expert on mercury toxicity. "Mercury is one of the most neurotoxic compounds known to man." Dr. Haley said some studies show people with amalgam fillings have four to five times as much mercury in their blood and urine as people without such fillings.

Mercury in Vaccines

The insidious avenue of mercury poisoning through the ethylmercury preservative in several vaccines has already been mentioned in

---

[18] Kupsinel, Roy MD, "Mercury amalgam toxicity," J. Orthomol. Psychiat, 13(4): pp. 140-57; 1984

both Chapters One and Two. In this section I will summarize more of the terrifying details of how this came about.

Thimerosal is 49.6% ethylmercury by weight and, since the 1930's, has been used as a vaccine preservative intended to protect against bacterial contamination in multi-use containers.[19] The Manufacturers' Safety Data sheet for thimerosal states that the substance is "highly toxic," and warns about the danger of "cumulative effects" and "prolonged or repeated exposure" to mercury. That is because a danger point for mercury toxicity occurs when the rate of exposure exceeds the rate of elimination. This "threshold effect" then results in a neurotoxic shock to the immune system which can show itself months after exposure. As suggested earlier, this may be why children diagnosed with the "regressive" form of autism experience normal development from birth, then suddenly start regressing after further insults to their immune systems with other vaccines, notably the live viruses in the MMR.

As we have stated, a great deal of evidence implicates thimerosal as one of the primary etiologic triggers responsible for the current epidemic of "regressive autism," a trend that rapidly accelerated in the early 1990s. Furthermore, the historical record clearly shows that what were once considered "safe thresholds" for known neurotoxicants have continuously been "revised downward" as scientific knowledge advances."[20]

Ironically, as knowledge about the neurotoxcity of mercury accumulated during the 20th Century and as concerns were raised about mercury's ubiquitous and increasing environmental presence, no one thought to question its safety in vaccines—not even after an expert FDA panel had concluded in 1982 that thimerosal was unsafe and should be removed from all over-the-counter products! In fact, during the Institute of Medicine's (IOM) thimerosal/autism hearing on July 16, 2001, U.S. vaccine official Neal Halsey, MD, apologized for not having realized sooner that thimerosal-containing

---

[19] Vaccine Fact Sheets, National Vaccine Program Office, Centers for Disease Control website http://www.cdc.gov/od/nvpo/fs_tableVI_doc2.htm (This so-called "fact sheet" also contains the blunt statement that "There is no evidence that children have been harmed by the amount of mercury found in vaccines that contain thimerosal."

[20] Greater Boston Physicians for Social Responsibility, May 2000, *In Harm's Way: Toxic Threats to Child Development*, p. 14.

vaccines contained dangerously high levels of ethylmercury. It is a tragedy that this toxic substance in vaccines was overlooked.

The situation got out of hand in 1991 when the Hepatitis B vaccination was mandated for every newborn. This vaccine was loaded with thimerosal. Infants got not one, but three doses of Hepatitis B vaccine and three doses of the thimerosal-containing Hib or Human Influenza B vaccine during the first six months of their lives. Not counting maternal exposures, for many infants the levels of mercury exceeded the EPA's guidelines for "safe" exposure *in adults.* The accumulation of mercury in their small bodies may have exceeded the threshold of their ability to excrete the toxin. Children who do not exhibit ASD symptoms may simply have had higher thresholds or stronger immune systems. Breast fed babies have been shown to be less susceptible to getting the disorder and some mothers have reported their child became autistic shortly after cessation of breast-feeding, which is known to convey many immunity benefits.

A reasonable person might assume that American health authorities would have learned from the experience of other countries. For example, over 15,000 lawsuits were filed against the mandatory Hep B vaccination program in France, which led to the French Minister of Health finally ending that program for all French school children in October of 1998.[21] However, it was not until late in 2001 that mercury was removed from the Hep B vaccine and most other vaccines in the U.S. By then an entire generation of kids had been put at risk. Yet this removal did not occur until after Bernard et al had sent their thimerosal/autism paper to officials at the CDC, FDA, AMA, and NIH. The long version of the paper contained more than 400 citations. It also contained the comparison table that described how mercury poisoning causes speech and hearing deficits, sensory disturbances including sensitivity to loud noises, aversion to touch, and cognitive and behavioral impairments (See Appendix B). These same deficits are present in greater or lesser degrees in children with autism and autistic spectrum disorder. In brief, medical literature about mercury poisoning includes all the traits that define autism (DSM-IV) and other traits that are associated with ASD generally.

---

[21] http://www.909shot.com/hepfrance.htm

The scientific justification was overwhelming. Ethylmercury should never have been injected into humans, regardless of age.

The Saga of Several Autism Parents and "Parent Power"

The role of vaccinal ethylmercury was first realized by several parents of autism spectrum children. Albert and Sima Enayati, Sallie Bernard, Heidi Roger, and Lynn Redwood heard the FDA's 1999 announcement that some vaccines contained thimerosal, realized that mercury poisoning may have contributed to their children's autistic regression, and with Teresa Binstock began researching and writing the report that became known as the "Bernard et al mercury/autism paper." As the research materials accumulated and the paper took shape, this group began contacting officials at the CDC, FDA, AMA, and NIH. Surprisingly, officials at each of these agencies met with the co-authors and some of their supporters. The paper had called attention to a potentially important danger. Within the first year after the mercury/autism paper's long version was made available, vaccine manufacturers began removing thimerosal from most vaccines, vaccinating neonates with the hepatitis B vaccine was restricted, and thimerosal's adverse effects were reviewed by the Institute of Medicine and through a Congressional hearing led by Dan Burton of Indiana and the House Government Reform Committee.

The dedication and persistence of this small group of parents alerted the world to the autism epidemic's probable connection with vaccinal ethylmercury. When the Bernard et al co-authors calculated the amounts of mercury a child received for each of his or her recommended vaccines, they found that infants could be exposed to levels of mercury that exceeded the EPA's guideline of 0.1 micrograms of methylmercury per kilogram of infant body weight per day. Sally Bernard, Lyn Redwood, Albert Enayati and Heidi Roger then went on to create an advocacy group called "Safe Minds," which steadfastly lobbies against mercury-containing vaccines.

Since the distribution and publication of the "mercury/autism paper," thousands of parents have come to believe that their children's regression into autism was caused or augmented by vaccinations containing mercury. For many such parents, this belief was reinforced after chelation related lab tests confirmed high levels of mercury in their child. In 1999 the FDA issued a letter to vaccine manufacturers asking, *but not ordering,* that mercury-containing thimerosal be removed from vaccines. Finally, in 2000, the FDA cited a joint statement by the American Academy of Pediatrics and the U.S. Public Health Service that "called for the removal of thimerosal from vaccines as soon as possible."[22] Even after all that, the nation's physicians and hospitals were allowed until late in 2001 to use up already purchased stockpiles of mercury-containing vaccines, including the Hep B vaccine. In other words, despite the known toxicity of mercury and its organic compounds, more children may have been injured during the two-year period following the FDA's admission that many infant and toddler vaccines contained high levels of ethylmercury.

It is interesting to note that, pursuant to federal drug-safety laws, a coalition of more than 35 law firms in 25 states filed a lawsuit in October 2001 to force drug companies to study how the presence of mercury has affected children.[23] In Texas and Florida other groups of lawyers are suing vaccine and thimerosal manufacturers for damages, medical costs, and nursing care for what they believe to be the thimerosal-caused autism of young children. The threat of lawsuits may have been a factor in finally persuading vaccine makers to remove mercury from most vaccines given to children. However, despite this flurry of litigation, the most important fact is that many autism spectrum children show incredible improvement in response to physician-supervised chelation when combined with gut healing and nutritional support. The lawyers' ads on television asking, "Could your child have autism because of vaccines?" have raised awareness in many parents previously ignorant of the saga surrounding vaccines and autism. This awareness has also increased the need for more doctors who are willing to biomedically evaluate these children—including ordering laboratory tests for heavy metal

---

[22] Letter from Center for Biologics Evaluation and Research, a department within the U.S. Food and Drug Administration, July 4, 2000.

[23] Bob Wheaton, "Mom Says Mercury in Vaccine Harmed Child." *The Flint (Michigan) Journal,* Oct. 22, 2001.

accumulation. These tests and others will be discussed in Chapter Four and also Chapter Seven.

Susceptibility, Timings, & Thresholds

Many questions remain: If the accumulation of toxic metals is an etiologic basis for many cases of autism, why are most similarly exposed children not affected? If a child's accumulation of toxic metals can induce autism spectrum traits, why is there so much variation from child to child? Might toxic metals be a contributing etiology in at least some children with PDD, Tourette's Syndrome, or ADHD?

As researchers, physicians, and parents begin to use laboratory test data to answer these questions, topics such as familial genetics and the timing of exposure to toxic metals naturally arise. Another factor is the child's health at the time a large initial or repeated exposure is experienced. The concept that winds through all of these explorations is *susceptibility*, which we have mentioned in previous chapters. At any given time in their young lives, some children may have increased susceptibility to a toxin such as lead or mercury and for various reasons. The child's increased susceptibility may have a genetic basis[24] and thus would tend to be chronic or ongoing. In contrast, various illnesses can weaken immunity, thereby impairing detoxification and increasing susceptibility. In other words, a sick child may be likelier to experience adverse reactions to toxic metals both immediate and/or delayed than would a healthy child. Variations in immunity, in detoxification status, and in nutritional level affect susceptibility along with exposure levels and the infant's or toddler's age at the time exposure occurred. In my opinion, this complex tapestry accounts for why some children are not affected, why others are autistic, or why still others enter the non-autistic portion of the ASD spectrum. Clearly vaccines, even those that do not contain thimerosal, should not be administered to children who have an infectious illness. Dr. Stephanie Cave, with Deborah Mitchell, has recently published an excellent book on vaccinations that I

---

[24] Westphal GA et al. Homozygous gene deletions of the glutathione S-transferases M1 and T1 are associated with thimerosal sensitization. Int Arch Occup Environ Health. 2000 Aug;73(6):384-8

recommend to all parents, entitled, "What Your Doctor May Not Tell You About Childhood Vaccinations."[25]

Increased susceptibility and toxic injury so early in life can open the door for a number of later adverse events, several of which appear to be etiologically significant within subgroups of autism spectrum children. Recall our discussion in Chapter Two where we described how mercury becomes an irritant to the intestinal mucosa. Mercury attaches itself to sulfur in the gastrointestinal tract, causing widespread disruption of transport mechanisms, peptides, and enzymes. This can lead to gut inflammation, inhibition of digestive enzymes and peptides, and difficulty digesting dairy and wheat products.

It all fits together. Mercury and other heavy metals can damage gastrointestinal tissues, alter immune function, and impair intake of nutrients necessary to feed the brain properly. All this leads to *children with starving brains.*

---

[25] Cave, Stephanie (with Deborah Mitchell), "What Your Doctor May Not Tell You About Childhood Vaccinatiions," Warner Books Sept 2001

PART TWO

Diagnosis and Treatment

FOUR

CLINICAL AND DIAGNOSTIC EVALUATION

To briefly summarize the first three chapters: I have described how autism spectrum disorder is a complex multi-system medical illness with immunological, gastrointestinal, and neurological issues. The disorder is being increasingly recognized as having a variety of etiologies, and precise mechanisms are still being studied for both the genetic and environmental issues involved. The more scientists learn about autism, the more complex the disorder appears. Many of us have come to accept that a common etiology arises from a genetic susceptibility that gets triggered by one or more environmentally based injuries, pathogenic insults, and/or toxic exposures in the womb or early childhood. Since ASD can involve so many major systems of the body, I believe an affected child should receive an intensive clinical and diagnostic evaluation to identify the affected body systems and underlying pathologies as a basis for subsequent treatment. In this chapter I describe my current evaluation and testing procedures.

Bio-Medical Evaluation

Parents need to know at the outset that the complexity of ASD means that diagnostics and treatment are neither easy nor quick. A great deal of devotion, time, patience, and hard work is required; the strains upon economic and emotional resources may be great. Prolonged treatment falls 24/7 on the shoulders of the parents, even when they have been fortunate enough to find a caring and knowledgeable health practitioner to guide their child's treatment.

A further challenge faces parents who are considering embarking upon the journey of biomedical approaches to ASD. That is, almost all but *not all* affected children improve. As of 2003, there is no clear way to determine whether a child will improve in a major way, or just a little, or not at all. However, the improvements that occur for many autistic children diagnosed and treated biomedically are likely *not* to occur if the parents and the child's primary physician fail to explore the possibilities available now.

When looking clinically at hundreds or even dozens of autism spectrum children, much variation is seen from child to child. These variations in medical history, health status, and biomedical profile call for a personalized evaluative approach for each child. The first step in my bio-medical evaluation of a new patient consists of preparing a thorough family and child health history in the form of an extensive questionnaire followed by an interview, preferably in person but possibly by phone for those living at a distance. These histories often provide important clues in determining whether the child fits into one of the autism spectrum's biomedical subgroups. Does the family have a history of autoimmunity or allergies? Are there indications of viral presence, heavy metal toxicity, or other special categories? Is anyone else in the child's family affected by an autism-spectrum disorder? Answers to these questions often help us design a treatment likely to be effective.

FAMILY AND MEDICAL HISTORY

Family

An extensive questionnaire should detail family history, especially regarding relatives with autism spectrum disorder (ADD, ADHD,

PDD, Asperger's, high-functioning autism), dyslexia, learning disorders, autoimmune disorders, Down Syndrome, Alzheimer's, mental retardation, mental illnesses such as recurrent depression, bi-polar disorders, and schizophrenia. Particular note should be taken of maternal health or toxic exposures, specifically:

Before conception: Mother's health (particularly autoimmune conditions and any indication of immune system impairment[1]), general nutritional status, genetic predispositions on either maternal or paternal sides of the family, maternal vaccinations near time of conception.

During gestation: Toxic exposures (e.g. mother's dental work done with amalgam placement or removal), ingestion of large amounts of mercury-contaminated fish, exposures to pesticides or other heavy metals such as lead, maternal malnutrition, Rh factors, viral or other maternal illnesses, pregnancy complications, medications.

During birthing and early infancy: Infant pre- or post-maturity, difficult labor, breast-feeding difficulty, milk or soy allergy in non-breast fed infants, feeding and digestive problems, vaccinations particularly with thimerosal, infections, antibiotic treatments.

Child

Delivery issues, labor and delivery problems, condition at birth, weight, APGAR score, and mother's age at delivery. Medical: breast-feeding experience, digestive problems, vaccination history with any noted reactions, infections, antibiotic use, seizures, other medications, allergies, surgeries, dental work. Further details are often extremely helpful. Specifically:

- **Development:** General: Eating patterns, toileting patterns, sleeping patterns. Size in relation to same age peers. Age walking began, speech began, speech delay, any regressions noted in language, peculiarities in speech, eye contact history.

---

[1] Comi A.M. et al. "Familial clustering of autoimmune edisorders and evaluation of medical risk factors in autism," J. Child. Neurol. 1999 Jun;14(6): 388-94, Johns Hopkins Hospital Div of Ped Neurology, Baltimore MD

- **Detailed vaccination history:** Dates given, number of shots given at one time, health status if known at time of vaccination, unusual reactions (excessive crying, fevers) noted. Many parents have documented the timings and amounts of ethylmercury injected during vaccinations, as well as incidents of multiple vaccinations per visit to their doctor.

- **Detailed dietary and stool history:** How long breast-fed, when milk/soy products introduced. Food likes and dislikes, allergies, need for and reaction to special diets. What kind of diet the rest of the family eats generally. History of diarrhea or constipation, reflux, presence of yeast infections, including treatments and results.

- **Personality:** Alertness, fears, phobias, repetitious activities, mood swings, hyper or hypoactive, temper tantrums, inconsolable crying spells. Attachment and relating issues: Closest bond, making and keeping friends, affection, reactions to other children, pets, baby-sitters, daycare, teacher reactions. Imagination pattern, motor development, handedness, eye contact, reaction to change, sense of humor, self-sufficiency. Need for special schooling, nature of any learning disabilities.

PRETESTING CONSIDERATIONS

Many parents usually go to a specialist in autism for a biomedical evaluation and treatment if they can find one. For these families, the primary pediatrician remains the person the child sees for general check-ups, routine vaccinations, and for treatment of infections, injuries, or chronic medical conditions. Many ASD children have already been tested to rule out the well-known genetic abnormalities before seeking help from an autism specialist.

For the autism bio-medical consultation, it can be helpful for the specialist to see the child with his/her family, noting the relationships of the child with siblings and parents. General observation of health, skin color, general tone, motor development, alertness, eye contact, fearfulness, speech patterns, handedness, and attachment and relating behavior helps the physician have a base line for comparison with later stages in the child's treatment and development. Watching the child play with toys is instructive; asking the child to write or draw gives a lot of information about language receptiveness as well as fine motor development and level of conceptualizing. Extent and quality of verbalization should be noted for comparison as treatment progresses.

In cases where the pre-testing evaluation (and perhaps follow-up treatment as well) is done at a distance, serial candid photographs of the child and monthly status report forms filled out by the parents are very helpful in documenting progress. For me, e-mailing has often been convenient, saves time trying to return phone calls, and leaves a dated record for the patient's chart for both me and the parents. E-mail has become one of my favorite ways to get progress reports from the parents and give them feedback on testing results and further treatment considerations. Besides the telephone being more disruptive and intrusive and less efficient than e-mail (if there is anyone busier than a doctor it is the mother of a special needs child!), this method of communication helps to avoid misinterpretation of my treatment intentions and instructions by having them all down on paper and dated.

New Diagnostics in ASD Based on Screening

The medical history and interview are followed by diagnostic lab tests to determine what biomedical issues need to be addressed. The new diagnostics in autism are based upon *screening*. Many biomedical irregularities in an autistic child are subtle. The lab tests are not intended to confirm an obvious illness, but to reveal underlying pathologies. The use of lab-based screening provides data that often reveals an imbalanced or even etiologically significant pathology that provides the basis for subsequent treatments.

For example, heavy metal screening is particularly important for children who received the Hepatitis B vaccination as neonates or young infants, between the years 1991 (the year it was mandated), and late 2001, (the year the CDC finally ordered thimerosal removed from the newborn Hepatitis B vaccine). Heavy metal screening is also recommended for autism-spectrum children whose mothers received RhoGam treatment during pregnancy or had amalgam removal or placement during pregnancy. Children in these categories have a higher risk of overexposure to the neurotoxic effects of mercury. Proper diagnostic testing for heavy metals is essential for determining appropriate and effective chelation treatments (see Chapter Seven).

Data from thousands of autistic children reveal the existence of "subgroups" of similar biomedical profiles. Which subgroup best describes a child is virtually impossible to know without a thorough evaluation. It takes medical histories, responses to several simple treatments, and lab-test data combined to provide a portrait of a child's biomedical characteristics. Despite the existence of subgroups of ASD children, each one has a unique profile.

Initial Strategies in Test Evaluation

As I have emphasized already, many autism spectrum children have intestinal problems, and in my experience most of those children respond favorably to a gluten-free or a casein-free diet. This is one of my first recommendations to most parents. Food hypersensitivity can occur even in the absence of obvious intestinal symptoms that are not usually the immediate allergic reactions tested by mainstream doctors. Also, a child may be sensitive to foods other than wheat and milk products. A food hypersensitivity test should occur early in the diagnostic sequence. Because many ASD children have food hypersensitivity or an intestinal pathology, many of them show improvements when prescribed various nutritional supplements.

After several months of a gluten-free and casein-free diet reinforced with nutritional supplements, another test may be warranted to assess if hypersensitivities have changed. Many children I see are already on the GF/CF diet when they come for their evaluation; a lot of time is saved when this is the case.

At the time of the child's first visit, I order a complete blood count and a metabolic panel so as to obtain a base-line for future reference. Because so many of these children have been found to have intestinal colonizations by pathogenic bacteria, fungi, or parasites, a urine test to check for fungal and bacterial metabolites and sometimes a fecal-culture evaluation is often ordered right away as well (see below).

MORE TESTS, A NEW PHILOSOPHY

Except for the basic routine screening tests that almost any local lab can do (CBC, Chemistry Panel, and Thyroid Panel), most insurance plans do not pay for all (or sometimes any, depending on the insurance plan) of the specialty tests needed for ASD children. A fairly complete lab-test panel can range in cost from $1,200 to $3,000 (depending upon which tests are ordered). It is important for parents to understand that even with all this medically useful data there is no absolute guarantee that it will always lead to a clear diagnosis and to treatments that invariably work.

In the long run, a certain percentage of children evaluated and treated biomedically make wonderful progress, and some have even lost their diagnosis as autistic. A larger percentage make major progress toward improvement but, to various degrees, remain somewhere "on the spectrum"; unfortunately another small group makes little or no progress. At this time, the only way by which parents can learn whether or not the biomedical approach "works" and was worth the investment is to have tried it.

After the medical histories are obtained, the GF/CF diet started, and some basic nutritional supplementation initiated, many options arise. A fairly complete battery of tests can be ordered if the parents are willing, or further lab-tests can be done sequentially, a few at a time. This depends on the parents' medical philosophy, awareness and knowledge about the biomedical approach, as well as their health insurance coverage and economic situation.

In making this decision, parents should know that when data are obtained all at one time, their interrelationships are often easier to recognize. The interrelationships among all major systems are so complex that comprehensive information is useful, if only to rule out certain conditions. When lab-tests are too scattered across time, they are less helpful in obtaining a good portrait of current condition. Therefore, the ideal situation is to have a child receive all the major testing at the time of the evaluation, although I understand this is not always possible or affordable. Sometimes a child will have had some tests done fairly recently by another doctor and understandably parents will not want to repeat those. Historical perspective is helpful, but current testing is usually essential to guide optimal treatment.

PARENTS, DOCTORS AND TESTING PHILOSOPHY

Often, biological pathologies are subtle and the child's underlying disease processes are not obvious. For instance, children with inflamed gastrointestinal tracts can amazingly have few or no symptoms of this problem, and it will not be learned until testing that they have pathogen overgrowth often accompanied by markedly imbalanced amino acid patterns or vitamin, mineral, and fatty acid deficiencies.

Parents differ in regard to testing their affected child. Some parents are very desirous of having many tests done to get as much diagnostic information as possible. Others so dislike the idea of the child having a venipuncture ("needle stick") that they will actually delay seeking a biomedical evaluation for this reason. Insurance company variabilities complicate matters further. For many of these children, "autism" or ASD may not be the diagnosis appropriate for their insurance applications. There often are underlying disease processes that are etiologically significant and that can be identified, treated, and coded, such as immune deficiency, gastroenteritis, heavy metal poisoning, viral infections, etc.

Doctors too vary in regard to testing. Some still think in accord with the "must be genetic" model and believe that biomedical testing is frivolous and unnecessary. Obviously, I disagree. In contrast, the growing number of physicians who are moving towards biomedical models for ASD are allowing those models to modify their clinical approaches. Let us consider several general approaches a physician might take.

Some physicians feel that they do not need to test the child very much and suggest treatments according to an intuitive assessment of the child's past history and current problems. Other physicians, particularly if pressed for time, may diagnose and treat in accord with an established protocol that may not reflect the unique biomedical nature of a particular child. In contrast, some physicians order a thorough set of lab tests early in the diagnostic process as a general principle. The latter approach can be very useful when the physician is experienced in the biomedical aspects of ASD and is capable of

interpreting a set of complex data. Sometimes physicians will cooperate with anxious parents who want extensive testing even if they
don't feel it may be necessary.

I have noticed a trend that provides a practical perspective on
testing. The longer a practitioner works with these children, the
more "streamlined" his or her assessment becomes, and less testing
is necessary—at least in early phases of the treatment regimen. Later,
if the child develops further problems or is not making progress,
then more extensive tests (along with more advanced treatment
protocols) can and should be considered. Since each child is unique
biomedically, parents should not be surprised if, for an exceptionally
challenging situation, a consultation with a neurological, immunological, endocrine or gastrointestinal specialist is recommended.
Examples of such complicated cases are the severe seizure disorders
or highly allergic children who might have a negative reaction to certain treatment regimes. Often these specialists do not know much
about autism in general (as yet!), but know a lot about a particular
child's medical problems related to their specialty.

My philosophy as a clinician is to order those tests which will
give me information useful in selecting and guiding treatment.
However, since lab tests are expensive and not always reimbursed, a
frank discussion with the child's parents is important. I try to find
out their philosophy and economic situation as regards their child's
medical care. I feel that timing is often quite important and some
tests have higher priority than others. Furthermore, the physical act
of holding an uncomprehending child down to obtain a blood test
is traumatic to both the child and the parents. Thus, I sometimes
order non-invasive (urine, hair, and stool) tests in the beginning and
try to have most of the initial evaluation work requiring blood tests
organized so that only one blood draw (with a "butterfly" needle so
that all tubes can be obtained with one venipuncture) is necessary
for the initial evaluation. A prescription for an anesthetic (lidocaine
2.5% and prilocaine 2.5%) cream to numb the venipuncture site
helps some children. They still don't like to be held down but at least
they learn that the "stick" doesn't hurt.

If the initial screening tests indicate the likelihood of heavy
metal toxicity, assessment of the child's readiness for oral chelation
treatment is very important. We have learned that gastrointestinal

health and nutritional status must be maximized before starting chelation for optimal outcome. I want to stress that chelation therapy in my opinion should not be done without active participation of a physician. Several types of lab tests are virtually mandatory. One type monitors metals presence and metals outflow. Another type of lab test will monitor the child's health during chelation. The medications used during the oral chelation detoxification process can be stressful to the liver. Some children need to have chelation halted temporarily if the child's lab tests so indicate liver stress or excessive pathogen overgrowth. That is why this treatment should be done under the supervision of a knowledgeable health practitioner who knows how to monitor the progress of these children through the most up-to-date tests available. Medically developed chelation protocols are available from the Autism Research Institute website online and are described in Chapter Seven.

Descriptions of Specific Laboratory Tests

NECESSARY PRELIMINARY SCREENING TESTS

- **CBC (Complete Blood Count) with Differential and Platelets**
- **Comprehensive Metabolic Panel**
- **Thyroid panel (T3, T4, TSH)**

These tests can all be obtained with one draw at any local laboratory in your vicinity and are often covered by insurance. These tests help us to check the child's general health for such conditions as anemia, liver or kidney impairment, or thyroid imbalance, all of which are not uncommon in ASD children.

- **Urinalysis**

Small children may need to have a urine sample brought from home in a clean glass jar; very young children can be fitted with a plastic urine collector to get a specimen. A urinalysis will check for bleeding, bladder infections, or evidence of kidney disease by the presence or absence of bilirubin, protein, or casts from the kidneys.

- **Hair analysis**

By now, many parents have heard about the heavy metal toxicity problem, and are willing to do a hair analysis. In my opinion, this is an informative non-invasive and inexpensive screening test. I highly recommend Doctor's Data Laboratory for this test. This laboratory has probably the world's largest database regarding hair analysis. Hair is an excretory tissue rather than a functional tissue. Hair element analysis provides important information which, in conjunction with symptoms and other laboratory data, can assist the physician with a diagnosis of physiological disorders associated with abnormalities in essential and toxic element metabolism. Toxic elements may be up to several hundred times more highly concentrated in hair than in blood or urine. Therefore, hair is the tissue of choice for detection of cumulative body burden and recent exposure to elements such as arsenic, aluminum, cadmium, lead, and mercury. With experience reading these tests, hair analysis results can often ascertain mercury poisoning. For example, in many cases the test can determine the presence of mercury poisoning, even though (except for recent large exposure) it will seldom show up directly as a high level of mercury on the test. The special discernment here is knowing what mercury does to the essential minerals in the body. Dr. Andrew Cutler,[2] a chemist who suffered for many years and was finally treated for mercury poisoning from amalgams, has been very helpful to the chelating community in teaching us his system of "counting rules" on the hair analyses to help determine mercury toxicity.

Hair analysis is basically a preliminary screen, however, and often needs to be followed by more specific blood and urine testing to validate those results. Recent as yet unpublished studies indicate that hair in autistic children often displays lower levels of toxic metals than their siblings and parents. This may actually turn out to be further evidence of impaired detoxification in our ASD children.

Blood tests must be viewed carefully as well. Physicians who are not familiar with heavy metal poisoning will often order a blood test for mercury, and when it returns with negative results, assure the parents that their child does not have mercury poisoning and does not need chelation. Blood tests only reveal recent large exposures,

---

[2] Cutler, Andrew "Amalgam Illness Diagnosis and Treatment," Minerva Labs, Jun 1999

and will show nothing of the mercury in the brain that is behind the blood-brain-barrier and no longer available for assessment in peripheral blood studies. I have had some disappointing experiences with colleagues who refused to participate in the investigation after ordering and receiving a negative blood test; parents need to know that the doctor who does this is not aware of the new biomedicine of mercury poisoning in ASD children.

Hair testing must be ordered by a health care professional. Doctor's Data Lab charges $42 if you send in payment with the hair specimen. Since insurance will rarely if ever pay for this test, I advise parents to send their payment along with the hair, because if laboratories have to bill insurance and wait to get money they may never receive, they end up billing the patient for all the extra paperwork and phone costs. Explicitly, if the hair analysis is billed to insurance without advance payment, the lab charges $76, which is billed to the client when insurance denies the claim. If insurance does pay, the patient is reimbursed. This is true for much of the testing and patients can often save a lot of money in lab testing by paying at the time they send in the samples. Though patients complain about this, it is understandable that the extra personnel and phone costs in handling insurance claims needs to be re-imbursed and creates a need for the lab to have differential charge policies. I personally feel parents should focus their efforts on insurance reform rather than anger at lab billing policies. (I do not receive anything from the labs I use, not even a discount for myself!)

Specialized Laboratory Tests as Individually Indicated

I recommend a basic blood count, metabolic chemistry, and thyroid panel be obtained as a base-line for all children. Special tests are ordered according to the symptoms and history of the child and often include immune system tests, tests for the presence and levels of viruses and fungi, and peptide testing for wheat and milk tolerance. I do the latter test now only for parents who are very resistant to going onto a gluten and milk-free diet, and want laboratory proof that their children are indeed intolerant of these large peptides. An extensive food tolerance panel and plasma amino acid panel are helpful to direct proper nutrition and nutrient protocols. These preliminary tests often indicate the need for treating Candida yeast or other pathogenic overgrowths in the gut and elimination of foods containing wheat, milk and often soy as well as one of the first steps. Treatments for these conditions are explained in Chapter Five. Blood, stool and urine studies can identify pathogens or pathogen metabolites and provide the basis for proper supportive and anti-pathogen treatments. Blood tests help target areas where the bio-chemistry can be improved by proper supplementation. Hair, urine and blood testing together can help determine whether heavy metal toxicity is present and then direct the removal and necessary mineral and nutrient support for chelation. Proper monitoring throughout the treatment process helps us fine-tune dosages of medications and nutrients and maintain optimal health of the children undergoing treatment.

There are multiple more refined tests for special cases as indicated by the clinical progress, but these listed below are the ones I most commonly find helpful in my practice during the initial evaluative phase. Some children who have a seizure issue may need to be referred to a pediatric neurologist to obtain 24-hour EEG studies if they have not already done so. Intractable infectious cases with major immunological derangement may need work with an immunologist or an infectious disease specialist. Some digestive problems are so severe that the child may need to be sent to a gastroenterologist for endoscopic studies. Rarely, a child may need to be referred to an endocrinologist for management of brittle diabetes or severe thyroid problems, or to an allergist for severe asthma treatment. Occasionally, such specialists may have been consulted even before the child is brought in for an autism-related biomedical evaluation. It is important for all the child's doctors to work as a team so that the treatments do not conflict, even though many mainstream doctors as yet know little about the biomedical approach to autism. Parents need to be prepared for some physicians to become threatened with information and treatments they do not as yet understand and so disparage the use of diet and nutrients in the treatment of their children.

URINARY PEPTIDE TESTS FOR CASEIN AND GLUTEN

This is a chromatographic test for the exorphin peptides, including the large peptides produced by wheat (gluten) and milk (casein). *Quantitatively accurate measurement of these peptides is still not yet in the realm of routine clinical testing, and results in terms of clinical application have been very confusing over the years.* Children with high values may show no gut symptoms or any benefit by removal of casein and gluten from their diets; many children with normal values may respond amazingly well to a GF/CF diet. I no longer routinely order this test for my clients unless the parents are extremely desirous of it, hoping it may free them from having to use the GF/CF diet. Still, no matter what the test shows, particularly if the child has a restricted diet and any bowel problems, I suggest that all of them undergo a trial of the diet if they are not already on it, since the great majority of children with autism benefit.

Parents are often surprised and pleased to see definite clinical improvements in most cases even before starting chelation. I have also found that the parents' willingness to adhere to the challenging task of keeping their children on this diet often indicates their willingness to go through the prolonged and grueling process entailed in healing their children. This includes getting their children to take multiple nutrients, observing strict chelation medication schedules, and procuring testing necessary to guide treatment.

ORGANIC ACID TEST (OAT-URINE)

The Organic Acid Test is one of the routine tests I order because of the ubiquitousness of the yeast problem and metabolic imbalances. The OAT test measures key components in the child's biochemical factory. Metabolic function testing by organic acid analysis provides indicators of how efficiently metabolism is functioning, how well it is converting food into usable products for health, and where problems may be occurring. It is especially important for revealing those microbial imbalances that cause the buildup of metabolic toxins that can be identified in overnight urine. As mentioned earlier, most cases of yeast infection result in symptoms of chronic diarrhea, constipation or an alternation of the two, as well as gas, bloating, abdominal discomfort, and foul-smelling stools. However, I have occasionally encountered children with yeast overgrowth as shown by lab tests who do not have any obvious bowel symptoms. Clinically, if children remain very picky about food, I suspect a chronic gut inflammation and pathogen colonization in spite of the lack of symptoms.

90-FOOD IgG ANTIBODIES TEST (SERUM)

Delayed or hidden food sensitivities are typically not noticeable for several hours or days after ingestion of a particular food. Frequently, these reactions reflect chronic exposures to the commonly eaten derivatives of corn, wheat, milk and egg. This comprehensive panel is a valuable tool in the clinical management of food allergic patients. For those children who are not benefiting from the GF/CF diet or who benefited at first but then regress, I order this test to make sure some of the common foods they eat are not affecting them. IgG indicates delayed sensitivity (not the IgE, or immediate allergic reaction that most allergists obtain), which afflicts the children with autism more frequently. In that sense, it is more a food sensitivity test than a true allergy test, indicating that even without an obvious allergic reaction, these foods are stressing the gut and contributing to its continued inflamed state. When these offending foods are removed children often make another leap in their healing process.

AMINO ACIDS, (PLASMA)

Amino acids are the building blocks of protein and are essential for many bodily processes. The digestive tract breaks down protein from food into individual amino acids, which are then absorbed into the blood stream. These amino acids:

- Build the structural proteins of muscle and connective tissue
- Make enzymes which control every chemical reaction in the body
- Make a variety of brain neurotransmitters and hormones
- Generate energy
- Stabilize blood sugar
- Aid in detoxification and anti-oxidant protection.

Because of poor dietary habits or inadequate digestion and absorption of proteins, most ASD children have amino acid imbalances. The vast majority of these imbalances seem to be related to maldigestion or disorders in the metabolism of methionine and cysteine, and often will indicate an insufficiency of taurine. Low taurine can affect both detoxication and uptake of essential lipids from the diet and can cause a deficiency of vitamins A, E, D, and essential fatty acids. To get a baseline test, the first amino acid analysis should be done with the child eating his/her usual diet but without taking nutritional supplements for 3 days prior to the test. Later testing can be done with the child using their usual food and supplements for fine-tuning their regimen. More information can be provided with a 24-hour urine amino acid study, but the specter of trying to collect 24 hours of urine from most of these ASD children is daunting and I and others usually use the the the fasting plasma analysis.

COMPREHENSIVE MICROBIAL/DIGESTIVE STOOL ANALYSIS

For children who continue to have bowel problems even though they are on the diet and use probiotics, this is a valuable test of the nature of the digestive tract to guide further treatment strategies. This analysis evaluates digestion, absorption, gut flora, immune status, and the colonic environment, and can evaluate for parasites using microscopic examination. A sensitivity panel for treating pathogenic flora is provided by some labs but must be specifically requested and costs extra, of course. However, the panel is invaluable in treating repeated bouts of pathogen infestation to make sure the proper anti-fungal or anti-biotic agent is being used.

FATTY ACID ANALYSIS (PLASMA)

ASD children typically have very poor diets and particularly diets that contain "good fats" found in vegetables, nuts, whole grains, and fish (which I now suggest not be eaten by the children in treatment with me because of mercury levels in most of the fish available.) The hydrogenation process used in modern food processing destroys important fatty acids and creates structurally altered fatty acids called trans fatty acids that may be harmful to the body. Please see more about fatty acids in Chapter Six on nutrients.

The plasma fatty acid test can measure over 30 different fatty acids in body stores——essentials and their derivatives, saturated, and trans fatty acids. This test is usually further along in my testing sequence unless malnutrition seems apparent at the outset of the evaluation; I always order it for ADD-ADHD or bi-polar children, as many studies are coming out showing the efficacy of treatment of these children (and adults) with fatty acids. This test helps me guide dietary modifications and supplements that can move the child toward a healthy balance of their fatty acid levels.

TESTS FOR METALLOTHIONEIN DYSFUNCTION

Dr. William Walsh at the Pfeiffer Treatment Center located in Naperville, IL believes that metallothionein (MT) dysfunction is one of the primary bases for ASD. 85% of children he studies exhibit elevated copper/zinc ratios in blood compared to healthy controls. He tests for plasma zinc, serum copper, plasma ammonia, urinary pyrrole, and ceruloplasmin to help him balance the body chemistry of his patients with minerals, especially zinc, and other nutrients.

MT protects cells from the harmful effects of oxidative stress, DNA damage, and toxicity of excess heavy metals. As it is an intracellular protein, only the cellular activity is important for the assessment of metal-induced toxicity; plasma analyses of MT levels are not relevant. I use the functional MT assay which analyzes the cellular level of MT expression before and after stimulation with metals as performed by Immunosciences Lab in Beverly Hills, CA to assess effectiveness of MT protection. This test along with hair analyses and RBC minerals guides me in determining the need for chelation work for my patients.

Like all of us working with ASD children, Dr. Walsh has found the greatest treatment challenge is the high incidence of severe gut problems. He reported ASD outcomes in his chemical rebalancing nutrient therapy protocols dramatically improved with regular use of special diets, digestive aids, probiotics, and sugar elimination.[3]

---

[3] Walsh, William J. et al., Booklet "Metallothionein and Autism." Oct 2001, Pfeiffer Trtment Cntr, Naperville, IL

Laboratory Testing in Chelation Therapy

The primary tests to prepare for chelation therapy (see Chapter Seven for a discussion of the chelation protocol) are:

- Standard preliminary tests as outlined above to check general health

- Urine and/or stool tests to make sure gut is healthy, e.g. OAT and CDSA.

- Hair analysis (see above)

- Red Blood Cell mineral analysis to help in mineral/nutrient plan

- Pre and post-challenge urine test for toxic elements

The challenge tests are often unnecessary and are ordered when desired by parents or the referring doctor who may not be convinced that the child would benefit from chelation therapy. A regular morning urine sample is taken (pre-challenge), and then two doses of the chelating agent are given, usually DMSA (Chemet, or 2,3-dimercaptosuccinic acid), as calculated per weight of the child and administered the night before and the next morning. The post-challenge is obtained by catching a urine sample within several hours of the morning dose. The chelating agent binds to the metals that are in the urine and the pre and post-challenge tests are compared to help see what the response to chelation may be. Further details of this test are given in Chapter Seven.

Immunology Testing

Because of its highly technical nature, the discussion of immunology testing is included in Chapter Eight where the immune system is discussed in greater detail.

Which Laboratories to Use

The question of which laboratory to use is an important one. The preliminary tests are pretty standardized and can be done anywhere.

If the practitioner has his or her own venipuncturist in the office that is ideal. If not, it is important to help the patient locate a lab nearby that is willing to draw blood for specialty labs and work with special needs children. These laboratories often specialize in autism, and perform tests not usually available locally. In this case, kits are either given to the patient by the practitioner or sent to them upon the doctor's request by the lab. The primary laboratories I personally use for specialty work are:

CALIFORNIA
Immunosciences Lab (ISL)   **310-657-1077**

GEORGIA
Meta-Metrix Lab (MML)   **800-221-4640**

ILLINOIS
Doctors' Data Lab (DDL)   **800-323-2784**

KANSAS
Great Plains Lab (GPL)   **888-347-2781**

NORTH CAROLINA
Great Smokies Lab (GSL)   **800-522-4762**

All of these labs are willing to send kits to the clients upon the doctor's request. Most send duplicates of results to the ordering practitioner so the patient can have one for their files.

I'm sure there are other good laboratories out there; each practitioner has to experiment and find the ones with which they like to work. Using the same lab for a certain test with all my patients helps me relate test results to the symptoms I'm seeing clinically. This approach also helps me become familiar with the lab personnel so I can get my questions answered. Ease of reading the reports, timeliness of getting results back, and the accessibility of the lab directors to talk to me about results are often important to me in choosing between equally good labs.

FIVE

GASTROINTESTINAL HEALING

Gastrointestinal Health is a Key Issue

The "take home" message of this chapter is that the majority of autistic children suffer from impaired gastrointestinal health. Many of our children are unable to verbally express the pain or discomfort they may feel, yet intestinal problems may be obvious from patterns of persistent diarrhea, constipation, abdominal pain with bloating or abnormally appearing stools. In some children, intestinal pathology may be less obvious and detectable only via appropriate lab-tests, (e.g. mild inflammation due to undiagnosed food hypersensitivity). Parents and physicians often focus on the more obvious cognitive impairments and may not realize that correcting their child's underlying intestinal imbalances can lead to significant overall improvement.

Among autism-spectrum children, self-restriction of their diet to a few usually non-nourishing foods is common. Yet even the rare child who is willing to eat vegetables and other nutritious foods may not be able to get these nutrients to benefit his/her brain adequately because of the inability to properly digest, absorb, and/or utilize the nutrients taken in. In some cases, nutrients may be prevented from nourishing the brain cells because of viral infestations or other toxins in the brain. PCR (polymerase chain reaction)-based studies have shown that certain viruses can migrate into small areas of the brain, remain dormant for long periods of time, and do so without generating an obvious encephalitis. Prolonged diarrhea could enable viruses to enter tissues of the gut in some children, from where they would be capable of migrating into the central nervous system.[1]

The impressive shift in cognition in many children during heavy metal chelation treatment definitely implicates toxic metals as interfering with the brain's ability to take in adequate nutrients for proper function. In nutritionally preparing children for chelation when laboratory tests indicate mercury poisoning, there is very often an obvious improvement in cognition and language with the nutrient program alone. A state of impaired nutrient status in blood, intestines, liver, and kidneys could allow for metals accumulation injurious to those tissues and, if the metals level is sufficient, then some metal may enter the central nervous system and disrupt neuronal function.

To repeat, unavailability of breast feeding, persistent colic in infancy, frequent use of antibiotics, certain immunizations, and inability to detoxify heavy metal or other environmental toxins are all known to contribute to impaired gut function. Food allergies, intolerance to wheat and milk products, evidence of immune impairment such as frequent ear infections in infancy, and chronic yeast or viral infections all point to a need to have the gastrointestinal system evaluated in our ASD children. Family history may implicate genetic or environmentally shared factors, since digestive disturbances are common in the parents and siblings of children with autism. Dysfunctions such as "leaky gut" syndrome (excessive permeability), fungal, bacterial and parasite overgrowth, malabsorption (incomplete uptake of nutrients), maldigestion, inflammation (enterocolitis), and liver detoxification impairment are frequently noted by the clinicians working with these children. Histological studies done on a study of 36 children with autism showed evidence of reflux esophagitis in 69.4%, chronic gastritis in 41.7%, chronic duodenitis in 66.7%, and low intestinal carbohydrate digestive enzyme activity in 58.3%.[2]

---

[1] Binstock, Teresa, Common Variable Immune Deficiencies, http://www.jorsm.com/ ~binstock/cvid.htm

[2] Horvath, K. et al., "Gastrointestinal abnormalities in children with autistic disorder." Journal of Pediatrics 1999 Nov., 135(5): 533-5

Some parents have related to me that when they asked their pediatrician for remedies for their child's bowel problems, they were told that "it is normal; it is a stage that will pass." Untreated, some of these children may gradually get better, but many of them continue severe bowel dysfunction into adulthood. On the other hand, when their GI ailments are treated successfully, most autistic/ASD children respond favorably, not only with improved digestive health and function, but also by exhibiting improved behavioral and developmental responses. Chronic diarrhea, constipation, gaseousness, and abdominal discomfort are obvious to the caretakers of these children. However, we are finding that many children even in the absence of these overt intestinal symptoms have significant gut problems that often must be addressed as the first step in their healing journey. Part of the challenge in dealing with the gut disorder is the inability of many children to tell us how they are feeling along with their commonly observed high pain threshold.

Research has shown that 60-70% of the immune system in humans is located within the intestinal tract and its digestive organs, easily making the gut the largest immune system organ in the body. Because the immune system is so involved with the gastrointestinal tract, intestinal pathology can contribute to immune dysregulation, and vice versa. Regardless of whether the immune impairment is acquired or genetic, many of these children are susceptible to multiple infections, especially ear infections, and are often repeatedly treated with antibiotics—without considering the possibility of viral otitis, for which antibiotics are ineffective. Antibiotics not only irritate the intestinal wall and cause gut inflammation, but also destroy the beneficial bacteria, creating an opportunity for Candida, (a yeast), Clostridia (an anaerobic bacteria) and other pathogens normally kept in balance by the "good bugs" to overgrow and cause further damage. Pioneering researchers including Dr. William Shaw have shown that many autistic patients tend to have elevated yeast levels in their intestines.[3]

As we have mentioned in earlier chapters, yeast overgrowth interferes with the absorption of nutrients (the yeasts take them for their own growth and multiplication, particularly the sugars); this is

---

[3]   Shaw, William PhD Biological Treatments for Autism and PDD, New revised 2002 edition

often the cause of the diarrhea and/or constipation. Yeast species can excrete chemical byproducts that are absorbed through the intestinal wall and enter the blood stream to circulate throughout the body. Furthermore, yeast cells can convert to an invasive colony form, imbedding themselves into the lining of the intestinal tract and, via secreted enzymes, destroy intestinal tissue. This type of injury creates "holes" in the intestine through which undigested food molecules can pass. This hyperpermeable state is called "leaky gut syndrome." In many children with leaky gut, the undigested food is apparently detected by the immune system, causing antibodies of both IgE (immediate reaction) and IgG (delayed reaction) to be produced. This process leads to greater allergic susceptibilities. Effective treatment of yeast or bacterial overgrowth often decreases or eliminates these allergic reactions.

Treatments That Can Be Implemented by Parents

THE GF/CF (GLUTEN, CASEIN FREE) DIET

As we indicated in Chapter Two, well-respected researchers have shown in their studies that casein, which is found in milk, breaks down in the stomach to produce a peptide known as casomorphine. Morphine is a powerful painkilling drug. The peptide casomorphine has "morphine"-like or opioid properties. Similar opioids called gluteomorphins are formed in the stomach when these children try to digest gluten from wheat and other grains like rye and oats. Though other researchers have not found the same results with their studies, and therefore dispute the "opioid theory" there is no doubt that parents often say of their children with autism that they appear "spacey" and that they don't seem to feel pain in ways similar to someone under the influence of opioids.

Scientific studies are pointing to inflammation in the gut being caused by gluten, casein, soy and other foods. This is not an "allergy" from the perspective of a traditional allergist, but what is called T-cell inflammatory response to these foods. In a study conducted by Dr. H. Jyonouchi from the University of Minnesota, it was shown that 75% of the children with autism spectrum disorder have T-cell reactivity to foods.[4]

Regardless of the theories, clinical experience of many DAN! physicians has identified the GF/CF diet as the single most effective action you can take on your own to begin to help your child. In my practice, I have found that almost every child with autism placed on this diet benefits from it. Many parents of my young patients have reported that their children's chronic diarrhea stopped and the appearance of formed stools began after successful implementation of the GF/CF diet, particularly when any current yeast infection was treated at the same time. Many other parents report that potty training was finally achieved within a few weeks after the child began a GF/CF diet.

Many parents also report that their children are better able to mentally focus and show improvement in their capacity to learn as a result of the diet. For instance, Janie, the mother of an autistic child named Kelly, told me, "We are having great results on this diet. Kelly is much more aware, alert, and curious about her environment. She also has better eye contact and is more affectionate since starting it." Improvements such as these may be due to the fact that intestinal pathology has an effect on brain function; gut-brain interactions have been well described by numerous researchers.[5]

When I first recommend the GF/CF (and recently, SF or soy-free) diet to parents, most mothers (and some fathers) protest, "My child will starve, he (or she) won't eat anything else." The majority of ASD children have very limited diets. They refuse most foods and fixate on only a few favorites, generally foods such as pizza, chicken nuggets, cakes, cookies, and ice cream, foods rich in gluten or casein. They seem to be addicted to exactly the foods they need to stay away from. I understand that it seems like an almost impossible task to change your child's entire diet, and I cannot deny it affects the whole family. However, many families find that the child is not the only person with hypersensitivity to gluten, casein or soy. Some families have ultimately found that they all feel better after eliminat-

---

[4] Jyonouchi H. et al., "Proinflammatory and regulatory cytokine production associated with innate and adaptive immune responses in children with autism spectrum disorders and developmental regression." J. Neuroimmunol 2001 Nov1;120(1-2): 170-9

[5] Binstock, Teresa, Medical Hypotheses, Volume:57, Issue:6, Dec. 2001 pp. 714-717 "Anterior insular cortex: linking intestinal pathology and brain function in autism-spectrum subgroups"

ing wheat, milk and soy products from their diet. This is not easy especially when there are older siblings who have established eating habits and resist changes. It took me nine months to finally convince myself and my daughter Elizabeth, Chelsey's mother, to initiate the GF/CF diet in 1998. However, she now swears by it. I encourage parents by assuring them that the benefits to the child will outweigh the difficulties, and hopefully as the children heal, they will be able to tolerate some gluten and casein. To repeat, the majority of the parents of my young patients report significant improvements in sleep patterns, behavior, language, eye contact, attention span and ability to focus and a decrease in "stimming" in their children after starting this regimen.

Many parents report seeing physical, emotional, or even cognitive improvements a few days after dairy is removed from their child's diet. Some parents make the same point about gluten. However, gluten takes longer to disappear from the digestive tract than casein. Urine tests reveal that casein can disappear from the body within three days, whereas it can take months before the gluten leaves. In fact, urine tests have revealed gluten in the urine of some children for as long as eight months after it was removed from the diet. However, if it shows up in the urine after that time, it may be that not all hidden sources have been identified. Some parents find their child didn't improve until hidden sources of gluten (or casein) were discovered and removed. When I used to ask parents to eliminate just casein and gluten, many children improved to a certain point and then plateaued. When a subsequent IgG food test showed other hypersensitivities, the removal of these substances would lead to a further spurt in progress. As more and more of the hypersensitivity food tests showed that soy was a frequent allergen, I suggest at the outset of the diet that soy also be eliminated, which has led to even better results.

A word of warning: Illogically, the U.S. Food and Drug Administration maintains that casein is not a dairy product. Therefore, many foods marked as "non-dairy" contain casein. It may be listed on food labels as sodium caseinate. Any food with that ingredient should be eliminated from your child's diet. Adhere to the diet strictly for at least six months. Almost all of the parents of my patients have reported improvement from the diet. As I have said, I have come to the realization that for most autism-spectrum children, until the inflamed gut is healed, pathogen overgrowth corrected, and nutritional status improved, other treatments will be far less effective.

How to Start the Diet

I recommend that parents start the process of a casein/gluten free diet slowly. Sometimes taking away the offending foods one meal at a time while gradually introducing new ones works the best for some families. Often, parents find that removing milk products is easier than the removal of wheat. Take straight milk away first, then over the course of several weeks, remove other milk and dairy products. Use substitutes such as rice, potato, almond, or coconut milks if food sensitivity testing has shown that your child is not allergic to any of these substances. Then start removing the wheat-based products. Have the rice or potato bread substitutes handy, and slowly let the children acquire a taste for them during the period of casein removal. Many mothers (and a few dads too!) learn to make breads from non-offending flours. I have recently begun recommending that parents avoid soy-based products completely unless a food sensitivity test demonstrates that the child is not allergic to soy. It used to be one of my standby substitutes until I learned from experience (lack of success on the diet with using soy as the main milk substitute) that soy comes high on the list of foods likely to cause adverse reactions, right after wheat and milk.

Be strict about the diet. Tell your friends and other family members not to weaken and give the child a regular cookie or cracker. Even tiny amounts of gluten or casein can cause a child to regress and have diarrhea for days. I learned that "Just a little can't hurt anything" can lead to a real setback until the gluten finally gets out of the system again. Not a few children learn that these foods will make them sick, and so will refuse them if offered by a friend or relative who just can't believe pizza or cookies are bad for anyone.

Unfortunately, we have learned that gluten is hidden in many products and ingredients. Therefore, when you go grocery shopping you have to be vigilant. Become a detective and ferret out hidden sources of gluten and casein. Be warned: Hidden sources of gluten will not be immediately recognizable by just reading the label of foods. For instance, many labels may state "natural and artificial flavors, food starch, malt, and vinegar." Those are only a few of the ingredients that can be derived from wheat.

Where to Get Help

So what are you going to do? Do not get discouraged. Manufacturers are very consumer conscious and the demand for foods free of casein and gluten is increasing steadily as more and more parents realize that curtailing these offending foods makes their children healthier. If you have any doubts, phone the manufacturer (most have toll-free lines) and ask the customer service representative to check if the suspect food or any of its ingredients contains gluten or casein. If they blithely and automatically claim that their product is GF/CF, explain that gluten or casein can be used in preparation of the labeled ingredients and specifically ask if they know for sure whether any of those ingredients have had contact with wheat or milk. If the customer service representative is uncertain, ask to speak to a supervisor and ask that he or she check with the food manufacturer's chemists. The more calls like that they get, the more conscious they will become about the issue. Although acquiring this knowledge and checking ingredients may at first seem overwhelming, once you invest the initial effort you will quickly learn which foods are safe and which are not.

You will also learn where to buy GF/CF foods. For instance, GF/CF foods like Heinz Ketchup, Bush's Baked Beans, Ore-Ida Golden Fries, and Starkist Chunk Light Tuna (although we are now recommending ASD children not eat tuna because of the mercury levels) are available at most local supermarkets. Other GF/CF foods such as Erewhon cereals and GF/CF-free yogurts can be found at local health food stores. Kosher markets that sell products marked "Pareve" are GF/CF. Many Internet and mail order sources sell GF/CF products. McDonald's has agreed to cook their french-fries separately from their chicken McNuggets and remains the favorite for most of these children for dining out.

There are two superb books that I recommend to all parents planning to put their child on the GF/CF diet. One, written by Karyn Seroussi, mother of a son formerly diagnosed as autistic who has now lost that diagnosis, is entitled, *Unraveling the Mystery of Autism and Pervasive Developmental Disorder: A Mother's Story of Research and Recovery*, published by Simon & Schuster, 2000. Another mother of an autistic child is Lisa Lewis, author of *Special Diets for Special Kids*, 1998, published by Future Horizons, Inc. Lisa Lewis and Karyn Seroussi also founded ANDI, the Autism Network for Dietary Intervention, an organization devoted to helping families get started and maintain the GF/CF diet. They produce *The ANDI News*, a quarterly newsletter with articles written by parents and health professionals regarding the diet. Contact ANDI at P.O. Box 1771, Rochester, NY 14617-0711, or email: AutismNDI@aol.com. Also check http://www.AutismNDI.com for similar information.

Another resource for help in implementing a GF/CF diet is *The Gluten-Free Baker Newsletter* which is published quarterly and provides recipes for flavorful baked goods. Write the newsletter for subscription information at 361 Cherrywood Drive, Fairborn, Ohio, 45324-4012. Still another resource is Autism Educational Services (AES) in New Jersey. Phone and ask for Nadine Gilder at 732-473-9482 or email her at ngilder@worldnet.att.net.[6] AES has developed a recipe book of GF/CF foods ranging from pancakes and waffles to mock Graham Crackers and has also developed a cassette tape, "How to Survive a Gluten-and Casein-Free Diet" that further explains why you should put your autistic child on such a diet. The tape contains many timesaving tips on how to maintain such a diet.

An excellent cookbook with delicious GF/CF recipes is *The Cheerful No Casein, No Gluten, Sugar Optional Cookbook* by Sally Ramsey, a professional chemist who is a gourmet cook. It is available from the Autism Research Institute, San Diego, CA.

Many parents ask me if their child should have certain testing done before going on the GF/CF diet to see if their child really needs this kind of special treatment. Tests for urinary peptides may sometimes be useful, though there have been many false negatives reported. A morning urine sample can be tested and will often identify peptides in the urine of these children if done before they start the restricted diet. These tests are not perfect, and as yet are con-

---

[6] Nadine Gilder, pamphlet, "The Importance of a Gluten-and Casein-Free Diet," Autism Education Services, published by Autism Educational Services, 1218 Steeplechase, NJ.

sidered "investigational." Studies show that at least 50% of people with autism who are tested appear to have elevated levels of these opioid-like peptides, thought by prominent researchers such as Paul Shattock in England and Karl Reichelt in Norway to result in abnormal stimulation of opiate receptors in the brain. The effects of this stimulation can be a reduction in pain threshold along with other opiate-like reactions such as impaired perception, learning and motivation. I believe a food-hypersensitivity panel is extremely useful for most of these children, though it does not check for peptides.

In my clinical experience, some children have produced negative results on these lab tests, but my assessment of the child was more correct as there was remarkable improvement when the child was placed on the GF/CF diet. I believe that even if the gut pathology has not progressed to the point of a leaking gut, there is still a lot of evidence that these foods irritate the gut and cause other digestive and immunity problems. The large peptides contained in wheat and milk are very similar. Many children do best when both gluten and casein are avoided. Yet for some children, gluten is the primary culprit; for others, casein must be removed, and for others, soy too offends. Each autism-spectrum child is uniquely individual, even at the level of food hypersensitivity.

The GF/CF diet is an important treatment that can be instituted by parents without any prior laboratory tests. At first in my practice, I accepted all of the families who sought my help. It took me a while to learn that the children who were on the diet generally responded to treatment more successfully than those who had not had the casein and gluten removed. Then I and other clinicians began realizing children with yeast overgrowth were not responding as well as we hoped for to the chelation therapy; in fact, the yeasts, clostridia, and other pathogens seemed to be thriving on the oral chelation agents and rendering our administration of them ineffective for detoxification purposes. These lessons clarified a general principle: *gut healing has to come first*, and gut healing cannot take place if foods that are not being properly absorbed and digested are keeping the gut inflamed. As this book goes to press, I have a waiting list of parents who want their children to be evaluated for treatment. One of the ways I screen my acceptance of new clients is by their parents' willingness to implement the GF/CF diet; that's how strongly I feel about healing the gut first. I have no way to prove that all the children have inflamed guts and need the diet, but research evidence is coming in steadily that the majority of these children studied do have inflamed guts. Clearly, removing irritants and toxins from the diet and environment as much as possible is the first step in allowing the gut to heal.

One way parents may do their own evaluation without any laboratory testing is to implement what we call the rotation diet. Foods or food classes are systematically removed for at least 4 days and then restarted with close observation of changes in behavior, toileting, or other parameters such as sleep patterns, learning capabilities, and eye contact. Through hard-earned clinical experience, DAN! doctors have found that each child presents a unique treatment challenge based on his or her biochemical status, immune needs and sensitivities to foods and chemicals. I ask parents to impose the diet for at least four and preferably six months strictly before abandoning it.

ENZYMES

Parents ask me: How long should I keep my child on the GF/CF diet? Several years ago, many of us working with these children would have said "Probably forever!" However, that hopefully may be changing as we are learning more. One of the factors affecting this change is the increased understanding of the importance of digestive enzymes as part of the healing regimen in ASD. Another encouraging factor is the observation that some of the children who have been undergoing chelation long enough to lower their toxic metal load have become able to tolerate previously offending foods. This treatment-related progression back to a more ordinary diet is being helped by the addition of enzymes to help reduce the inflammation in the intestinal lining that can be associated with the leaky gut syndrome. Digestive enzymes diminish both the number and size of inappropriate molecules which in turn tends to reduce inflammation. Reducing inflammation helps heal the leaky gut that was initiated by yeast-excreted enzymes that allow the organisms to burrow deeply into intestinal tissue. Impairments in digestion and absorption (often accompanied by gut inflammation) contribute to the child's impaired nutritional status, which can in turn contribute to and further impair immunity, detoxification and brain function. Furthermore, the proper breaking down of foods minimizes the residue of undigested food that encourages the growth of pathogenic organisms.

Many researchers have done studies showing the incomplete breakdown of protein peptides from casein and gluten (Shattock[7], Reichelt[8]); other researchers have shown the inflammation of the gut lining (Wakefield[9], Horvath[10]) found in the majority of ASD children studied. These as well as further studies have documented and described enzyme deficiencies.[11] The studies reveal a complex range of enzyme deficiencies: pancreatic enzymes, stomach lining enzymes, and brush border membrane enzymes secreted by the small intestine.[12] These and many other studies suggest that these enzyme deficiencies and especially carbohydrate malabsorption may explain many of the significant intestinal problems that the ASD children have.

Regardless of whether the deficiency of pancreatic enzymes starts with a toxic injury such as a mercury-laden vaccination at birth, arises from antibiotics or adverse colonization, or derives from a difficult to define genetic predisposition, the bottom line is that the gut impairment clearly needs to be treated for these kids to improve. There are many different enzyme formulations to handle the special needs of ASD children. Trial and error with safe plant-based enzyme preparations is the best way to find out what most benefits your child. I advise parents in the beginning of the gut-healing program to use enzymes only for dietary infractions that are likely to occur during large family gatherings and birthday parties at friends' houses where restriction is difficult. When the new improved enzymes

---

[7] Shattock, P., Lowdon, G., "Proteins, peptides and autism, Part 2: Implications for the education and care of people with autism." Brain Dys 1991;4(6): 323-34

[8] Reichelt, K.L. et al. "Gluten, milk proteins and autism: dietary intervention effects on behavior and peptide secretion." Jour Applied Nutrition 1990;42(1); 1-11

[9] Wakefield, A.J. et al. "Enterocolitis in children with developmental disorders." American Jour Gastroenterology 2000 Sep; 95(9): 2285-95

[10] Horvath K. et al. "Gastrointestinal abnormalities in children with autistic disorder." Jour Pediatrics 1999 Nov;135(5): 533-5

[11] Brudnak, M. "Application of Genomeceuticals to the Molecular and Immunological Aspects of Autism", Medical Hypotheses, 2001

[12] Beck, Gary and Victoria, Rimland, Bernard "Unlocking the Potential of Secretin", Autism Research Institute, 1998, San Diego CA

started coming out, parents were enthusiastic and began replacing the diet with enzymes, with some children becoming very ill. My current approach is to use enzymes in combination with dietary restrictions until children are well on the road to intestinal health. I do not agree with enzyme makers who advertise that enzymes can replace dietary control. My clinical experience early on indicated that in the beginning of treatment for the children where I tried enzymes alone I found only 50% improvement over what a restricted diet based upon food hypersensitivity testing achieved. Before the gut has at least partially healed, some enzymes may be irritating. I advise parents to start with very small doses given just before meals, working up to an optimal level and sometimes with every meal or snack. Many children benefit by removal of items such as soy and corn along with casein and gluten products; enzymes may help them handle these foods if total removal is difficult. For at least some children, appropriate use of digestive enzymes may eventually supplant or even replace dietary restrictions, but not without considerable gut healing first according to my experience.

I find that most children benefit by a broad-spectrum enzyme formulation. My current recommendations (2004) are Klaire Labs, recently improved Vital-Zymes Complete high-potency broad-spectrum digestive enzyme formulation[13], and Kirkman Labs, Enzym-Complete with DPP-IV, also a broad-spectrum formula.[14] Both formulations are SCD compliant and both were created by Dr. Mark Brudnak, (see p. 100). As all children are unique, I advise parents always to try different formulations to see what works best for their child.

PROBIOTICS

Probiotics are beneficial microorganisms ("good gut bugs") that normally inhabit the healthy intestine. Probiotic supplements are often used to prevent or counteract the overgrowth of pathogenic organisms in the gut such as yeast, bacteria, and parasites. We try to "crowd out" the pathogenic bugs ("bad gut bugs") by giving large numbers of beneficial ones. For most autism-spectrum children with intestinal challenges, probiotic supplements are important in bring-

---

[13] Klaire Laboratories, www.Klaire.com, 866-216-6127
[14] Kirkman Laboratories, www.kirkmanlabs.com, 800-245-8282

ing the diseased gut back to health. Clinicians becoming more aware of the increasing incidence of yeast infections regularly recommend that patients taking antibiotics also take probiotics, which can minimize the likelihood of overgrowth by pathogens. Fortunately there are numerous preparations available of these essential gut denizens that have proven effective in diminishing diarrhea and constipation, particularly in conjunction with a GF/CF diet. Clinically, probiotics are effective in reducing allergic symptoms, regulating bowel function, and enhancing the immune system. They are remarkably safe and can be purchased by parents without a prescription.

However, a few parents have reported adverse effects of probiotic supplementation, particularly when the gut is severely inflamed. Apparently probiotics can increase gut inflammation in some children. Your child may respond well to one kind or brand of probiotic and negatively to another. It is a case of trial and error, based on astute observation of the child's responses, always starting with small doses and gradually building up. I routinely recommend a broad-spectrum formulation; my favorite is Klaire Labs' new high-potency Ther-Biotics Complete, which contains 12 synergistic colonizing and transient probiotic strains that provide a high degree of intestinal support. This product needs to be mixed with cool (not warm or hot) beverages or food such as pear sauce before meals to retain the new InTactic technology for delivering far higher functional potency than other probiotic formulations.

Nutritionist Mark Brudnak, formerly a consultant to Kirkman Labs' Technical Staff, believes probiotics play a pivotal role in detoxification. He provides scientific support regarding the ability of probiotics to detoxify methyl mercury by sequestering it and propelling it along the gastrointestinal tract toward elimination.[15]

Generally, commercially available formulations contain the most well recognized strains of probiotics that address those various populations of pathogens that might be causing or contributing to the gut problems. Though some manufacturers state their probiotics need not be refrigerated, I recommend they always be kept cold to

---

[15] Brudnak, MA, "Probiotics as an Adjuvant to Detoxification Protocols." Medical Hypotheses, July 2001

maintain maximum potency. It is also important to keep track of expiration dates and use only fresh products.

Yogurt is a good natural source of the Lactobacillus acidophilus strain of bacteria that research studies have shown counteracts yeast overgrowth and reduces the toxic by-products that overgrowth produces. Many health-conscious adults ingest yogurt regularly, but since almost all of the children in my practice are on a milk-free and usually soy-free diet, parents need to make sure that the probiotic formulations they use are dairy and soy free as well.

Numerous studies have been published showing the role of probiotics in promoting the immune function of the gut, both by strengthening immunological barriers and stimulating immune function.[16] This is not surprising when we understand the huge part the gut plays in regulating the entire immune system.

Both animal and human studies have shown that infants are much more susceptible to persistent yeast infections than adults. In very persistent infections, large doses of probiotics are essential to help crowd out the offending pathogens and help the child's immune system combat the infectious process. When yeasts colonize the gut, they produce toxins that can get into the blood stream and travel to other organs such as the brain. These circulating toxins create even more damage to the gut, producing substances such as ammonia and phenols that need to be counteracted in the child's overall nutrient program.

BASIC NUTRIENT SUPPLEMENTATION

Though choosing supplements that directly address deficiencies targeted by laboratory testing is ideal, parents should not wait for these tests to start supplying their ASD children with the basic nutrients they are likely to need. Before any testing is even necessary, I believe parents should give their child a good Basic Multiple Vitamin and Mineral—without copper—at least daily; Vitamin B6 in the P5P+Magnesium form, 50mg once/day; Vitamin C 100-1000mg, as much as you can get your child to take in divided doses (Vit C does not stay in the body very long) without causing loose stools;

---

[16] Cross ML. Microbes versus microbes: immune signals generated by probiotic lactobacilli and their role in protection against microbial pathogens. FEMS Immunol Med Microbiol. 2002 Dec 13;34(4):245-53.

and Calcium 500—1000mg per day. Dimethylglycine (DMG) is an important non-toxic supplement and comes in a small sublingual form (125mg) that tastes good, as glycine is naturally sweet. In some children, DMG will start activating greater language ability. Every child should be given a trial of DMG, starting with one a day always given in the morning, building up to three or four all taken at once in the morning if hyperactivity isn't a problem. Giving folinic acid 800mcg along with DMG will often prevent hyperactivity. DMG does double duty in providing the brain with a valuable and important amino acid, and also helps raise immune system efficiency. In about 15% of children, DMG causes agitation as well as hyperactivity, even with folinic acid. Some parents have found that TMG (trimethylglycine) is more tolerable, even though the compounds are very similar, and a few children can tolerate neither DMG nor TMG. (Folinic acid is the biologically active form of folic acid.)

In the next chapter called "Feeding the Starving Brain" I will describe in more detail tests that help target your child's specific nutrient needs, and will also describe those nutrients I have found to be helpful for most autism spectrum children.

In summary, parents need to educate themselves about these treatment modalities that help most autism-spectrum children along the road of recovery—even before finding a physician qualified in autism. Besides *diet restriction* (eliminating casein, gluten, soy and all refined sugars) and *appropriate supplementation* with plant-based digestive enzymes, almost all ASD children need probiotics and a good basic nutrient program. Often, parents who have read about and studied the biomedical-treatment options may know more than their family doctor or pediatrician, whose views about autism are likely to have been formed in medical schools that taught the "must necessarily be genetic" model of autism. So I advise parents to do the homework. As outlined above, you can pursue initial aspects of your child's healing yourself; this saves you money and time, and allows the doctor to focus on testing and prescription medications that may facilitate further treatments. If these preliminary steps are already well along, then lab-tests and treatments that require medical supervision such as anti-fungal, anti-viral, and detoxification protocols can be instituted much sooner.

When you do start the dietary, probiotic, nutrient and enzyme treatments, don't try everything at once. I advise you start one thing at a time and give each a good week to stabilize before you add anything else to the regimen. Keep a journal of what you are doing and how the child is responding. Record the dates and doses of nutrients, so if there is any reaction it will be easier to find the culprit. Record the dates of diet changes, infractions and their consequences. Learn to keep good records of your child's progress and insist on getting a copy of every test taken to keep for your medical files.

Gastrointestinal Treatments That Require Physician Participation

As described in the last chapter, when treatment moves beyond the GF/CF diet, digestive enzymes, probiotics and basic nutrients, laboratory tests that must be ordered by a doctor are needed to guide your child's further treatment. It would be ideal if every family could find a sympathetic and knowledgeable doctor to guide the healing program. However, the fact of the matter is that the complex needs of these children, the newness of the biomedical approach and the epidemic proportions of autism have created a drastic shortage of such physicians. Thus, as I have emphasized, parents must become not only their children's educational advocates but their medical advocates as well. It is imperative that parents read, study, join support groups, peruse the incredible resources now available on the internet, and start the child's healing work even while searching for the doctor oriented towards the biomedical aspects of ASD children.

If parents have already implemented a restricted diet supported by a program of probiotics and enzymes, started a good basic nutrient program, and have been willing to cut out excess sugars and junk food, the child will be well along in the healing game by the time a physician needs to participate in further stages of evaluation and treatment. Yet in moving beyond the child's initial phases of healing, not only must the tests be ordered and interpreted by the doctors, but the prescriptions for advanced drug therapeutics such as anti-fungals, anti-virals, antibiotics, chelation, and specialized medicines for behavior, seizures, and sleeping difficulties if indicated require a doctor's participation.

Learning from the internet and from books is helpful. However, in my opinion some treatments should NOT be tried as home remedies. Chelation is one such treatment. Some parents have felt they can't afford chelation or have been unable to find a physician who will supervise the process and have tried going it alone. This course of action is unwise as behavioral deterioration (i.e., regression) is possible if the child gets a severe gut pathogen infestation. Chelation must be supervised by a physician and augmented by appropriate lab tests.

ANTI-FUNGAL TREATMENT

Along with foods that act as toxins, the accumulation of mercury and other heavy metals also stresses the gut and opens the door to yeast overgrowth. As I have emphasized, for many autism-spectrum children, injury by vaccinal ethylmercury may have been the trigger that set off the whole cascade of problems—including the child's chronic susceptibility for gut dysfunction. The oral chelation agents which I will describe in Chapter Seven have unfortunately shown themselves to be an encouragement for yeasts and anaerobic bacteria such as Clostridium difficile. I have found my biggest delays in the chelation process are caused by the necessity of stopping chelation to treat these pathogenic overgrowths.

Just as the gut needs to be as healthy as possible to start the chelation process, similarly dietary approaches that minimize the yeast burden need to be enacted before starting anti-fungal medication. For example, eliminating foods with sugar should be done for at least two weeks before starting an antifungal medication. Why take medicine to kill the yeasts and feed them their favorite food (sugar) at the same time? Sucrose, glucose, fructose, galactose, honey, brown sugar, maple syrup, rice syrup, etc. are all sugars that feed yeast, and therefore are not beneficial for kids with yeast infestations (or perhaps any kids, certainly in excess or at the expense of healthier foods!). In my opinion, aspartame is not good for anyone, and especially not for ASD children. Nothing is without its drawbacks, but at the moment the sugar substitutes I recommend are stevia and xylitol. Unfortunately, fruits contain high levels of various sugars and must be strictly limited or preferably cut out altogether when yeast is an issue. This includes fruit juices, except for pear juice which yeasts don't seem to crave as they do apple and grape products. Dr. Bruce Semon in his book *Feast Without Yeast*, says "In clinical experience, apples, apple juice, grapes and grape juice wreak havoc in children sensitive to yeast. Pears substitute well for apples; fresh berries substitute well for grapes."[17] Semen only recommends cranberry and pear for fruit sauces. Other clinicians and I have wasted precious time trying to treat yeast with anti-fungal remedies while the child continues to feed the yeast colonization by eating sugary foods, fruit, and fruit juices. Anything that negatively affects immunity is likely to help yeast overgrowth, and sugar (by any other name!) is well known to be injurious to the immune system, especially to one that is already impaired.

In addition to being willing to restrict sugar, parents have taught me that rotating natural anti-fungals such as Lauricidin, grapefruit seed extract, oregano, garlic extract, and undecyn can often help in keeping children free of yeast overgrowth. Homeopathic treatments along with continuous probiotics are often a part of this alternative or "natural" yeast control. Inspired by this, I have for many months been working with Klaire Labs on a potent natural anti-yeast formulation that has a lot of promise, CandXFactors, and we will be starting clinical trials on this agent soon.

When we start anti-fungal treatments, natural or prescription, parents need to know that their child may experience what are called "die-off" side-effects. In medical lingo this is called "the Hexheimer reaction." As the yeasts are starved by lack of sugar and/or are killed by anti-fungal agents there's abnormal release of toxic by-products, creating side-effects that often seem like those of "flu." Symptoms may include fever, irritability and body aches and pains as well as an increase in hyperactivity, "stimming," and other autistic behaviors.

Even though these natural remedies can be quite effective, severe cases of fungal colonization often require a prescription medication; both need to be accompanied by probiotics and sometimes enzymes.

---

[17] Semon, Bruce MD & Kornblum, Lori, *Feast Without Yeast*, Wisconsin Institute of Nutrition, LLP, 1999

Nystatin is the most well-known prescription anti-fungal medication. It is very safe as it does not enter the blood stream but stays within the gastrointestinal system. Besides safety, readiness of most doctors to prescribe it and insurance companies' willingness to pay for it (relatively inexpensive) are a few of Nystatin's best features. Some of its worst are that it works best if given four times a day and is much less effective for more serious infestations than some of the systemic anti-fungals. For the child who cannot swallow capsules, Nystatin powder tastes quite bitter but can be mixed with stevia and dye-free flavorings by a compounding pharmacist.

The prescription anti-fungal that I have found the most useful is Diflucan (Fluconazole), reported to have the best central nervous system penetration. Though all systemic anti-fungals present a small possibility of liver toxicity, I never have seen that in my practice. I order a CBC and Comprehensive Metabolic Panel before starting any prescription anti-fungal other than Nystatin, which is not absorbed by the gut except in rare cases of extreme gut inflammation. If tests are within normal limits, I prescribe 4-5mg/Kg a day of the Diflucan divided into two doses, and administer for 21-30 days. There is a 40mg/ml variety which is most convenient, as it creates a smaller amount that has to be given per dose. I obtain an OAT (organic acid test) to check for yeast in the week following this course of treatment unless the child still has obvious clinical symptoms of yeast infestation. If the latter is true, I give one week off and ask the parents to obtain another serum chemistry with liver enzymes to assure that the liver is not showing stress from the treatment. If this test is normal I do not have to check again for two months unless there is some clinical indication of liver stress.

The other prescription anti-fungals I use are Nizoral (Ketoconazole) and Sporanox (Itraconazole), but only if treatment with Diflucan does not seem effective and if lab-tests indicate the child's colonization would be more responsive to other agents. Sporanox is one of the few antifungals that eradicate Candida parapsilosis, a dangerous pathogen. If rarely the child has elevated liver enzymes on the "safety" blood tests, I resort to the safer Nystatin while giving nutrients to strengthen and regenerate the liver. Note that liver health is extremely important regardless of other treatments.

OTHER GUT PATHOGENS AND TREATMENTS

Sometimes extremely large amounts of probiotics are required to crowd out the yeasts and bacteria, especially Clostridia. Clostridia are anaerobic bacteria commonly present in small amounts in the gut, but capable of creating a dominant colonization. Unfortunately, Clostridia overgrowth can be very resistant to treatment and very destructive to the gut wall. Some children have been noted to have an amazing improvement in their cognition and behavior during a treatment course of the antibiotic Vancomycin, which kills Clostridia. However, because it is spore-forming, the child's impairment almost always returns after the course of antibiotics is completed. When a child has severe Clostridia, even more strict adherence to diet and probiotics is in order. I have learned that clostridia must be treated before or concomitantly with anti-fungal treatment when both are present, as it has been noted that when one is treated, the other can sometimes flourish with less competition for the food available. I have recently started the use of anti-bacterials and anti-fungals concomitantly for several months at a time along with high potency probiotics such as Klaire's Ther-Biotics Complete, a frequent combination being Diflucan with Vancomycin or Flagyl.

Flagyl (Metronidazole) is a powerful antibiotic that is effective against bacteria such as Clostridia and protozoa or other common parasites. This medicine is very bitter, although a compounded form tastes somewhat better. Heavy use of probiotics upon cessation of the drug is recommended as Flagyl will destroy "good bugs" too. In extremely resistant cases of Clostridia, the antibiotic Vancomycin HCl just mentioned is very effective, but also must be followed by adequate probiotics to replace the good flora that this medicine destroys.

Anything that enhances the immune system helps the child combat yeast overgrowth. Anytime a child starts erratic and unusual behaviors (and there is no obvious cause such as starting a new nutrient or a dietary infraction), yeast or other pathogenic overgrowth should always be suspected, tested for, and adequately treated.

Anytime a child acts "drunk" you can bet they have the "auto-brewery syndrome"—alcoholic intoxication due to the overgrowth of Candida albicans in the G.I. tract.

The Secretin Story

Parents are the experts for their own children in most ways. I have noted that if a mother has an eating disorder herself she may find it doubly hard to deny her child the foods that are part of her addiction, especially sugar. Yet I continually see the nobility in parents who supersede their own limitations and do what helps the child, no matter how hard it is. Here's a real-life story.

The desire of one mother to get a certain test for her child with autism led to the development of a useful treatment for a substantial subset of autistic children and provided even more convincing evidence that autism is a gut-related illness. This mother (not a patient of mine) is a guiding light, someone who was not willing to accept her child's severe gastrointestinal problems as something to be disregarded just because he was autistic. The "secretin story" provided important evidence that helped many professionals to recognize that in autism the gut and the brain are connected.

Secretin is a natural hormone that has been used as a diagnostic tool to check pancreatic function. Victoria Beck, the mother of an autistic child troubled by severe diarrhea and gut pain, had read about this test. She convinced a medical doctor to give an infusion of secretin to her son, Parker, to see if it would yield a clue as to why he had constant bowel problems. It only takes 10 or 15 seconds for the infusion to go in. After just that small amount of time, Parker startled both the medical doctor and his mother by speaking directly and coherently to his mother. Victoria's son had not spoken for months.[18]

Victoria was totally elated. The medical practitioner, K. Horvath, MD, of the department of Pediatrics at the University of Maryland, was totally mystified, but intrigued and decided to study the hormone further. After years of exploration he now postulates that secretin helps the leaky guts of some autistic children at least temporarily. In one double-blind, placebo-controlled study, Dr. Horvath and colleagues measured the intestinal permeability of

---

[18] Victoria A. Beck, *Confronting Autism: The Aurora on the Dark Side of Venus —A Practical Guide to Hope, Knowledge, and Empowerment,* 1999, New Destiny Educational Products, Bedford, NH

20 autistic children after a single dose of secretin. "Double-blind, placebo-controlled" simply means that a similar number of patients were infused with a fake hormone and neither the researchers nor the patients knew who was getting the secretin until after the study was over. Thirteen out of 20 autistic children who had exhibited high levels of intestinal permeability showed significant decreases in gut leakage after the infusion of the real hormone.[19]

Research is continuing. In November of 2001, at the annual meeting of the Society for Neuroscience and the International Meeting for Autism Research, scientists reported animal studies demonstrating that secretin specifically activates neurons in the amygdala, a part of the brain known to be important in social interactions. Several studies in other laboratories had previously established that people with autism do not show normal activation of the amygdala when engaged in such social interactions as recognizing emotions from facial expressions. A long-held theory about secretin is that the hormone stimulates proper digestion and assimilation of foods, which may help to increase a child's detoxification potential while enhancing the availability of nutrients necessary for proper brain function.

Though studies have repeatedly shown that secretin therapy is safe, it is recognized that only a subset of autistic children may be significantly responsive. Younger children aged three or four seem to be more responsive than older children with a few notable exceptions. Among the findings presented at a recent international medical meeting:

A. Dr. R. Sockolow and colleagues from the department of pediatrics at Winthrope University Hospital, Mineola, NY, conducted a six-week study on 34 autistic subjects to assess the safety of secretin treatment. Each child had two secretin injections and no serious side effects were seen immediately after the treatments nor during the six-week follow-up. Four of the patients showed "dramatic improvements" in

---

[19] K. Horvath, R. H. Zieke, R. M. Collins et al., "Secretin Improves Intestinal Permeability in Autistic Children." Presented at the World Congress of Pediatric Gastroenterology, August, 2000.

sociability. All four had had low baseline secretin levels before the therapy.[20]

B. In another 12-week double-blind, placebo-controlled study, Dr. Cynthia Schneider and her colleagues at the Southwest Autism Research Center, Phoenix, AZ, evaluated the effects of a single dose of secretin on 30 children with PDD. The children, ages two to 10, were randomly assigned to receive either a high or a low dose of the hormone. Again, neither the researchers, the patients nor their parents knew the size of the dose each child received. The children were given psychological, language and GI assessments at the beginning of the study and at three, six, and 12 weeks after the infusion. The researchers reported that the children who had the most severe PDD symptoms exhibited greater improvements at the six and 12-week points with the high-dose, rather than the low-dose of secretin. Single doses of secretin were generally ineffective in children with mild or moderate levels of autism.[21]

C. When a study is not "blinded", it is called an "open-label" trial. J. R. Lightdale and his colleagues evaluated the effects of single-dose secretin on the gastrointestinal functioning of 20 young autistic children who had a history of GI problems. Prior to treatment, 80% of the children had loose stools. Parents of 15 of the 20 children reported fewer and more normal stools during the five weeks following secretin treatment. Although not confirmed by clinical testing, 83 percent of the parents reported moderate to significant language improvement in their children following the treatment. Lightdale and his colleagues concluded that a subset of autistic children may indeed suffer from pancreatic dysfunction.[22]

---

[20] R. Sockolow, D. Meckes, K. Hewitson, and V. Atluru, "Safe Use of Intravenous Secretin in Autistic Children." World Congress of Pediatric Gastroenterology, August, 2000.

[21] C. K. Schneider et al., "Synthetic Human Secretin in the Treatment of Pervasive Developmental Disorders." World Congress of Pediatric Gastroenterology, August, 2000.

[22] J. R. Lightdale et al., "Evaluation of Gastrointestinal Symptoms in Autistic Children." World Congress of Pediatric Gastroenterology, August, 2000.

Unfortunately, a roughly equal number of studies have failed to find positive effects from secretin infusions. Still, an increasing number of parents claim that secretin helps their children. Why do so many researchers continue to do studies that show negative results? Dr. Bernard Rimland suggests a "negative placebo effect" may be occurring. A "negative placebo effect", he explains, "is the tendency for researchers who believe that a certain treatment doesn't work to conduct research that "proves" just that. As an example, Dr. Rimland cites a study published a few years ago in the *New England Journal of Medicine* in which the researchers reported they found no benefit to autistic children after administration of secretin. Yet, the same authors reported that 69% of the parents wanted their children to be continued on the hormone. Could the parents be better at seeing improvements in their children than the researchers?

I'm a firm believer in parent wisdom. If parents say that their child is improving on the therapy, I'll bet they are usually right. Research on secretin is continuing, and I believe that it will prove to be an effective therapy for about 25% of autistic children.

While secretin is a promising treatment to some children with autism, it obviously isn't a "magic bullet" for all. We keep finding out that there is no one treatment that works for all ASD children. However, secretin was the first treatment to appear in a long time that had such a dramatic effect. Hopes in the ASD community ran high about secretin until we reluctantly realized that most children didn't have the amazing response exhibited by a few. However, the secretin story gave us more clues to the importance of healing the "leaky gut" and helped inspire a lot of investigation into the gut-brain connection that is continuing to this day. Of course, for the small population that benefits by secretin therapy, it is used regularly and in a cyclical manner. When parents who have their child on this treatment see their child revert to earlier or regressive behaviors, these symptoms are signaling that another secretin treatment is needed. Some parents have continued having IV injections given to their children every 5-6 weeks for over 3 years now, and many others continue to use the transdermal form nightly or a few nights a week.

The secretin story is important because it illustrates the value of parental observations and because secretin's efficacy calls attention to the importance of healing intestinal pathologies and leaky guts.

Summary—Gut Health and Healing

In my opinion, when all biomedical factors are considered, restoring intestinal health is a primary key to healing the autistic child's immune system and brain function. A leaky or permeable gut allows peptides, those incomplete proteins that are short chains of amino acids, to leak through the intestines and invade the bloodstream. The bloodstream carries them throughout the body to locations where they are not supposed to be including the brain. Some of the peptides seem to act as opioids that apparently "drug" our children. However, even non-opioid peptides can be dangerous. The body may perceive those peptides as neurotransmitters. These peptides can bind to normal neurotransmitter receptor sites and block, or at least impair, normal transmission of nerve signals. Naturally, this adversely affects brain cognition and development.

Leaky gut syndrome is a subset of intestinal pathology, and not all autism spectrum children have demonstrated increased permeability in their evaluation. Many children do not show the elevated peptides on the tests we now have available, but when they are elevated it is always an extra incentive to the parents to place their child on the restricted diet. However, other types of gastrointestinal pathology can induce the gut inflammation and nutrient deficiencies described previously in this chapter and further in Chapter Six. We know that the leaky gut syndrome causes a long list of vitamin and mineral deficiencies because the inflammation process damages the various carrier proteins normally present in a healthy GI system. My own clinical experience and study after study has shown that these children are deficient in various vitamins, minerals, amino acids, essential fatty acids, enzymes and co-enzymes. That's why I recommend a comprehensive program of nutrient supplementation in conjunction with the GF/CF diet. Besides replacing depleted nutrients, a more recent addition to my supplementation program consists of enzyme therapy to improve the gut's ability to break down proteins. Even on a strict diet there are peptides in foods other than milk, soy and wheat that do not get broken down properly in many children's diets. Many parents are starting to supplement the diet with the use of enzymes and several nutrient companies are working to make better enzyme compounds that are helpful for differing needs. Many parents use them only for dietary infractions, some use only enzymes in conjunction with a regular diet, and others use both. The use of both diet and enzymes at this point appears to be the most beneficial, though some children who are losing their autism diagnosis through chelation and other bio-medical interventions are gradually converting back to a regular diet with the transitional help of enzymes.

For some children who do not respond to the GF/CF/SF diet and continue to have gut problems, parents have gone on to implement even more restricted diets. One of these, the Specific Carbohydrate Diet (SCD) is based on Elaine Gottschall's book, "Breaking the Vicious Cycle," originally intended for those suffering from Crohn's Disease, Ulcerative Colitis, Celiac Disease, IBD, and IBS.[23] This diet is a strict grain-free, lactose-free, sucrose-free dietary regimen that works by severely limiting the availability of carbohydrates to intestinal microbes leading to the formation of acids and toxins which can injure the small intestine. SCD is based on the principle that specifically selected carbohydrates requiring minimal digestion are well absorbed, leaving virtually nothing for intestinal microbes to feed on. At the present time, some ASD parents are transitioning their children from GF/CF/SF to SCD with generally good and some exceptional results. Adjustments have had to be made for the autism population, as many parents found they could not rapidly give their children dairy and honey until after a period of several months or more on the SCD. A website with much information on this diet as well as recipes and lists of "legal" foods is available[24].

I have found that parents who have been using restricted diets, perhaps for years, do not usually return their children to the SAD (Standard American Diet) as they recover. Such parents have learned so much about food and what is good not only for their ASD child

---

[23] Gottschall, Elaine, "Breaking the Vicious Cycle: Intestinal Health Through Diet," Kirkton Pr, Dec. 1994
[24] www.pecanbread.com

but the rest of their family that they avoid the SAD in its embrace of fast, often greasy foods augmented by excessive carbohydrates, non-food items such as coloring agents, and lots of sugar and salt. A setback in their child's hard-earned recovery is not worth the risk and, in the process of implementing and carrying out the diet, most parents have become convinced of the importance of nutrition for overall good health.

I will have more to say about the important role of nutrients in the next chapter. However, I want to again emphasize that the GF/CF/SF and sometimes SCDiet may be the most effective initial action parents can take (before the doctor comes, who may or may not know anything about the importance of diet in autism) to start helping their ASD child move along the road to maximal recovery.

SIX

FEEDING THE STARVING BRAIN

Vital Nutrients

It is now generally accepted that vitamins, minerals and other supplements have important roles to play in promoting optimal health, reducing the risk of chronic disease, and extending the life spans of adults. It thus escapes me why anyone would question the vital role nutrients have in healing the ailing gastrointestinal systems of children with autism spectrum disorder, especially when laboratory tests have revealed vitamin and mineral deficiencies in almost all of the children tested. I will continue to emphasize that children with autism almost always have underlying physical medical problems, especially gastrointestinal problems that must be treated. A child's state of health reflects his or her state of nutrition. When minerals, vitamins, amino acids, or enzymes are deficient in a child's system, the result can be a "disturbed biochemical homeostasis" or imbalance that causes impairment of nutrition to all parts of the system, including the brain. This, in turn, can cause an inability to focus, concentrate, and stay on task. Unfortunately, many mainstream physicians still tell parents that diet changes or supplements are of little use. Many doctors remain locked in a paradigm that says treatment means prescription drugs; once out of formal medical training physicians depend primarily on the pharmaceutical industry to provide their continued medical education.

Woody McGinnis, MD, a leading autism researcher from the Tucson, AZ area conducted a study of ASD children and found that 69% of the children suffer from esophagitis, 42% suffer from gastritis, 67% suffer from duodenitis, and 88% suffer from colitis. The frequent nighttime awakening of ASD children is thought by some clinicians to be due to irritating reflux problems; persistent bowel problems are obvious in years-long intractable diarrhea, constipation, or both at various times in the child's history.

A common denominator in all these conditions is gut inflammation. For example, duodenitis is inflammation of the duodenum. Colitis is inflammation of the colon. Esophagitis is inflammation of the esophagus, and yes, gastritis simply means inflammation of the stomach.

If mainstream medicine will not provide relief for our ASD children suffering from those chronic conditions, we must turn to alternative medicine. By the way, just because "alternative medicine" includes the modifier "alternative," one shouldn't necessarily think of it as "lesser medicine." Although the popular press has made a big deal about the dichotomy between so-called "mainstream medicine" and "alternative medicine," this artificial division blurs considerably if one takes the long view. Many treatments once considered "alternative" have become "mainstream" once their effectiveness became proven. The use of antibiotics to cure ulcers is one example. Furthermore, some therapies once considered "mainstream" are now considered "alternative." The use of herbal therapies is one such example. For hundreds of years, mainstream doctors used herbs as the mainstay of their treatments. It was only with the rise of modern pharmaceutical companies that herbal preparations fell out of favor. Ironically, some herbal therapies may be on the way back to the mainstream. Two examples are the use of the milk thistle herb to strengthen the liver, and the use of St. Johns' Wort, sometimes referred to as "herbal Prozac" for the treatment of depression.

University researchers tell us that the "gold standard" for evaluating medical therapies is the double blind, placebo-controlled study —the type of study where neither the patients nor their treating physicians know which is the treatment being evaluated and which is the placebo. However, as anyone who is familiar with the history of medicine can attest, most medical treatments in current use were originally validated over a period of time by the "silver standard" of clinical trials without the rigorous double blind, placebo-control study to back it up. Once a treatment is known to work it often becomes unethical (especially in lifesaving situations) to do a double blind, placebo-controlled study because one segment of the population being tested will get the placebo, not the needed treatment.

In the absence of large scale, double-blind studies, how does one separate the wheat from the chaff in treating this complicated disorder we call ASD? There are reasons DAN! practitioners take a pragmatic view in prescribing the treatments they do. A large number of biochemical and biological abnormalities have been identified in autistic children and adults and, as James Laidler, MD, a medical colleague, pointed out, "Treatments directed at these abnormalities are likely to be helpful." And they are. One of my inspirational and favorite mottos is Dr. Bernard Rimland's emphatic "Do what works!" Many of the successful DAN! treatments were learned through trial and error, since few researchers have been interested in looking for funding for studies on nutritional deficiencies, nutrient supplementation, special diets, or detoxification protocols. (However, NIH has recently funded two studies on thimerosal's possible role as a neurotoxin for the immune systems of newborns, which is certainly a step in the right direction). Informed parents and concerned physicians are not willing to wait until extensive formal studies are done to use methods that are safe, make a lot of sense and are already showing benefit for many children.

NUTRITIONAL DEFICIENCIES
IDENTIFIED IN OUR CHILDREN

What are the biochemical imbalances generally present in ASD children? According to a DAN! study on the "Nutritional Status of Autistic Children,"[1] most autistic children demonstrate the following abnormalities:

---

[1] Reported by Woody McGinnis, MD, during presentation at October, 2001 DAN conference, San Diego. For a review of published medical studies on the nutritional status of autistic and ADHD children see www.autism.com/mcginnis

- Low vitamin B6 levels and poor B6-binding combined with low or low-normal amounts of intracellular magnesium

- Low intracellular zinc

- Low blood levels of vitamin A

- Low biotin, B1, B3, and B5 function, according to micro-biological assays

- Low urinary vitamin C

- Low Red Blood Cell (RBC) membrane levels of eicsapentae-noic acid (EPA is a derivative of omega-3 fatty acids)

- Elevated RBC membrane levels of archidonic acid (one cause of inflammation)

- Low levels of taurine (vital to nerve cells)

- Elevated casomorphine and gliadomorphine levels (opioid peptides)

- Elevated urinary yeast metabolites

- Elevated IgG antibodies to milk

- Imbalance of the bacterial flora of the gut

In addition, many autistic children demonstrate:

- Low serum selenium (50% of subjects)

- Low folate and B12 on microbiological assay

- Elevated Red Blood Cell membrane trans fatty acid levels

- IgG antibodies to grains

- Elevated urinary bacterial metabolites (50% of subjects)

- Overly acidic stools

Furthermore, studies by Dr. William Walsh, Dr. William Shaw and others reveal that large numbers of autistic children are deficient in Zinc, B6, and GLA (Gamma Linolenic Acid), as well as low methionine levels usually due to poor-quality protein intake.

THE USE OF VITAL NUTRIENTS

The above listed imbalances are what I and many other DAN! practitioners are attempting to treat with biomedical protocols that use specific vitamins, minerals, and other nutrients. Although these treatments have not been formally evaluated by large double-blind, placebo-controlled trials, the vital nutrients employed have been used safely for years to treat these and similar abnormalities in patients with other ailments. In other words, we know from long-term clinical practice that these supplements are safe and effective. Still, it is important to point out here that often a great deal of trial and error is involved in determining optimal nutrients and appropriate dosage levels for each child. Even though we know certain substances may be deficient in most of the children in the spectrum, individual tolerances and sensitivities require that we start with low doses, build slowly toward what we feel are adequate levels to correct deficiencies, and observe closely for reactions. In very sensitive children, occasional testing must be done to evaluate specific deficiencies and help guide us in our nutrient program. There are even brand sensitivities in some children, and certain additives or tablet coverings can sometimes make the difference as far as tolerability for a particular child.

The vast majority of my patients, particularly the younger ones, show enormous benefits from their nutrient/vitamin/mineral program. Typically ASD children's food choices have been so limited that almost all of them have long-standing vitamin and mineral deficiencies. If they were not using vitamin supplements before, the reaction is sometimes quite dramatic, taking the form of greater speech, more eye contact, and better behavior and sleeping patterns within days to a few weeks after starting their nutrient program. My advice to parents is to start with low doses, using one new nutrient at a time until the child adjusts to the recommended dose before starting the next nutrient, all the while carefully observing and recording reactions.

Parents are often dismayed at the number of nutrients they are asked to give to their children, and some creative ways have been devised by vitamin dispensers and parents to hide bad flavors. Giving the child a feeling that they are doing a very important job in getting them down (and resisting making a face when you smell them yourself!) often helps. Sometimes nothing but a compassionate but firm, "There's no choice; we have to do this, so let's get it over with" approach is necessary. Following the nutrient brew with a favorite drink or a favorite chewable clearly in sight is sometimes helpful. There is a lot of incentive for the parents to teach the children how to swallow capsules, which makes life easier for everyone. To facilitate this, parents may purchase very small empty capsules at their pharmacy and practice with these to get the child used to swallowing small objects before moving on to the regular or large sized capsules.

When parents fully understand the seriousness of their child's nutritional deficiencies, it makes this daunting task of taking supplements more tolerable, just as in the case of the GF/CF diet when parents recognize the damage certain foods are doing to their child's gastrointestinal tracts and brains. Some parents who felt that their children did have a fairly good diet were quite surprised at the beneficial reaction to the nutrient program. These cases demonstrate that due to maldigestion or malabsorption problems even a child that is not so picky still may not be providing the proper nutrition to the brain because of his or her gut inflammation.

PRIMARY RECOMMENDED SUPPLEMENTS

Primary

- Vitamin B6, preferably the activated form P5P`, 50mg under 5yrs/day, 50-100mg over 5yrs/day

- Magnesium, glycinate form is most absorbable, 200-400mg/day. (I also advise the Vit B6 in the activated P5P` + Magnesium)

- Zinc, picolinate form is most absorbable, but I also give zinc monomethionine and zinc citrate at certain times and for certain children: 20-50mg/day (up to 1mg/lbs + 20)

- Calcium, at least one gram daily divided into several doses

- Selenium, doses up to 150-200 mcg daily for the larger children; 75-150 mcg under 5 (unless testing shows levels very low—high doses can be toxic)

- Vitamin A, 2500-5000iu/day (part may be as Cod Liver Oil); beta-carotene does not convert to A in most children.

- Vitamin C, up to 1000mg/day to tolerance, better given 3 or 4 x/day (doesn't stay in the body very long)

- Vitamin E, 200mg/day for under 5yrs, 400mg/day for over 5yrs

- Essential Fatty Acids, Omega-3's 750-1200mg, essential for all–750mg EPA, 250-500 DHA/ and GLA 50-100mg/day

- DMG (125mg caps or sublinguals 1-6/day) or TMG (500-2000mg/day + Folinic Acid (800-1600mcg/day)

- Vitamin B12 as methylcobalamin 750-2500mcg injectables (75mcg/Kg) 2X/wk

Miscellaneous

- Additional Minerals e.g. Manganese, Chromium, Molybdenum, Boron, Vanadium

- B-vitamins e.g.Thiamine, Riboflavin, Niacin, Biotin, Pantothenic Acid

- Amino Acids, essential and non-essential

- Minerals, B-Vitamins, and Amino Acids are usually included in a comprehensive multiple vitamin/mineral compound. With amino acid testing, some children receive an individualized formula, which is optimum, but usually balanced formulas are available that serve many children adequately.

- Specific nutrients may sometimes be given based on test results showing deficiencies or in special circumstances such as chelation which may require extra nutrients to compensate losses. Special nutrients may include those with strong antioxidation benefit, such as idebenone. (The biological form of CoQ10.)

- Most children are low in L-glutathione; reduced L-gluta-thione in capsules and transdermal creams are available and advised for some children. For children who do not have elevated cysteine (about 15%), reduced L-glutathione precursors are good preparation for chelation and actually begin the process slowly and safely.

- Milk thistle compounds for liver health and immune enhancers or modulators such as transfer factor or arabinogalactans are utilized for children whose immune impairment results in frequent illnesses.

Metallothionein Dysfunction

Dr. William Walsh at the Pfeiffer Treatment Center in Naperville IL has been working on metallothionein dysfunction in ASD children and reports significant improvements in nutrient programs designed to correct this dysfunction. (see Causation Models in Chapter One and Testing in Chapter Four). His medical system includes extensive laboratory testing, diagnosis of chemical imbalances, identification of nutrients that are in deficiency or overload, and biochemical therapy aimed at balancing body chemistry. Though some of his nutrient protocols are patented and presently not generally available except to those working with his staff, he has shared some of his findings. He states that "45% of our autistic population exhibit undermethylation which can be effectively treated with supplements of methionine, magnesium, DMG, SAM(e), and calcium, along with strict avoidance of DMAE and folic acid. In contrast, 15% of autistics exhibit overmethylation and benefit from liberal doses of DMAE, folic acid, and B-12, along with strict avoidance of methionine and SAM(e)."[2] Undermethylation is thought to be the predominant state in most ASD children. What seems like "over methylation may indicate a trap in the complex folate cycle where important enzymes and co-factors are not available to keep the cycle functioning properly. See Appendix D4.

---

[2] Walsh, William J. et al., Booklet, "Metallothionein and Autism," Pfeiffer Trtmt Ctr, Naperville IL, Oct. 2001

The Rationale Behind the Use of Specific Nutrients

B6 AND MAGNESIUM

Bernard Rimland has for many years championed Vitamin B6 (pyridoxine) and magnesium as effective treatments for ASD children deficient in those substances. According to Dr. Rimland, 18 studies evaluating vitamin B6 as a treatment for autistic children have provided positive results. Dr. Rimland collaborated on two such studies; in one double-blind, placebo-controlled study with Drs. Enoch Callaway of the University of California, San Francisco, and Pierre Dreyfus of the University of California, Davis, 16 autistic children were treated with B6 and magnesium. The magnesium was added because it enhances the effects of B6 and protects against possible B6-induced magnesium deficiency.

There were statistically significant positive benefits to children who were on daily doses of between 300 and 500 mg of B6 (8 mg of B6 per pound of body weight) combined with several hundred mg of magnesium (3 or 4 mg of magnesium per pound of body weight). The benefits included increased eye contact, less self-stimulatory behavior, more interest in the world around them, fewer tantrums, and expanded speech. While no patient has been "cured" with the vitamin B6 and magnesium treatments, many parents report the treatments produced calming effects and resulted in improved, more normal behavior.

In a survey of over 3,500 parents of autistic children, the parents were asked to provide rating on a variety of treatments and interventions. Among the biomedical treatments, the use of vitamin B6 and magnesium received the highest rating from 318 parents with 8.5 of them reporting behavioral improvement to every one reporting behavioral worsening. Those results were better than what parents reported for drug treatments.

ZINC

Zinc is present in over 200 body enzymes, and its deficiency results in a weakened immune system. It is well known that most ASD children are deficient in zinc and excessive diarrhea is known to be one of the leading causes of zinc depletion. In fact, at the 2001 DAN! conference biochemist William Walsh, PhD reported that a study of 503 children with autism revealed that 85% had high copper-zinc ratios. In other words, they had abnormally high levels of copper and low levels of zinc in their bodies. Zinc is an essential micronutrient that the human immune system needs to function at peak performance. Zinc deficiency affects a range of functions including growth, immunity, and brain development. Controlled trials have shown that zinc supplementation is associated with improved growth, particularly among stunted children. Zinc also reduces the severity and duration of both acute and chronic diarrhea. In fact, the World Health Organization recommends giving zinc supplements to children as part of managing severe protein energy malnutrition and persistent diarrhea.[3] Though a dosage of 25-50mg of zinc is usual, in those with high copper levels, higher doses may be needed to oppose and get the copper level down. Zinc is so important that when I have children in chelation and their copper levels are high, I usually suggest 1mg per pound of body weight or more depending on test levels. Levels may need to be monitored for certain children to keep their levels within a normal range.

CALCIUM

Calcium is a major constituent of bones and teeth, and is crucial for nerve conduction, muscle contraction, heartbeat, blood coagulation, the production of energy, and maintenance of immune system function. A calcium deficiency can contribute to ADD/ADHD behavior. Children deficient in calcium are more likely to exhibit irritability, sleep disturbances, anger, and inattentiveness. According to the American Academy of Pediatrics, the current dietary intake of calcium by children and adolescents is well below the recommended optimal levels.[4] The first signs of a calcium deficiency include nervous stomach, cramps, tingling in the arms and legs, and painful joints. Children need from 800-1200mg of calcium daily, particularly those on the GF/CF diet.

---

[3] Statement at the WHO Conference on Zinc and Human Health, Stockholm, 14th June 2000.

[4] Policy Statement, American Academy of Pediatrics, in the journal *Pediatrics,* 104, Number 5, November 1999, pp. 1152-1157.

SELENIUM

Selenium is a mineral with antioxidant properties that works with vitamin E in preventing free radical damage to cell membranes. Selenium deficiency causes depressed immune function and a resulting increase in susceptibility to infections due to decreased levels of white blood cells and natural killer cells. Selenium is antagonistic to heavy metals in the body, and is an important mineral to supplement especially during chelation therapy. Care must be taken not to overdose since it can be toxic in excess and the multiple mineral supplements usually already contain selenium. I recommend 100 to 200mcg/day total intake.

VITAMIN A

Vitamin A is an antioxidant and general immune enhancer, specific against measles. Current RDA's for A are probably far too low generally and more so for our population, though rare cases of A can be toxic, usually in long-sustained high doses or mega-doses in the millions. Some parents are currently using a 2-day mega-dose to combat gut measles in their ASD children. Infants and many children are not able to convert non-toxic beta-carotene to A, so though important for itself carotenes cannot be relied upon as a source of A. Vitamin D can be toxic in large doses, so only up to 5000iu of A daily should be obtained from Cod Liver Oil; mega-dosing with Vitamin A must be done with the palmitate (or fish oil without D). My criteria for mega-dosing (400,000iu for 2 days in a row every six months) are: Elevated IgG serum rubeola titers, evidence of auto-immunity per high myelin basic protein and other neural elements antibodies, history of regression after MMR, and persistent gut problems, (and if possible to obtain, elevated salivary IgA secretory antibodies).

Dr. Mary Megson, a pediatrican in Richmond VA, showed that certain children susceptible to autism are genetically at risk from a G-alpha protein defect. She posits a progression of injury in these susceptible children starting with exposure to wheat, followed by exposure to measles antigen, and then addition of the pertussis toxin, which takes them into a disconnection of the G-alpha protein path-ways. The retinoid receptor pathways are critical for vision, sensory perception, language processing and attentiveness. Sideways glancing may indicate poor rod function and may be a tip-off to the G-alpha protein defect, especially if family history shows others with night-blindness and hypothyroidism. A trial of Cod Liver Oil followed by a trial of Urecholine for stimulating acetylcholine receptor blockage (shown by decreased bile and pancreatic secretions) might be therapeutic in this subset of ASD children.

VITAMINS C AND E

Vitamins C and E are important antioxidants which work together to fight free radicals, those unstable oxygen molecule outlaws that can literally pierce cell walls and oxidize or destroy brain cells. Since brain cells are very vulnerable to oxidative stress, adequate supplies of both vitamins C and E are essential. The body cannot manufacture Vitamin C so it has to be taken in through food or supplements, Vitamin C also protects against the harmful effects of pollutants and enhances immunity. Mothers of autistic children with constipation will be happy to learn that Vitamin C also helps regularize bowel movements because of its cathartic properties. In fact, Vitamin C is so important that we ask parents to increase it to gut tolerance, determined by increasing the dose until it causes diarrhea, than backing off just a little. We suggest parents give C in divided doses, as it does not stay around very long in the body. Vitamin C works synergistically with Vitamin E, so these two should be given together. C is recommended up to 1000mg or more/day and Vitamin E from 200-600IU/day according to the size of the child.

Vitamin E is an especially important antioxidant, protecting cell membranes from oxidative damage. This important vitamin promotes proper metabolism and reception of vitamin D and calcium, improves circulation, and repairs tissue. E also prevents cell damage by inhibiting lipid peroxidation and the formation of free radicals.

ESSENTIAL FATTY ACIDS

Factors contributing to an almost universal shortage of essential fatty acids in most Americans are: Soil depletion, excessive food processing, (e.g. chemical processing and refinement of foods with removal of certain oils to extend shelf life), and the widening use of antibiotics with the consequent alteration of intestinal flora. Children with attention problems and autism have been shown to be more deficient in essential fatty acids as a group than neurotypical children. Fish oil is rich in a special type of fatty acid called Omega-3. These fatty acids are labeled "essential" because our bodies don't make them. They must enter the body through our diets or from supplements. Furthermore, many autistic children have defects in fatty acid metabolism. Fish oil supplements work to correct that deficiency and are recommended for all children, not just those in the ASD spectrum. Cod Liver Oil supplies both Omega-3's and Vitamin A, but many children find it offensive to swallow. New deodorized forms of fish oils are becoming available, so it is important for parents to experiment until they find one their child will tolerate. I recommend 500-1000mg EPA/day and 250-500mg of DHA/day. Some children also need GLA 50-100mg/day; some forms of fish oil supplements contain all three of these together.

Omega-3 fatty acids are vital for normal brain development and the maintenance of neurotransmitter, cellular, and membrane integrity. Neurotransmitters affect behavior and learning. Any neurotransmitter deficiency or blockage will have a dramatic effect on a child's (or an adult's for that matter) ability to learn and function optimally. These essential Omega-3 fatty acids also help improve the immune response, work against inflammation in the GI tract, and help keep the blood flowing by preventing blood clots.

Please see information on testing for fatty acids deficiencies in Chapter Four.

DMG AND TMG

DMG (Dimethylglycine) benefits about half of the ASD children who take it, with notable language improvement in some after only a few days or weeks. Since it is non-toxic and also known to be an immunity enhancer, I suggest all parents give their child an experimental DMG trial. I prefer the small sublingual 125mg tablets because the children usually love glycine's natural sweetness, (I am always looking for nutrients the children like.) Morning dosages are preferable as some children show some hyperactivity until they get used to it; I suggest starting with one tablet and working up to 6 or more (all taken in the am) if benefit is shown. The hyperactivity that occurs with DMG in some children can be moderated by giving folinic acid along with it up to 2400 mcg/day. If the hyperactivity persists even with the folinic acid, the DMG should be discontinued, as approximately 15% of children are reported to be intolerant of methylating agents such as DMG and TMG (the "overmethylators.") Some mothers state that TMG does not cause the hyperactivity that DMG does; TMG is DMG with one more methyl group, increasing serotonin through a precursor called SAM(e) (S-Adenosylmethionine), an enzyme important in acetylcholine synthesis. However, other mothers report that when they changed from DMG to TMG they noticed hyperactivity and returned to the DMG without problem. Children's chemistries are so unique that trial and error with these non-toxic substances is the only way to find out whether they are beneficial. Both DMG and TMG have a tremendous safety record. See Appendix D4.

B-VITAMINS

The B vitamins are coenzymes involved in energy production and help to maintain healthy nerves, skin, eyes, hair, liver and mouth as well as muscle tone in the gastrointestinal tract. B vitamins should be taken together as they work as a team, but a larger amount of any one may be given additionally when necessary, such as B6 or folic acid.

A. **B1 or thiamine** is important for blood formation, the production of hydrochloric acid, and carbohydrate metabolism.

B. **Vitamin B2 or riboflavin** is necessary for red blood cell formation, antibody production, and is essential for the metabolism of tryptophan.

C. **Vitamin B3 or niacin, niacinamide, or nicotinic acid** is necessary for proper circulation. It plays an important role in the formation of tryptophan in the liver. Niacin aids in the metabolism of carbohydrates, fats, and proteins and in the proper functioning of the nervous system.

D. **Vitamin B5 or pantothenic acid** is known as the "anti-stress" vitamin. It is important in the production of the adrenal hormones, the formation of antibodies, and helps convert fats, carbohydrates, and proteins into energy. B5 is essential for production of vital steroids and cortisone in the adrenal glands.

E. **Vitamin B6 or pyridoxine (in its biologically activated form, pyridoxal 5' phosphate, or P5P)** is involved in more bodily functions than any other single nutrient. This vitamin maintains sodium and potassium balance, promotes red blood cell formation, and is necessary for normal brain function and the synthesis of RNA and DNA. These are the nucleic acids containing genetic instructions for the reproduction of all cells and for normal cellular growth. Multiple studies have shown the importance of Vitamin B6 for ASD children. Magnesium enhances the absorption and reduces hyperactivity which some children show with B6; I prefer the P5P compounded with magnesium for optimum benefit.

F. **Vitamin B12** is necessary for cell formation, proper digestion, absorption of foods, protein synthesis, and metabolism of carbohydrates and fats. A B12 deficiency is most often due to a defect in absorption and not a dietary lack except in strict vegetarians, since it is only available from animal sources. Deficiency is common in those with digestive disorders. Symptoms of deficiency include abnormal gait, memory problems, eye disorders, and anemia. Many ASD children show a mild anemia which can be caused by other nutrient deficiencies, especially zinc, as well as heavy metal intoxication. If the anemia is mild, I try to rebalance with nutrient support and gut healing before giving iron, which can increase oxidative stress. If more severe, insufficient B12 levels as a cause can be tested by a urine or blood measurement of methylmalonic acid (MMA), but there is no completely reliable test for Vitamin B12 adequacy. A trial with a methylcobalamin injection showing a good response qualifies as a positive test. If doses are adequate, we will usually see a positive response within the first few days. If the initial B12 shot does benefit the child, parents can be taught to administer the injection in varying schedules depending upon how long the benefit lasts. After a while parents can experiment to see if high oral doses will accomplish the same results. (See Appendix D3)

G. **Folic acid (folate):** Folic acid functions as a coenzyme in DNA synthesis and is essential for the formation of red blood cells. It works best when combined with Vitamin B12. The anemia caused by folic acid deficiency is similar to that of B12 deficiency, "large cell" or macrocytic anemia. Folic acid deficiency is common in those with chronic diarrhea, and does not store in the body for many years as does Vitamin B12. Folinic acid is the biologically active form.

AMINO ACIDS

Amino acids are fundamental building blocks for muscle and brain tissue and for hormones, neurotransmitters, hormones, and digestive enzymes. They are molecules connected together to form peptides or proteins, which can contain hundreds to thousands of amino acids. When vegetable or animal proteins are ingested, our digestive tract breaks them down to single, free-form amino acids or to very short-chained peptides (two or three aminos) which can be absorbed through the mucosal cells of the small intestine. Further digestion takes place by peptidase enzymes in the blood, liver, kidney and other organs. The resulting pool of free-form amino acids can then be reassembled in specific sequences to make human proteins and peptides used for tissue growth and repair and for a multitude of physiologic functions. The essential amino acids are: leucine, isoleucine, valine, methionine, phenylalanine, tryptophan, lysine, and threonine. Important nonessential (meaning the body can make them) amino acids especially in autism are taurine, cysteine, and glutamine. It is estimated that at least two-thirds of ASD children show abnormal amino acid patterns as shown by urine or fasting plasma amino acid analyses. Some of these abnormalities are of genetic origin, such as Phenylketonuria, but most of them seem to be related to maldigestion and subnormal uptake. Some labs which perform the amino acid analysis offer a customized amino acid powder to address the deficiencies, and adequate B-Vitamins and essential minerals must be provided with these supplements.

ADDITIONAL MINERALS

Vitamins and minerals are cofactors that activate amino acids and fatty acids in metabolic processes; they catalyze reactions in the mitochondria of the cells and are synergistic, meaning there is a cooperative action among them. Calcium, magnesium, sodium, potassium and phosphorus, are the "major" minerals and are needed in larger amounts than what are called "trace minerals": zinc, iron, copper, manganese, chromium, selenium, molybdenum, boron, germanium, sulfur, vanadium and iodine. Except for specially tested deficiencies or extra needs due to absorption problems or chelation, minerals are usually given in a multiple compound designed for the typical balance needed.

Nutrient Interactions

Although I have listed each of the above nutrients individually and explained the principal roles of each, it must be emphasized that there is a synergistic interaction or "dance" between the various vitamins, minerals, and other nutrients. In this dance, vitamins, minerals, and other nutrients partner with each other, changing partners often as they work together to enhance the health of the body and mind. That's why deficiencies in one vitamin or mineral often affect the role other vitamins and minerals play. For instance, deficiencies in Vitamins A, C, E, or of the B vitamins niacin, panothenic acid, B6, and folic acid and/or deficiencies in minerals like zinc, magnesium, calcium and selenium impact on numerous gastrointestinal and neurological processes. In particular, deficiencies in any of the vital nutrients just discussed can interfere with the body's ability to metabolize essential fatty acids. That can affect the immune and gastrointestinal systems and interfere with neurons, the message signaling transmitters to the brain. Study after study has revealed that not only autistic children, but also children with ADD and ADHD are lacking in key nutrients. When these nutrients are not present in the body or diet, cognitive function and behavior is adversely affected. If parents want their child to get better, it is absolutely vital to identify and correct nutritional deficiencies that interfere with the metabolism and functions for which certain nutrients are known to be necessary for optimal functioning.

Testing for Nutritional Deficiencies

Testing, as described in Chapter Four, usually starts with a routine complete blood count, urinalysis, a metabolic profile, and thyroid panel. This helps me see an iron deficiency as well as overall kidney, liver, thyroid and general health status. I list here again the particular tests that help to determine the optimum nutrient program for the ASD child (together with the medical and dietary history and clinical assessment):

- Fasting amino acid analysis (plasma)
- Organic acid analysis (OAT—urine)
- Fatty acid analysis (plasma)
- IgG (delayed) 90-food sensitivity test (serum)
- Red blood cell essential minerals (whole blood)
- Metallothionein dysfunction (see Chapter Four)

Red cell membranes can also be tested for fatty acid levels, but since we know almost all of our children are deficient, it is sometimes more prudent to provide the fatty acids and clinically observe the child's reactions. An RBC essential minerals analysis is performed as a monitoring test every few months when the child is undergoing chelation to make sure the mineral levels remain properly balanced. Occasionally, specific elements must be checked in a certain child such as cysteine, sulfates, and stool pH to help us fine-tune their supplement intake. Hair analysis is useful as a screen and can show overall imbalance patterns; this test serially can then be corroborated with more specific urine and blood testing if the child is not responding to the nutrient program in the way we had hoped.

Parents Say Nutrients Help Their Children

Some of the parents who come for evaluation seeking detoxification for their children from mercury reluctantly agree to the nutrient program when they find out it is a prerequisite to get to the magic "chelation therapy" they have heard about (see Chapter Seven). Many children improve so much on the nutrient program that some parents have questioned whether their child needs chelation. Actually, we know that the body will begin a detoxification process as the metabolism starts getting balanced, but this may be a very long process for most children. Since the parents want to maximize brain-healing without being required to indefinitely create special diets and give large doses of nutrients, almost all go on to a full supplement program to prepare their children for chelation. As they are also required to maintain the optimum diet for reducing gut inflammation and yeast overgrowth as well as administer probiotics regularly, they find the combination of this regime plus the supplements provides noticeable improvement in bowel function, cognition, and overall behavior. These parents did not realize the extent to which their children's brains were starving!

Here are some comments from just a few of those parents:

Sarah, the mother of 5 year-old Aaron reports, "In the past five or so days Aaron has taken a large leap forward. We see this mainly in language and abstract thinking. We are amazed at some of the things he is coming up with. We find ourselves just looking at each other with each new comment that he makes. We feel it is due to the supplements."

Janice, mother of 3-1/2 year old Terry, "We are faithfully following your recommendations since Terry has done nothing but improve dramatically since starting the supplements. He has been responding very well, with increased verbal skills which are surprising all of his therapists. He is listening better, repeating what I say as if he's absorbing new learning. It's very gratifying. Pronunciation is still rough, and he still has attention and processing issues. It will be exciting to see if we get even better results with the chelation process."

Darlene, mother of 4 year old Danny: "I think with all these supplements, Danny's overall performance has improved a lot already. Just this week, he started to use his gestures when he talks. This is something we have trained him to do for so long, and he just couldn't do before."

Joan, mother of 3 yr old Julia: "Within a week to ten days of starting the supplements, Julia has added 50 new words to her vocabulary. Her teachers are amazed and every day she seems to be coming up with new words we didn't even know she knew."

Marilyn, mother of 5 yr old Jimmy: " I never thought I'd be able to get all these pills down Jimmy, but once he knew he had to do it, he's being surprisingly willing. I think it's because he feels better and cares more about pleasing me and relating to all of us more than he ever has. He's definitely trying to talk more since we started the program. We are so pleased."

In summary, nutritional supplements can help alleviate the deficiencies so common in autism spectrum children. Nutritional imbalances are known to contribute to immune system abnormalities, pathogenic intestinal overgrowth, and impairment in detoxification. For those parents who do not choose to test their children, there are excellent neutraceutical companies that provide vitamin and mineral supplements specifically for ASD children. Supplement mixes are already made up that cover the most frequent types of deficiencies in the doses appropriate for the child's age, and I encourage all parents to get their child started on basic nutrients. Kirkman Laboratories is a company that worked with Dr. Bernard Rimland over 20 years ago to develop a compound called Super Nu-Thera (SNT) that continues to improve over the years and works well for many children. Kirkman's has dedicated itself to working with the autistic community to provide nutrients especially for this population. Kirkman's also provides a website with a marvelous compendium of autism information that may be downloaded for free. Dr. Michael Lang, a nutritionist with two autistic children himself, also has worked for many years to put out an excellent small line of vitamin and mineral supplements called BrainChild Nutritionals that are targeted for ASD children, (831) 465-0104. I recommend both of these companies, as well as other excellent neutraceutical firms that make a range of specific supplements needed by individuals and sub-groups of ASD children. The nutrient companies I personally use the most are: Thorne Laboratories, Ecological Formulas, and Klaire Laboratories. Vitamin Research Products, NF Formulas and Tyler Formulations also carry some specialty items I often recommend. I am sure there are many good products and neutraceutical companies that I have not tested, but over the years I have worked out nutri-ent programs that experience has shown me will help most of the children I evaluate using the sources mentioned. Supplementation is emerging as an increasingly important means of treating autism, as we are learning more about the role of the affected gastrointestinal tract in this disorder.

SEVEN

REMOVING THE HEAVY METALS

Heavy Metal Toxicity

Imagine you are standing on a pier. Your child is drowning (he or she has developed autism or one of the other autism spectrum disorders) and you can't swim. You desperately look for help or a life preserver (a physician or treatments that might work). You find a rope tied to the pier (special diets, nutritional supplements, anti-fungal/anti-viral treatments, secretin, chelation for heavy metal toxicity—all of which you have learned are safe and help many of these children). However, authorities warn you not to use it because it has not been proven that the rope is strong enough (the treatment option has not received final approval by "authorities" who are waiting for reports of completed scientific studies appearing in peer-reviewed journals). Meanwhile your child is still drowning (exhibiting autistic/ASD symptoms).

If you were that parent on the pier you wouldn't wait for the completion of double-blind clinical trials to assure you that that rope is strong enough. You would pick it up and throw it to your child. The worst that could happen is that the rope would break with your child closer to the pier! In real life, numerous parents, some of whom are physicians, have been finding that removing toxic metals is an effective treatment for their children. Parents of ASD children cannot afford to wait for approval of the guiding agencies appointed to protect our children's health to try treatment options these agencies consider "alternative medicine," particularly when the "traditional experts" have nothing better to offer. This is especially true as the parents learn that the very actions they dutifully followed on the recommendation of these authoritative agencies may have been the cause of their child's autism, such as accepting the mandate that their newborn be vaccinated with unsafe levels of ethylmercury via the HepB vaccine. The case for mercury-triggered ASD has been made in Chapter Three; further details are provided in Appendix B.

As we discussed in Chapter Three, many and probably most ASD children have impaired detoxification capability. This means that the child has reduced ability to sequester and/or eliminate toxic substances. Heavy metals merit special concern because they are present in increasing amounts in the environment of our technological society. The child's impaired detoxification appears to derive from several possible sources, including early immune injury and "mild" or not so mild intestinal pathologies with subsequent effects on nutritional status and immune function. Chelation-efficacy studies already presented to the Institute of Medicine and at an international conference support a new model: many autism-spectrum children have impairments causally related to the child's excessive accumulation of toxic metals. Also important is the fact that, along with removing excess accumulation of heavy metals, many children's biomedical profiles often reveal other underlying pathologies that, when treated, improve the child's gastrointestinal health, immunity, and capability for further detoxification.

A Practical Approach to the Removal of Mercury

Although occasionally described as an "alternative" therapy, oral chelation has been well studied and found to be both safe and effective for children. However, many physicians are not even aware that detoxification mechanisms are impaired in almost all autistic children, and very few are trained to oversee a chelation protocol. Chelation of ASD children should always be preceded by gut-healing, nutritional correction, and as much general improvement in the child's immune system as is possible. In fact, the preparation for chelation often enables the detoxification mechanisms to start improving on their own. I have seen this happen many times in my practice; the desire for this kind of treatment will finally motivate the parents to do a strict diet and place their children on the nutritional supplements they need to start getting better. Almost all children improve on the preparation process even before actually starting chelation.

Currently, DMSA[1] is the primary substance that I and other DAN! practitioners use to remove mercury and other heavy metals from our children if testing shows they are heavy-metal poisoned. DMSA binds toxic metals and enables them to be eliminated from the body, primarily through the urine. Also known as Chemet, the prescription form made by Sanofi Pharmaceuticals, DMSA was approved in 1998 by the FDA for the removal of lead from the bodies of children; its safety in children is well studied and documented. Fortunately, DMSA also binds other heavy metals, particularly mercury, although the process must be carried out with caution, since chelation also may remove other essential minerals needed by the body. If a child's medical history supported by laboratory testing indicates the presence of heavy metals, I use a protocol of oral chelation with DMSA in the first phase of the detoxification process. The child needs to be well mineralized prior to starting; during chelation, nutritional status and metal-profiles are monitored with regular lab tests.

I was moved to start using chelation therapy in my practice after hearing reports about the success that Dr. Amy Holmes was having in improving the health and behavior of autistic children through the removal of mercury and other metals by chelation. The mother of an autistic son, Dr. Holmes left retirement not long after her son was diagnosed with autism to join Dr. Stephanie Cave's medical practice in Baton Rouge, LA.

In October 2000, Dr. Cave spoke at an autism conference prompted by Bernard et al's autism/thimerosal paper (see Appendix B) and hosted by the National Institute of Environmental Health

---

[1] DMSA, trade name Chemet made by Sanofi Pharmaceuticals, is 2,3-dimercaptosuccinic acid

Sciences. The meeting's primary focus was the possible role of mercury in the causation of autism. She told the group that in her experience over a number of years of treating over 400 autistic children with various modalities, she had found no treatment more effective in a great many of those children than removing toxic metals via chelation.[2]

I had been corresponding by e-mail with Dr. Holmes about other treatments we were both using or considering around the time she was starting to chelate her own son and was impressed with her candor and courage as well as her careful and scientific approach to this new and exciting protocol. I knew she would not do anything that would harm her son who was her first chelation patient. Dr. Holmes inspired me to start chelation therapy with my granddaughter Chelsey, who was my first chelation patient and already six years old by that time. Evidence indicates that the older the children are, the slower they excrete the metals, but I believe it is better late than never to get their toxic load down as much as possible. Chelsey's progress was slow compared with the very young children I began chelating subsequently. We are still using chelation with Chelsey, with several long breaks along the way for other treatments.

Detoxification is not simple, and though there are various chelation protocols available for adults, there were no well-known chelation protocols in place for treatment of children prior to 1999 except for lead removal. Despite Stephen Edelson's 1998 study, only a few people were beginning to realize that mercury probably played a role in our epidemic of "regressive" autism.[3] In response to that situation, Dr. Bernard Rimland, director of the Autism Research Institute (ARI), convened a Consensus Conference on the Detoxification of Autistic Children in Dallas, Texas, February 9-11, 2001. The attendees included 25 carefully selected physicians and scientists knowledgeable about mercury and mercury detoxification, including Dr. Holmes and Dr. Cave. The fifteen physicians present included seven who were parents of autistic children who had

---

[2] Autism Research Institute: DAN! Mercury Detoxification Consensus Group Position Paper, May 2001, Background and Introduction by Bernard Rimland, PhD Director of ARI http://www.autism.com/ari/mercurydetox.html

[3] Edelson, S.B., Cantor, D.S., "Autism: xenobiotic influences." Toxicol Ind Health 1998;14: 553-563

detoxified their own kids with excellent results. The physicians present had treated well over 3,000 patients for heavy metal poisoning, about 1,500 of them being autistic children. The chemists, toxicologists, and other scientists present had a combined total of almost 90 years of experience in studying the toxicology of mercury. The purpose of the meeting was to arrive at a consensus document that would delineate the safest and most effective methods for detoxifying autistic children.[4]

The chelation protocol I have been using is based on the consensus information gathered at that conference. It is called simply the DAN! protocol for chelation. Of course, since each autism-spectrum child is unique, I use the protocol as a guide. Each physician needs to integrate the protocol's guidelines with considerations specific to the child being chelated. In other words, this consensus-protocol was written as guidance, not as law. I make allowances for differences in response and individual circumstances in the child's history and current medical status to alter the protocol as my clinical judgment dictates. The chelation-protocol's authors emphasize that the treatment of autism is in a state of continual flux and recommendations concerning the protocol will continue to evolve as more is learned about autism's various biomedical subgroups. As mentioned before, I ask the reader to take the recommendations in this book in the same spirit. The protocol document also states that the evidence that chelation is beneficial is largely based on clinical experience although the theories and medical models on which the therapy is based are being vigorously studied by a number of researchers.

Even if the child's initial evaluation indicates the presence of mercury, I do not initiate chelation therapy right away. Often parents hearing of this treatment want to bring their child in to just "get the metals out." Sometimes they are impatient when they find that much work has to be done to ready the child for this kind of treatment. The child's intestinal health, nutritional status, and immunity must be optimized. These goals need to be achieved before the child can be considered for chelation. Many of us have painfully learned

---

[4] ARI DAN! Mercury Detoxification Consnsus Group Position Paper, May 2001, Background and Introduction by Bernard Rimland, PhD Dir. of ARI http://www.autism.com/ari/mercurydetox.html

that unless the child is free of gastrointestinal pathogen overgrowth when we start, chelation with DMSA is likely to make the situation worse (as sulfur agents support yeast growth), to the point of making our chelating efforts unsuccessful. This effect of the overgrowth of yeast and other intestinal pathogens is one of the factors leading to a search for other means of handling the toxicity issue and will be discussed further at the end of the chapter. For the children with more mature gastrointestinal systems who do not succumb to gut pathogen overgrowth problems in the process, I still believe at this time that the process I am about to describe is the fastest way to get the metal load down in a way that leads to improvement in most children given this treatment.

Pre-Chelation Testing

I often include the hair analysis with the routine tests I order for the evaluation. The CBC and Chemistry Panel must be repeated just prior to starting chelation unless they have been done within the previous two months and results are within normal limits. If there is any evidence of abnormal values, these must be corrected prior to starting the detoxification process, e.g. the use of milk thistle to regenerate liver, iron supplementation for severe anemia, and mineral replacement for any other deficiencies. In addition to the routine evaluation tests (if not already done), I recommend the following:

- **Hair Analysis**: This is an informative, non-invasive and inexpensive screening test ($42 if paid when sample submitted). I order this from Doctor's Data Lab (DD) for several reasons: They have the biggest data base of hair analyses in the world, and Dr. Andrew Cutler taught me how to interpret their particular way of reporting. Dr. Cutler's reading is based on what is known about heavy metals' effects on essential minerals in the body. As a screen, if the lab results do not concur with what I am seeing clinically and historically, I can use further testing to corroborate the finding. *Anecdotal data from Dr. Holmes' large data base indicate that many ASD kids have lower levels of toxic metals in hair as compared to siblings and parents, which may turn out to be an indication of impaired detoxifica-*

tion. This would corroborate mineral evidence of toxicity with no or little mercury showing in the hair.

Technique: Parents are given a kit with a small scale they use with very clear instructions about what hair to cut. The hair sample is mailed directly to the lab for analysis. Doctor's Data will send reports to the ordering physician, who receives two copies, one to give to the parents for their child's medical file.

- **Pre- and Post-Challenge Urine Toxic Elements Test**: This testing is not actually necessary for most children, but it can be convincing for parents who doubt that their child could possibly have mercury poisoning. It also may serve as evidence to an insurance company to encourage their willingness to pay for treatment for heavy metal poisoning. Urinary testing is more reliable than hair, which can pick up environmental contaminants in shampoos, for example, or copper in swimming pools.

Pre-Challenge Technique: A urine sample is collected in the morning in the kit provided by the lab and placed in the refrigerator.

Post-challenge: A one-time dose of DMSA (10mg/kg) is administered orally and urine collected for six hours in a large orange plastic bottle, carefully measured and recorded. A portion of the urine is placed in the small bottle in the second kit and both bottles clearly labeled are put back into the kits along with the physician's requisition specifying which tests are wanted. All samples are kept refrigerated until Airborne Express comes to pick them up in the plastic bags provided in the kits by the lab.

- **RBC Essential Elements:** Many ASD children are depleted in essential minerals. This test helps assess whether the child is low in magnesium, selenium, zinc etc. and helps guide the nutrient program. The child needs to be well mineralized prior to starting chelation and monitored periodically (every 3-6 months) during chelation. Meta-Metrix and Doctors Data Labs do this test.

- **Cysteine:** This can be done as part of a Great Smokies Lab Detoxification profile and helps determine whether the child would benefit from glutathione, N-acetyl cysteine (NAC), or high sulfur foods in the diet. Those with high cysteine levels may have negative reactions to sulfur compounds and sulfury foods and sometimes to oral or transdermal glutathione. For those low in cysteine (the majority of ASD children) there is much benefit from NAC because it can rapidly elevate intra-cellular glutathione levels which are essential in detoxification processes.

Gut Readiness Before Starting Chelation

In Chapter Five we discussed the high occurrence of intestinal yeast colonizations and other intestinal pathologies in ASD children. In fact, medical histories suggest that early immune impairment is almost ubiquitous among these children, as indicated by repeated ear infections and/or gut dysfunction. In the DAN! chelation protocol document it states that attempting heavy metal detoxification before the patient's underlying gastrointestinal and nutritional problems are corrected will likely be disappointing. Please refer to Chapter Five for details about treating gut dysfunction.

- **Organic Acid Test (OAT):** If the child has had overgrowth of yeast or other pathogens, he/she will already have been placed on a strong dietary and probiotic program to get this controlled. A repeat OAT is highly recommended just prior to starting chelation to make sure the gut is in good shape for the process.

- **Comprehensive/Digestive Stool Analysis:** If difficulties in overgrowth of pathogens occurs, stool studies will reveal sensitivities and help determine which anti-fungals, anti-bacterials, and anti-parasitic medications are appropriate for the child's treatment. Earlier in my work with ASD children, if the OAT (Organic Acid Test) was normal (which is unusual), I would not usually order fecal studies unless the child had bowel dysfunction in the form of diarrhea, constipation, excessive gas or bloating, reflux, or stomach pain. However, I have recently had some cases where this testing showed parasites that do not put out known metabolites in the urine as yeast and many bacteria do, and more often now I may routinely order this in my evaluation. ASD children tend to put things in their mouths excessively and are apt to pick up parasites that can set up residence in the already compromised gut; these infestations need treatment.

Nutrient/Mineralization Readiness

Children with mercury or other heavy metal accumulation need early bio-medical intervention to help their gastrointestinal, immune, and neurological systems to heal and begin functioning properly. As I have explained in previous chapters, this often means special vitamins and minerals are needed to offset the chemical aberrations associated with the mercury-induced injuries and the subsequent neurological dysfunction. Because of poor nutrition and absorption, many ASD children have numerous mineral deficiencies, zinc and selenium being two of the most important ones.

- **Zinc** needs to be given prior to, during and after detoxification therapy along with all the other vitamins and minerals. (Please see Chapter Four for specific recommendations and specific testing to guide supplementation.) Supplementation with 1-2mg/kg/day of zinc is recommended; more may be needed if testing shows a marked deficiency. Many children are worked up to one mg per pound plus 15-20mg of zinc a day in preparation for chelation. The RBC essential minerals test allows such judgments to be made more precisely. It is preferable for zinc to be given alone (not with calcium or other minerals) for most efficient absorption.

- **Selenium** is one of the few nutrients that can cause toxicity if given in excess and should be limited to 1-4mcg/lb/day unless there is laboratory evidence of a profound deficiency. Again, occasional RBC minerals lab-tests allow monitoring of selenium levels and staying at or under 200mcg a day is safe.

- **Other minerals** may be deficient in ASD children. Molybdenum, manganese, vanadium and chromium, along with zinc, can be obtained in a multi-mineral supplement. For a comprehensive trace mineral product I use Thorne's Pic-Mins. Excessive copper is neurotoxic and often elevated in ASD children. Any multiple vitamin should be free of copper. Extra molybdenum along with adequate zinc may help children with high copper levels. There are many good multi-vitamin/mineral supplements; my favorite is Ecological Formulas Hypomultiple (without copper or iron). Iron levels are often somewhat low in many of these children, but unless excessively so, I do not usually supplement it, as too much iron can stress the oxidative mechanisms and the deficiency is seen by some as the body's way to conserve energy.

  To repeat: All supplements important to a good and balanced nutritional program should be well in place prior to chelation. If nutritional deficiencies have not been corrected, important physiological mechanisms that support detoxification may not function properly. Because the ASD child's diet is often limited, mineralization with supplements becomes even more important as some necessary minerals may be taken out of the body through the chelation process.

- **Vitamins:** Many ASD children are deficient in vitamins for the same reasons they are low in minerals: poor diet, and poor absorption. Tests show that many children are deficient in Vitamin B6, B12, folic acid, and niacin. These should be given routinely, beginning with the child's preliminary work-up (after testing) recommendations. Please see Chapter Four for guidelines. Vitamins C, E, and B6 and other B vitamins are particularly important to keep well supplied during chelation. Vitamin C is known to be an aid to detoxification and is non-toxic other than causing loose stools; I usually recommend C be given at least 3X/day in as high a dose as tolerated short of diarrhea. I usually give buffered C in a high-potency powder combined with Larch

Arabinogalactans, which is a very beneficial and safe plant immune enhancer (from NF Formulas).

Chelation for Heavy Metals, the DAN! Protocol

Though DMPS (2,3 dimercaptopropane sulfonate) is known to be a good mercury chelator, it has never been formally tested on children. Therefore until safety testing has been done on DMPS, DMSA is the chelator recommended by the DAN! Protocol for Phase I of the chelation process and the agent I routinely use. DMSA is safe, effective, and has been tested rigorously for use in children. However, I have occasionally used oral DMPS with good results in some of my older children whose progress has slowed down on DMSA, sometimes with a notable spurt in mercury elimination per urine testing. I inform parents DMPS has not been tested on children, but many parents have done their own research and want to try it anyway. In any event, I use very conservative doses, usually 50mg orally every eight hours. DMPS must be prescribed by a physician, made by a compounding pharmacy, is not paid for by insurance, and is expensive. In contrast, DMSA often will be covered by insurance, particularly if Chemet is prescribed. However, Chemet comes in 100mg capsules and I prefer (if the parents do not have to rely on insurance) that individualized capsules be compounded to get exactly the dose needed for their particular child, especially when he/she cannot swallow tablets. Many parents in my practice have been able to get their insurance to pay for compounded DMSA.

After DMSA has cleared the body of "loose" mercury or other toxic metals as shown by lab testing (usually urinary), we begin Phase II of the chelation therapy by adding another chelator, Alpha-lipoic acid (ALA) in an amount usually 1/6 to 1/2 of the dosage of DMSA. Unlike DMSA, ALA is believed to cross the blood brain barrier (BBB) and bind with mercury to remove it from the brain. ALA is a nutrient in many foods and can be purchased from any good health food store, although I usually have it compounded in exactly the strength I want for the weight of the child. Currently, most DAN! practitioners feel that ALA should not be used prior to DMSA chelation, because ALA can bind to a toxic metal in the body's periphery, some of the ALA-bound metal may cross the blood-brain-barrier, thereby possibly reentering the child's brain. In other words, ALA therapy should follow thorough DMSA chelation. It is important to point out that some practitioners do not agree with this and prefer to give ALA throughout chelation; some parents (usually those who do not have access to a supervisory doctor) have chosen to use ALA only, without clearing out the body mercury with DMSA. ALA has been noted to cause more side effects of hyperactivity or increased "stimming" in some children.

- **Phase I, DMSA (Di-mercaptosuccinic Acid) Dosages and Timing**: I basically use the 3 days on, 11 days off schedule for chelation except for special situations. This allows the parents to give the first dose on Friday around noon for children who are not in school, and in the afternoon for those who are, continuing either every 4 or 8 hours as directed for the particular child. There is some difference of opinion as to which of these timing schedules are the best, with some very substantial arguments by knowledgeable persons advocating each timing. I find myself often using the more frequent timing with smaller doses for smaller children and the lower frequency with larger doses for larger children, unless side effects or lack of progress indicate it may be better to give more frequent doses. I usually explain the different points of view to the parents and let them decide since there is evidence that both schedules work. I make it clear that we can always change the timing if experience indicates more frequent dosing might work better or longer periods between doses (much easier for all concerned) will work just as well. Again, there are differences of opinion about dosing; I tend to start very low and gradually work upward to the suggested amounts in the protocol per clinical results and lab testing, based on weight of the child. The point of Phase I is to remove as much body mercury and other toxic metals as possible, as DMSA cannot cross the blood brain barrier to remove it from the brain; the latter is done in Phase II using A-lipoic acid.

- **Dosages, DMSA:** Doses based on weight for 8 hour schedules are as follows for three days on and eleven days off: (Divide in half for 4 hour dosing frequency)

20-40 lbs. : 100mg.	50-60 lbs. : 250mg.
(especially for the	60-70 lbs. : 300mg.
smaller children,	70-80 lbs. : 350mg.
I start with half)	80-100 lbs. : 500mg.
40-50 lbs. : 200mg.	>100 lbs. : 500mg.

- **Lab Monitoring, Phase I:** I recommend urine testing (Urine Toxic Elements done by Doctor's Data Lab) after the 1st or 2nd two-week cycle, then every 3rd or 4th two-week cycle done on the 2nd day of the 3-day cycle several hours after the morning dose. I have found the random urines are as useful as the 6-hour collections I used to get, and much easier on the parents and child. Urine collection bags must be requested from the lab for children that are not potty-trained. This testing continues until the body mercury or other toxic metals are gone or extremely low and it is safe to give ALA without the danger of carrying ALA-bound toxic metal or "loose mercury" back into the brain. Usually after 10-12 two-week cycles the child's body is free of mercury, some are free after 7-8 cycles, and some take longer than 12 cycles. If pathogen overgrowth occurs, chelation must stop until that is addressed.

  Every 2-3 months while chelating I require "safety" testing: a CBC and Chemistry Panel performed to make sure blood, liver, kidneys etc are not being harmed. An RBC Essential Elements Test is helpful every 2-6 months throughout the process to help monitor mineral status; this can be done along with the routine tests every 2nd or 3rd time. (When aluminum is high, the nutrient Malic Acid is reported to be very effective in reducing aluminum levels; food from metal cans is to be avoided.) ALA is the best chelator for arsenic.

- **Readiness for Phase II: Adding A-lipoic Acid (ALA):** It is time to go on to Phase II when little or no more mercury is coming out as assessed by the Urine Toxic Elements test. DMSA pulls out most heavy metals in no particular order. If there are large amounts of lead or tin coming out, DMSA should be used until these are not being excreted in large amounts, as they may be "hiding" mercury and have been shown to slow down Phase II if not reduced to low level before starting the ALA. (If very large amounts of lead are starting to come out, sometimes showing up only after quite a few cycles, I sometimes give a long course of DMSA (19 days straight) to get the lead down before proceeding to Phase II. It is important that the parents become detectives to make sure their child is not being exposed to lead anywhere in his or her environment.) In addition to the metals mercury, tin, and lead being low, the child must have good metabolic test results and the gut must be in good shape, because ALA is notorious for "feeding intestinal pathogens," and severe yeast and Clostridia overgrowth can take place if not carefully monitored. Signs of pathogen overgrowth include bowel dysfunction or plateau or even regression in chelation effects. In my experience diligent probiotics, GF/CF diet, and sugar removal from the diet really pay off in terms of shortening the time for the chelation process. Many children have to endure long delays to take care of the "bad gut bugs." (See my comments at the end of this chapter about some recent developments that deal with this problem.) Recently I have started using transdermal ALA in Phase II to try to help prevent the overgrowth of pathogens; the few children on it seem to be doing very well, but it is too soon for me to report if this is as effective as the oral form. DMSA is quite unstable and not amenable to being made into a transdermal form as yet.

- **Phase II, Laboratory Monitoring:** DMSA dumps metals into urine, making lab testing fairly simple with the Urine Toxic Metals test. Once we add ALA, most metals are sequestered into the bile and then excreted through the stool. During the ALA phase, urine tests tend not to show mercury any more; thus the best way to test for excretion is through the Fecal Metal test also done by Doctor's Data Lab. Stool transit times vary and catching the metal output by stools is difficult. The test is done on Day 4, the 1ˢᵗ day after completing the three day cycle. Once children are out of diapers and particularly with bigger children, collecting stool samples can be fairly daunting for the parents. However, we only ask parents to do this test every 4-6 months. Recently I have been using serial hair analyses for the Phase II testing and, though it is less accurate than the stools test (if you happen to catch a sample at the right time!), I get useful information that combined with assessment from the parents and teachers help us to see what is happening. "Safety testing" is done every few months routinely. As time goes on I mainly do testing when there is a plateau in improvement or a regression (often caused by gut bugs). In addition to the lab test data, other useful information often comes from parents and teachers, whose assessments of the child's behavior and learning abilities provide an additional monitor about the effectiveness of the child's chelation therapy. Occasionally, a child experiences a regression while undergoing chelation. Many clinicians report that the regression is most likely due to a resurgence of intestinal pathogenic colonization. Albeit rare, other regressions have been noted for which we have no ready explanation. Parents and physicians need to be alert throughout the chelation process.

For ALA doses, use 1/6 to 1/2 the amount of DMSA for the child's weight; ALA and DMSA are given together either every 4 hours or every eight hours as the parents and I have agreed, 3 days on and 11 days off.

- **Completion of the Chelation Process:** Chelation is usually terminated when the child has "plateaued" and is no longer showing obvious changes in behavior and language. For some autism-spectrum children, this improvement is sufficient so that the child can be "mainstreamed" in school. Some children have even outgrown their diagnosis as autistic. However, chelation is so new that relatively few children have actually completed the process, the exceptions being very young children who seem to excrete their heavy metals much faster than older children. We usually say the detoxification work takes six months to two years and maybe longer for older children. Parental and clinical assessment is more important here than mercury excretion dropping below detectable limits as measured by lab testing.

On rare occasions, an autism-spectrum child undergoing chelation experiences an unexplainable but sustained regression. Though this may be confused with regressive episodes or traits (mainly hyperactivity, increase in self-stimulatory activity) at the beginning of DMSA treatment and also at the beginning of the ALA treatment, there are often improvements in language and sociability simultaneously that make parents want to keep going. Several children in my practice (as in those of other clinicians) have had difficulty when starting ALA; our first thought was that metals were being moved around. We came to discover that the most common reason was pathogen overgrowth, though we were not certain of this being the cause in every case. Sometimes we just cannot find out why the children stop improving and start regressing to previous levels, reminding us that there is still a lot unknown about this complex process. Treatments to eradicate pathogens in difficult cases can take months, and parents who had been seeing remarkable gains with their children prior to the pathogen invasion find themselves impatient to get on with the chelation. New therapeutic substances are being explored and created as fast as possible, such as the development of a "child-specific" transfer factor to get specific immune factors operating against a particularly difficult pathogen (e.g. Clostridium difficile).

Obviously the younger the children the easier it is to treat them and the faster they are able to excrete the metals. Sometimes the gains are uneven; some children become more sociable as their first improvement, others show expansion of language capabilities with receptivity (understanding what is being said to them) being one of the first improvements that many parents report. Expressive language and improvements in pronunciation seem to be the most difficult to achieve as noted in many other ASD treatments. It is very helpful to compare reports by the child's teacher as a check on the parents' and doctor's assessment as to progress.

In the name of safety, chelation, as we are learning to do it right now, needs to be a long, sometimes drawn-out process. Though I usually tell parents it may take from 6 months to two years for the younger kids and longer for the older children, every child is so different that this period varies considerably. Several of the children I am working with currently have improved so much that the parents and I feel they are well on their way to recovery. Some children respond very quickly, others move much more slowly. I cannot predict how any particular child may respond. Presently most of the children I have started on chelation are still in process (though sometimes with extended breaks). I have completed the chelation process for three high-functioning older children, one in middle school, one in high school, and one who just left home to go to college. Chelation along with many other treatments helped them improve considerably. All three of them were well enough to say something on the order of: "I'm tired of doing this; my friends think I'm nuts to have to take all these pills," or, "I'm on the team and doing well; I'm stopping this for now," or the girl who went off to college, "I'll take my vitamins morning and night only; I don't want to carry pills around with me in school!" I'll accept those signs of neurotypicality, gladly!

Summary Comments on Detoxification Treatment

Although it would be great to have a number of conclusive research studies to direct each of the protocols we use, neither I nor parents of ASD children are willing to wait for such research if a treatment makes sense and is safe. In the case of chelation, preliminary data are too compelling to wait for long-term verification studies. Many of my patients are drawing on every tool I have in my armamentarium that we think will help them. I'm constantly on the lookout for even more information and new treatments to help Chelsey and the other ASD children to have a better life.

In the beginning of my learning curve about chelation I discovered, through a process of trial and error, that if certain children developed an overgrowth of yeast or other gut pathogens, positive effects would plateau or even in some cases they would start to regress. Dr. Amy Holmes was the first to help me realize that the chelating agents we were using not only seemed to be feeding the yeast, but even encouraged bacterial overgrowth, especially Clostridium difficile, an anerobic bacteria very difficult to eradicate. (The OAT test identifies Clostridia through elevations in urinary metabolites such as HPHPA [dihydroxyphenylpropionate][5]). We knew all along that chelation might remove some needed nutrients, so we have been very diligent in making sure each child is properly mineralized and nutritional deficiencies corrected as much as possible. We also follow a conservative process of chelating for only a few days and giving the child's system (and the parents!) a rest of at least as many days off as on. Generally now with a few exceptions I follow the 3-days on, 11-days off cycle, which seems to provide a safe steady course to which most children respond positively without any evidence of harm. If there is evidence of "bad gut bugs" as shown by diarrhea, constipation, or severe regression in behavior—or if the child's metabolic signs deteriorate—chelation is stopped until the problem is taken care of by appropriate testing and treatment. I have come to immediately regard a plateau in improvement as a tip-off that gut pathogens may be affecting the child's ability to respond and take appropriate measures to correct the situation.

In my chelating experience, the children suffering the most with gut pathogens during chelation have been those not on the GF/CF diet. Recent studies support evidence that 75-80% of children with ASD have immune reactivity to dietary proteins including soy, milk, and wheat. Dr. Harumi Jyonouchi, pediatric immunologist and allergist at the University of Minnesota, has tested the immune responses of autistic children and compared them to healthy controls. Her scientific research supports parents' claims that autistic

---

[5] Shaw, William, 2002, New revised edition of Biological Treatments for Autism and PDD

children have abnormal immune responses to gluten, casein, and soy.[6] I have begun requiring the GF/CF and often SF (soy-free) diet as a prerequisite to chelation for children with delayed onset or "regressive"ASD, particularly those who received the HepB vaccine as newborns, very likely triggering the early gut and immune injury, frequent infections, antibiotics, and "leaky gut."

Confusion has arisen in the autism community at times over the dosing and frequency of administration of chelating agents. Studies have shown DMSA or DMPS do not cross the blood-brain-barrier, nor do they release the mercury once they bind to it, so mercury removal as shown by urinary testing during chelation is presumed to come from body stores other than the brain. Yet thousands of ASD children have unarguably improved with chelation. Suggestion that "redistribution of metals" causes damage with longer dosing intervals is scientifically unproven, yet clinical experiences show us that about 50% of children do better with 4 hr dosing and lesser amounts of chelating agents vs 8 hr intervals with larger doses. Many of us doing this work now believe that there are other as yet unproven mechanisms at work relating to the sulfation/methylation chemistry and provision of sulfur by the chelating agents for its various uses in the body, including formation of cysteine and its role in helping the body detoxify itself. I tend to give smaller more frequent doses to younger or more damaged children and every 8 hr larger doses to the older kids, with readiness to move to the 4 hr dosing if side effects or lack of improvement dictate; either schedule works for some children.

In a recent query to some of the practitioners who wrote the Mercury Detoxification Consensus Group Position Paper in 2001, I learned that several prefer now to only use DMPS (oral or IV), feeling it is a better chelator with less incidence of gut pathogen overgrowth than DMSA. Several prefer only the 4 hour schedules, a few more only use the 8 hr schedule, and most vary schedules according to the individual situation. Many doctors (including myself) are using transdermal TTFD (allithiamine) instead of or as an accelerator

---

[6] Jyonouchi H, Sun S, Itokazu N. Innate immunity associated with inflammatory responses and cytokine production against common dietary proteins in parients with autism spectrum disorder. Neuropsychobiology 2002;46(2):76-84

or adjunct to our usual chelating agents. (See later and also Appendix D) I want to emphasize once again that safety is of the utmost concern. Appropriate testing to monitor the status of the blood and urine should be done periodically. In addition, periodic urine and/or fecal tests to determine which metals are being re- moved are helpful in guiding treatment. Chelation therapy for ASD children as put out by the DAN! group is new and much is still to be learned by all of us in this field. Most but not all children undergoing chelation have benefited, and to the best of my knowledge, there have been no reports of irreversible medical damage from this treatment using DAN! guidelines.

In the rapidly expanding field of ASD treatment new medications and protocols will continue to arise either as variations or improvements in existing approaches, or as new possibilities. An example of the latter is a drug recently developed for use with early Alzheimer patients that is now being used in low doses effectively for a subset of ASD children. Dr. Michael Chez, Pediatric Neurologist in Lake Forest IL, has conducted many research projects for autistic and epileptic children, and has pioneered the use of the supplement carnosine, an amino acid dipeptide made up of histidine and alanine. In June 2001 Dr. Chez began a study using carnosine to determine whether it enhances seizure protection in children with recurrent seizures despite being on standard anti-convulsant therapy. Not only did he find that many children improved their seizure condition with carnosine but, unexpectedly, a pattern of gains in cognitive domains—including language, alertness, energy levels, and even gross motor ability—were reported in parental diaries of the children in the study. Some children showed more fluent language, better eye contact and more interest in the environment. A follow-up double-blind placebo controlled study with carnosine was begun by Dr. Chez, with results indicating clinically meaningful changes in many aspects of autistic features in the majority of children in the group, including expressive and receptive language. Though these are preliminary and small studies, there is no evidence so far of toxicity in the use of this nutrient. As a naturally-occurring amino acid found within the human body, the deep frontal part of the brain (entorhinal cortex) is believed to be a site where carnosine tends to accumulate. It may interact with zinc in that area, as well as having effects on GABA, a brain neurotransmitter, which by a complex chemical reaction forms homo-carnosine. Though there are many questions still to be answered, to Dr. Chez' credit he is not keeping his work to himself until he can get it published in a "peer-reviewed" journal. In the meantime, some of us have started to use carnosine with our children, and though it is early, there are some promising reports, along with some reports of hyperactivity in the beginning of treatment. We are learning that starting slowly and building up to the recommended dose (400mg twice a day) is probably better as is the case with most of the nutrients we use. Since carnosine has been used extensively in anti-aging group treatments, it can be purchased in several places over the internet. Dr. Chez has worked with a company that has created a compound called Carn-Aware consisting of 200mg of Carnosine, 25 IU of Vitamin E, and 2.5mg of Zinc that is available by calling 847-295-0748. Their recommendation is to work up to two capsules twice a day.

During chelation therapy, the overgrowth of pathogens occurring in the response of a sizeable number of children inspired Dr. Amy Holmes and other practitioners to look for new approaches for these "gut-bug prone" children. She had begun working with Dr. William Walsh (see The Metallothionein [MT] Theory in Chapter One) at the Pfeiffer Treatment Center in Naperville IL to learn more about his nutritional supplement programs aimed at inducing and promoting the normal MT functioning that is thought to play such a vital role in the normal detoxification of heavy metals. Although this may be a slower process, the long delays in the present DMSA-ALA protocol caused by the need to heal stubborn gut infections may end up taking longer for some children than the phased nutrient approach explored by Drs. Holmes and Walsh. For those children who do not have the gut infection problem, the DMSA/ALA protocol as outlined above is probably still the "fast track" to reducing metal load.

Those of us who have been using the DAN! protocol have noticed that many children improve when we begin with a strong nutrient program even before introducing the chelation agents. It is possible that we have been helping the child's own detoxification mechanisms to function better through improved nutrition even without understanding all the underlying cellular mechanisms. It is well known that MT function and glutathione are related, and improving glutathione levels will improve detoxification. The large amounts of cysteine required for MT syntheses can be supplied in the form of oral glutathione which breaks down in the G.I. tract with minimal side effects for most children. I usually start my nutrient program with anti-oxidant vitamins such as A, C & E, calcium, and mineralization (usually including extra zinc, an avoidance of copper, and P5P' plus magnesium). Once those are in place, I add other B vitamins, omega-3 oils, and oral and transdermal reduced glutathione with a glutathione precursor formula including NAC (N-acetyl cysteine), ALA, glycine, L-carnosine, inosine and selenomethionine as a preliminary "natural" chelation. I start this very cautiously as some children cannot tolerate too much NAC. Some practitioners have started administering IV Glutathione to ASD children with many showing great benefit; the glutathione-zinc relationship is known to be an essential aspect of effective MT function, along with adequate selenium to support the delivery of zinc to cells and the sequestering of mercury and other heavy metals.

At the present time Dr. William Walsh and his medical staff at the Pfeiffer Center in Naperville, IL describe a phased nutritional therapy to promote MT function in the gut, brain, and elsewhere. Their protocol is based on 1200 previously published articles describing MT synthesis and activation. Best clinical outcomes have been achieved using a two-phase protocol: (1) preloading with zinc and augmenting nutrients, followed by (2) cautious, gradual introduction of MT promotion nutrients. The scientific literature studied by the Pfeiffer staff indicated to them that most of the body's MT is induced by zinc, with glutathione needed for its loading and redox exchange. The net result of the delivery of zinc to cells is that the zinc-MT appears to be a "magnet" for toxic metals. MT proteins are composed of 14 amino acids and zinc, yet in the early trials some ASD children were unable to handle the cysteine portion of the formula. Later formulations substitute oral glutathione to provide the large amounts of cysteine required for the MT synthesis usually only with minimal side effects. The Pfeiffer Center has patented various MT-promotion formulations and, because of the need for medical supervision and regular testing, these formulations are available by prescription only from the Pfeiffer Clinic Pharmacy.

The Pfeiffer Center recommends MT-promotion therapy for any child with disturbed metal metabolism. Key lab tests to assess this include serum copper, plasma zinc, and serum ceruloplasmin. In healthy individuals, the Cu/Zn ratio usually ranges between 0.8 and 1.2; the amount of free copper (unbound by ceruloplasmin) ranges from 5 to 25 mcg/dL. A new test for MT function is now available from Immunosciences Lab. in Beverly Hills, CA (See p. 83).

The primary or "zinc loading" phase takes from 4 to 8 weeks with the zinc dosage build-up being accompanied by augmenting nutrients. After the zinc loading phase, the second or "MT promotion" phase is begun, with a very gradual introduction of the specially formulated compound of 13 amino acids plus glutathione (in place of cysteine) and selenium in what Dr. Walsh calls a "pulsed" protocol (i.e., 3 days on, 4 days off). Along with the MT-promoter, continuation of the primary phase nutrients, GF/CF diet, probiotics, and behavioral and other ongoing therapies is recommended. Chelation therapies which deplete zinc stores (DMSA, DMPS, etc) should be alternated with the MT promoter program. Recent evidence points to fewer adjustment problems in those children who have done DMSA chelation to get the heavy metal load lowered prior to starting the MT promoter. An important recent addition to my detoxification regiment is the use of transdermal allithiamine (TTFD) or thiamine tetrahydrofurfuryl disulfide. Early studies are showing this to be an effective and gentle steady detoxification agent I am finding useful in those children who have a strong tendency toward developing pervasive yeast infestations from the use of DMSA and DMSA/ALA. Please refer to Appendix D for full details.

As in all our detoxification protocols, these therapies aim to eliminate toxic metals, protect against future toxic exposures, normalize the gut, improve immune function and behavior, and enhance development of brain neurons and synaptic connections. Dr. Walsh stresses that early intervention is critically important for the latter, especially for speech and cognitive advancement. The process goes much slower with older kids, but he believes that with parents' patience the older ones also can benefit greatly from this treatment. He advocates behavioral therapies which shower the brain with impulses and promote neuronal development in conjunction with the MT promotion therapy. Actually, this is advisable no matter what is being done biomedically for our ASD children.

As has been emphasized, much of the DAN! chelation protocol and my personal approach to treatment includes healing the gut and obtaining optimal nutritional status. This approach supports the glutathione/metallothionein interaction as described by Dr. Walsh. Recently, some reports from the Pfeiffer Center show that children with heavy metal toxicity who have previously been chelated to get the heavy metal load down often respond more favorably and with less side effects to the metallothionein promotion program.

Clearly, further research and documentation is needed and is occurring. At this time, the bottom line is that many children are being helped by the protocols delineated in this book. As the data already presented to the NIH and IOM indicate, the earlier detoxification therapies as well as behavioral therapies are begun—simultaneously with gut healing and nutritional support—the likelier the child will significantly improve.

Questions and challenges relating to detoxification continue. Opinions on optimum frequency and dosage amounts of chelating agents continue to differ among well-respected practitoners. More doctors are using DMPS than before even though it has not been formally tested in children. Many of us agree that small oral doses are safe and effective; opinions vary on the safety of the IV route. Discovering new ways to turn on the detoxification mechanism inherent in all of us is definitely exciting research which we will learn more about in the months to come. Some children beset by intractable gut infections may benefit more by the slower phased nutritional approach Dr. Walsh and others advocate. I would venture to guess that some children using a primarily nutritional approach may still have to undergo some chelation to reach maximum healing. I suspect that even after successfully going through chelation or MT-promotion treatment, it still may be necessary for some ASD children to continue certain nutrients to prevent metal accumulation recurrence. Clearly, the jury is still out on these issues, and different subsets of children according to age, gut status, toxicity level and other factors may respond more favorably to one or another protocol as we are finding for most bio-medical treatments for ASD children.

EIGHT

IMMUNITY, AUTOIMMUNITY, AND VIRUSES (Or Other Pathogens)

An Overview of Immune Dysregulation in ASD Children

GENETICS

In 1997 when I first began searching for information about the biomedical aspects of autism, most of the medical literature referred to this disorder as genetic and stated that autism begins in the womb. My explorations revealed an enormous diversity for the etiologies of autism and acknowledgment that the underlying pathologic mechanisms were unknown in most cases. I found there was no clear proven identification for any one exclusive chromosome carrying a gene for autism, though several studies showed that 5% of autistic children possessed an identifiable array of chromosomal aberrations. Still, there is general consensus among researchers and clinicians working with the autistic spectrum disorders that family and twin studies give enough evidence to indicate that hereditary factors play a role. In Bernard Rimland's 1964 study of monozygotic (identical) twins with autism, he concluded that genetic components seemed strong, yet were significantly affected by the existence of modifying factors.

IMMUNE ABNORMALITIES

The infectious and toxic etiologies would seem to be exceptions to the genetic influence. However, an individual's susceptibility to such injuries can be heightened by genetic predisposition, as well as by environmental factors, so that the timing of an insult can be crucially important. In an informal survey of one of the internet autism groups in which I was a participant in 1999, 30% of the mothers of children with autism who participated reported having autoimmune diseases, which is consistent with Comi, et al. Such studies have shown an increased incidence of hypothyroid disease and diabetes as well as rheumatoid arthritis in the parents of children with autism compared to parents of matched controls.[1] Many immunological studies of individuals with autism have found atypical immune function of one type or another, the results often depending on the age of the individuals in the particular study. Such studies included:

- Abnormalities in T cells and T cell subsets (Stubbs, et al. 1977, Warren, et al. 1990, Yonk, et al. 1990. Warren, et al. 1995, Gupta, et al. 1998)

- Depressed responses to T cell mitogens (Stubbs, et al. 1977, Warren, et al. 1986) decreased natural killer cell function (Warren, et al. 1987)

- A lower percentage of helper-inducer cells (Denney, et al. 1996)

- Elevation of interleukin-12 (Singh 1996)

- Elevation of interferon-gamma (Singh 1996)

- Elevation of alpha-interferon levels (Stubbs 1995).

Immunological signs of food allergy have been found to be higher in patients with autism compared to healthy controls.

The major histocompatibility complex (MHC) has a group of genes that control the function and regulation of the immune system. One of these genes, the C4B gene, encodes a product that is

---

[1]   Comi A.M. et al., "Familial clustering of autoimmune disorders and evaluation of medical risk factors in autism." J. Child Neurol 1999 Jun;14(6): 388-94

involved in eliminating pathogens such as viruses and bacteria from the body. A deficient form of the C4B gene, termed the C4B null allele (meaning no C4B protein produced) has an increased frequency in autism, ADHD, and dyslexia.

AUTOIMMUNITY AND AUTISM

In a review of the literature in the emerging field of "psycho-neuroimmunology" van Gent et al hypothesize that autoimmune and/or viral processes in some way affect the nervous system and alter central nervous system activity.[2]

Antibodies to myelin basic protein (MBP) and neuron-axon filament protein (NAFP) have been found to be positive in children with autism compared to healthy controls.[3] Singh et al have reported that positive measles virus or HHV6 titers were related to autoantibodies, especially those of anti-myelin basic protein in children with autism but not in controls.[4]

PATHOGENS AND AUTOIMMUNITY

An infection with a pathogen that triggers an abnormal immune response to self-tissue can be an important component of the development of autoimmune disorders. Some infectious diseases identified in autistic children are rubella, herpes simplex encephalitis, varicella, cytomegalovirus, and roseola (caused by the HHV6 virus). In very young children, an inherited but mild deficiency of the immune system may prevent the patient from clearing a pathogen in a timely and normal fashion without the child necessarily seeming to be very ill. This situation places him or her at higher risk for the pathogen to interfere with brain development or function and/or to trigger autoimmune responses, both of which are strongly identified as major ASD symptoms.

---

[2] van Gent T. et al., "Aurism and the Immune System," J. Child Psychol Psychiatry 1997 Mar;38)3): 337-49

[3] Hassen, A.N. et al., "Neuroimmunotoxicology: Humoral assessment of neurotoxicity and autoimmune mechanisms, Environmental Health Perspectives Vol. 107. Sup. 5 Oct. 1999

[4] Singh, Vijendra K., "Abnormal Measles Serology and Autoimmunity in Autistic Children." J. of Allergy Clinical Immunology 109(1):S232, Jan 2002, Abstract 702

Uta Frith says in her book, *Autism: Explaining the Enigma,* "If the central nervous system becomes infected at a critical time, either before or after birth, autism may result.... Of special interest are certain types of virus called retrovirus, which totally integrate themselves in genetic material in the body cells. Other viruses that have been suggested as possible causes of Autism are herpes and cytomegalovirus. These can remain dormant for years but from time to time can be reactivated."[5]

GASTROINTESTINAL DISEASE AND AUTISM SPECTRUM DISORDER

MMR and Development Regression

Dr. Andrew Wakefield, formerly a research gastroenterologist at Royal Free Hospital and School of Medicine in London, and the Inflammatory Bowel Disease Study Group there, have identified measles virus (MV) particles in the ileal lesions of some children with autism. The complicated politics with the vaccine industry and the official rejections of Wakefield's excellent research that led to his departure from Royal Free Hospital would make a dramatic movie. Recently, important parts of Wakefield's work have been duplicated by Dr. Timothy Buie of Harvard, who identified a group of autistic children with ileal hyperplasia. Subsequently, a respected virology group in Japan used a DNA/RNA sequencing technique to demonstrate that the MV present in the children with ileal inflammation was indeed the vaccine strain.[6] This finding leaves little doubt in the minds of many parents and professionals that a certain subset of children are susceptible to developmental regression from the MV component of the MMR. Dr. Wakefield has said all along that there was no need for all the furor. All the vaccine makers had to do was to separate the three components (Measles, Mumps, and Rubella) and allow them to be given as separate single vaccines spaced in time,

---

[5] Frith, Uta , p. 79-80, Autism: Explaining the Enigma, 1989, Blackwell Publishers Inc, Malden, MA 02148

[6] Kawashima H., et al., "Detection and seqencing of measles virus from peripheral mononuclear cells from patients with inflammatory bowel disease and autism. Dig. Dis. Sci. 2000 Apr;45(4): pp. 723-9

with the parents taking care to make sure their children were not suffering from some infection or illness at the time of the shot.

Fungal Infections and the Immune System

Cell-mediated immunity has been shown to be an important host defense mechanism against Candida albicans infections. A switch from Th1 to Th2 type responses has been noted to increase susceptibility to mucosal candidiasis.[7] Several studies have documented Th2-like shifts in certain groups of autistic children.

ATYPICAL ELEVATIONS OF COMMON VIRAL TITERS

Examples of these include Epstein-Barr Virus, Cytomegalovirus, Herpes Simplex Viruses 1 & 2, HHV6, and MV. Although interpreting viral-titer lab data is complex, the various titer elevations suggest to Teresa Binstock and others that an ASD subgroup has chronic, low level viral infections that are etiologically related to the child's autism.[8] These children have enough overall immunity to keep from appearing sick, yet they have an underlying immune-impairment that permits an atypical chronic infection to exist. During the 1990s, polymerase chain reaction (PCR) studies demonstrated that certain viruses can invade and migrate into small areas of the central nervous system without necessarily generating an obvious encephalitis, where they can remain dormant for long periods of time even as cell function is altered.

It has been shown in rats that the ubiquitous Herpes Simplex Virus (HSV) is capable of entering gastrointestinal nerves and of migrating into the spine from various peripheral locations. Furthermore, Gesser et al showed that this migration could occur all the way into the amygdala and that HSV's migration in humans can follow the same pathway as identified in rats.[9] We hypothesize that,

---

[7] Romani L., "Cytokine modulation of specific and nonspecific immunity to Candida albicans. Mycoses, 1999; p. 42 Suppl 2: pp. 45-8. Review. Also, Romani L., Immunity to Candida albicans: Th1, Th2 cells and beyond. Curr Opin Microbiol. 1999 Aug;2(4): 363-7. Review

[8] Binstock T., Intra-monocyte pathogens delineate autism subgroups. Med Hypotheses. 2001 Apr;56(4): 523-31

[9] Gesser R.M., Koo S.C., "Oral inoculation with herpes simplex virus type 1 infects enteric neuron and mucosal nerve fibers within the gastrointestinal tract in mice. J. Virol. 1996 Jun;70(6): 4097-102

in at least some autism-spectrum children who respond favorably to acyclovir or Valtrex, HSV may have migrated into crucial brain regions and done so intraneuronally, without creating an obvious encephalitis. This model is consistent with the amygdala's role in anxiety, emotions, appetite, the processing of sensory information, and reaction to faces. In fact, the amygdala have neurons specific for eye contact and are linked with seizure disorders and certain emotional nuances of language.[10] Other autism-spectrum children who respond favorably to acyclovir or Valtrex may have HSV persisting within other tissues such as the pancreas, liver, and spleen.[11]

ALLERGY AND IMMUNITY

In babies that are bottle fed, a milk-based formula would cause children allergic to milk to have very early gut inflammation and indigestion problems. Breast fed babies generally have better immunity because they receive antibodies from their mother's milk and are rarely allergic to it. Some mothers have reported their child's descent into autism began shortly after cessation of breast-feeding and the introduction of cow's milk into the diet. Of course, other events may take place around that time also, like the injection of toxin-laden vaccines, but there is a lot of evidence that breast-fed babies generally fare better in ASD than bottle-fed babies. These findings would seem to corroborate the growing realization that casein is toxic to many and perhaps most ASD children when taken together with all the studies that have shown a higher incidence of allergies in ASD children than in controls.

CHRONIC LOW-GRADE INFECTIONS

A long-standing model of autoimmunity posited that autoimmune syndromes could be induced in some individuals by a "hit and run" pathogen (since ordinary laboratory studies at the time could find no evidence of the pathogen). However, more recent PCR-

---

[10] Binstock T, "Fragile X and the amygdala: cognitive,interpersonal, emotional, and neuro-endocrine considerations," Dev Brain Dysfunction 1995 8: pp. 199-217

[11] Berkowitz C. et al., "Herpes simplex virus type 1 (HSV-1) UL56 gene is involved in viral intraperitoneal pathogenicity to immunocompetent mice." Arch Virol 1994;134(1-2): 73-83

based evidence increasingly demonstrates that several subgroups of multiple sclerosis patients may have reactivated or chronic, low level infections.[12] Similarly, clinical lab data suggest that there are subgroups of ASD children in whom a low-level or a reactivated infection may be etiologically significant.[13]

When considering an individual child (not in the context of a general epidemic), it is always difficult to know whether he or she is part of the ASD infection-subgroup because of a predisposition due to mild immune impairment, because the infection was prenatal or congenital, or whether lingering infection continues to inhibit immune capacity.

Diagnostics–Immune Testing

"What tests to order" in immunologically diagnosing ASD children is not easy for several reasons. This is a relatively new field for clinicians, and it is difficult for parents to find a doctor willing to order and evaluate the lab data. Understandably, parents do not appreciate unnecessary tests for children who are not able to understand why they are being held down and "tortured." Insurance often will not pay for these "non-mainstream" tests; a full array of diagnostics can be quite expensive, with no guarantee that the results will lead to effective treatments. Still, there are many parents who are willing to invest in such testing and there is a growing amount of clinical lab-test data to help us understand more about dysregulated immunity, impaired detoxification, and seemingly subclinical infections. In addition to the CBC, metabolic panel, and other tests already described, the following are helpful in immunologically evaluating ASD children—the first three listed are in my practice the minimum. The Comprehensive "Premier" Panel includes the three of these plus important other tests that give a much better immune/viral overview to guide treatment.

---

[12] Tomsone V. et al., "Associatioin of human herpesvirus 6 and human herpesvirus 7 with demyelinating diseases of the nervous system." J. Neurovirol 2001 Dec;7(6): 564-9

[13] Singh V.K. et al., "Serological association of measles virus and human herpesvirus-6 with brain antoantibodies in autism." Clin Immunol Immunopathol. 1998 Oct;89(1): 105-8

COMPREHENSIVE (HERPES) VIRAL SCREEN #3

Elevated antibody titers to viruses are often found when ASD-children undergo immunological testing. This viral screen differentiates the IgG (indication of past exposure or chronic activation) and the IgM antibodies (indication of very recent infection or recent reactivation) of herpesviruses such as HSV1, HSV2, Varicella Zoster virus (VZV), EBC, Cytomegalovirus (CMV), and HHV6. Impaired immune function along with impaired detoxification and ever increasing environmental toxins may predispose toward chronic viral infections otherwise normally immunosuppressed. I usually also order IgG Rubeola antibodies in addition to the herpes viral screen with this panel.[14]

NATURAL KILLER CYTOTOXICITY TEST

Immunological cytotoxicity is a principal mechanism by which the immune response copes with and often eliminates foreign material or abnormal cells such as viruses or other microorganisms. If viral titers are high and NK cytotoxicity levels are low, we have a strong indication of viral presence that may be contributing to autism symptoms.

MYELIN BASIC PROTEIN (MBP) ANTIBODIES

Myelin is a multilamellar membrane surrounding nerve fibers in both the central and peripheral nervous systems, derived from the plasma membrane of the oligodendrocyte in the CNS and the schwann cell in the peripheral nervous system. Antibodies (IgG, IgA, IgM) against MBP have been observed in a high percentage of ASD children. Positive tests are an indication of autoimmunity.

COMPREHENSIVE ASD VIRAL/IMMUNE PANEL

Working with Aristo Vojdani, PhD, director of Immunosciences Lab., I have found the following tests useful for immunologically evaluating ASD children and guiding me to effective treatments.

---

[14] Hayney M.S. et al., "Relationship of HLA-DQA1 alleles and humoral antibody following measles vaccination. Int. J. Infect Dis. 1998 Jan-Mar;2(3): 143-6

PREMIER AUTISM PANEL, ISL[15]

- Streptococcal Peptides (M5, M12, M19) (IgG)
- Gliadin Peptides Antibodies (IgG, IgM, IgA)
- Casein Peptides Antibodies (IgG, IgM, IgA)
- Antibodies to Hg Binding Antigen (Fibrillarin) (IgG, IgM, IgA)
- Dipeptidylpeptidase (DPP IV) Antibodies (IgG, IgM, IgA)
- Anti-Myelin Basic Protein Antibodies (IgG, IgM, IgA)
- Anti-Neurofilament Antibodies
- Metallothionein (Cellular Level)
- NK Cell Activity
- Measles Antibodies (IgG, IgM)
- Immunoglobulins (IgG, IgM, IgA)
- VIRAL SCREEN #3:
- Varicella Zoster Virus (IgG)
- Cytomegalovirus (IgG, IgM)
- Epstein-Barr Virus or VCA (IgG, IgM)
- Herpes Type 1 & 2 Virus (IgG, IgM)
- Herpes Type 6 Virus (IgG, IgM)

Cost $1544, 50% Off as Panel = $772 Pre-Paid (as of 3/2004)
Blood Required: 2 yellow tubes (10cc each), 1 red tube (10cc)

Case History–Suzie

In 1998 I was asked to work with a high-functioning 16-year old autistic girl whose mother thought she might have a "brain virus." I told the mother I had never treated anyone for a brain virus before and suggested she see another doctor in the area known for his work with immune dysregulation and viruses as causes of autism—but she was persistent. I will always be grateful to this parent as well as other devoted parents who have challenged me to learn more in order to help their children. I went back to the textbooks, research articles, and some new sources such as Teresa Binstock's published and informal writings on pathogens, viruses, and autoimmunity. Getting ready to work with Suzie, I began to learn all I could about these complicated issues.

---

[15] Immunosciences Lab., Inc., Beverly Hills, CA 90211 Tel: 310-657-1077, Fax: 310-657-1053 www.immunoscienceslab.com, immunsci@ix.netcom.com

Suzie was (is) a beautiful, petit young girl who I would have guessed to be about fourteen rather than sixteen years of age. The mother, a teacher/writer who became a full-time mother when Suzie was born, described a crew of daily tutors (including week-ends), and other enormous efforts made through the years to keep her daughter in public school. Having managed to stay at her grade level, Suzie was a junior primarily by struggling extremely hard to please teachers and parents. However, socially she was isolated, had no friends, and no boys had ever shown interest in her even though she had nice features and an attractive though somewhat immature body. She seemed a bit dreamy and distracted, yet could answer factual questions fairly well. She had strange eating patterns, having refused to eat with her family for years, and liked only a few foods. In taking the medical history, her mother told me that Suzie was normal until around age four when she got roseola, a usually mild and transient childhood disease caused by the HHV6 virus and typically presenting with a widespread rash. After the disease was over, she began behaving differently and, though she never lost speech, did not seem to learn as well as other kids in her classes. The mother showed me pictures of Susie through the years in which occasional breakouts of what looked like brief recurrences of the roseola rash would show on her limbs. (It appeared that she had a chronic low-grade HHV6 infection that occasionally reactivated.)

I conducted routine screening tests which all were within normal limits and placed Susie on a nutrient program (which she agreed to) and suggested dietary modifications (with which she had trouble cooperating). It is much easier to get three and four year olds on a GF/CF diet than a teenager! I conferred with Dr. Ari Vojdani, the director of Immunosciences Laboratory in Beverly Hills, who has been another wonderful resource in helping me begin to understand more about viruses and the immune system. He advised me to order a comprehensive viral panel and a natural killer cytotoxicity test in addition to the CBC, Chemistry Panel, and Thyroid Panel I had already done. Her tests came back with positive IgG (past or chronic infection) and IgM (current infection or reactivation) of HHV6 (the roseola virus). She also had very low NK (natural killer) cytotoxicity function, meaning that her immune system was impaired in its first line of defense to combat viruses. I was surprised; Susie's mother was not. She is one of the many wise mothers I have met since starting to work with these "special needs" children.

I had already started Susie on a small dose of an SSRI hoping to alleviate some of her social anxiety, which seemed to help her be a bit more outgoing. She had been on the SSRI and the nutrient program for several months by the time I started her on acyclovir (the antiviral useful against many strains of HSV and VZV, and with varying degrees of effectiveness against EBV and HHV6). Soon we moved to a modified acyclovir, called Valtrex, which has a different rate of assimilation and is said to be approximately 6 times more potent. I had used Valtrex for many adult herpes patients through the years and knew it as a very safe drug.

After just a week to ten days of the Valtrex, the change in Suzie was amazing. Her eyes brightened, she was more "present," became wittier and more expressive generally, and was starting to acquire friends. It was as if her classmates had never seen her before. Within three months she was on her way to becoming a normal, rebellious, typical teen-ager, totally mystifying her parents and surprising tutors who had been working with her for years. Soon, she started rebelling against spending so much time with the tutors and, as she let most of them go, pleasantly surprised her parents by maintaining her B and C grades. She started attracting boys for the first time in her life and began the usual dramas of high school "thrills and heart-breaks" so characteristic of neurotypical kids. She still exhibited some learning difficulties, but the positive change in all areas of her life was noticeable to anyone who had known her before the treatment. Her parents were enormously delighted and grateful for her "emergence." The mother felt her "inner certainty" that Suzie had a medical problem had been vindicated in the face of Suzie's physician-father who had steadfastly attributed her traits to learning disabilities that needed to be handled by educational psychologists (as had been done with her older sister).

Suzie stayed on the SSRI's for just a few months and the Valtrex (1500mg per day) for 18 months; her viral titers kept going down while her NK values kept going up. At various times in her course of treatment, she took 4-Life Transfer Factor and also the natural anti-viral Monolaurin (Lauricidin). Even after being stabilized, her mother was reluctant to take her off the Valtrex even though Suzie hated the routine "safety" blood tests we needed in order to make sure her liver was not being affected by the treatment. (It wasn't.) Finally, we did phase her out of all her medicines as she approached graduation. She also became weary of taking so many nutrients as she started to feel better. She still maintained her somewhat eccentric eating habits as she left home last fall to attend a small private fine-arts college a few hours away, but we all gratefully accepted that. A few months ago, the parents called to inform me that Susie was maintaining a B average in school and had a steady boy friend the parents liked. I consider her free of the diagnosis of autism, even though she retains some of her eating idiosyncracies. Interestingly, I find her erratic diet not terribly different from many young women in her age group who place a greater investment in staying thin than they do on good nutrition.

Treatment Considerations

Needless to say, the success with Suzie thrilled me and inspired me to obtain viral panels on all the children I evaluated (including Chelsey), starting them on anti-virals with any sign of elevated titers to the herpes family of viruses. However, though many younger children gradually improved, none had the startling and immediate success with the anti-virals that I had experienced with Susie. I was reassured soon after that my results with Suzie were not anomalous when I discovered that other physicians (eg, Michael Goldberg & Sidney Baker) were describing in conferences and on internet websites a subgroup of children for whom anti-virals induced major improvements. I was using anti-virals along with implementing other treatments with the younger kids such as GF/CF diet, secretin, vitamins, nutrients, etc., so the source of any improvement was not so obvious as it was in Suzie's case. Then, in the summer and fall of 2000, I started hearing of the improvement in children undergoing chelation for heavy metal toxicity, particularly mercury, and began actively investigating and using this therapy in my practice.

The heavy metal issue brought a lot of things together for me. I could understand that mercury impairs the immune system, interferes with certain enzyme systems, and allows yeast, colonizing bacteria, and perhaps even some viruses to get a firm hold on the gut tissues. These factors—along with food hypersensitivity—would interfere with nutrient transport across intestinal membranes and would make it chronically difficult for the child to receive adequate brain nourishment. Furthermore, inadequate availability of nutrients can reduce immunity and make it difficult to heal the opportunistic infestations that are so common in ASD children. I began to see that many ASD children seem to have entered into a vicious cycle of intestinal pathology, suboptimal nutrition, and weakened immunity, all of which needed treatment. Impaired detoxification and the subsequent accumulation of toxic metals seem easier for me to understand and treat than the immune, autoimmune, and viral issues. It seemed reasonable to me—and to other physicians who have subsequently presented evidence to the NIH, the IOM, and the FDA—to try and get the toxic metals out of the child so that other simultaneous or subsequent treatments would be more effective.

Chelation seemed especially important in the light of chronic intestinal pathology since the anti-virals do not affect bacterial or fungal colonizations. In fact, we were all discovering at that time that yeast kept coming back and that gut issues remained a serious problem in some kids no matter what we did. If lab-testing and an initial chelation treatment indicated heavy metal poisoning, my view was—and still is—that healing the gut, optimizing nutritional status, and removing heavy metals may be sufficient for boosting the child's immune system to the point where it can do its job of suppressing viruses and other pathogens wherever they may be. As I have repeatedly emphasized, we know chelation should not be instituted until after the gut healing is well under way, otherwise it may be ineffective or even make the gut situation worse.

If—after gut healing and nutritional restoration—diagnostic studies do not indicate heavy metal poisoning, or after progress in chelation has plateaued with no known explanation before full healing, I proceed to the investigation of the immune system by doing more specific immune and viral studies to detect atypical presence of pathogens as an etiologic factor in the child's disorder.

TREATMENTS TO ENHANCE THE IMMUNE SYSTEM

The immune system is intimately related to the gastrointestinal tract, as I have said repeatedly. In addition to its role in defense, the gut-associated lymphoid tissue prevents systemic immune responses to food antigens and plays an important role in maintaining tolerance to self. More immunoglobulin is synthesized and secreted (secretory IgA antibodies) into the digestive tract each day than is produced anywhere else in the body. Immunoglobulin in the intestinal tract may help protect against autoimmunity and the initiation of autoimmune diseases. It is impossible to know which starts the pathology in these children, the gut injury or the immune impairment, as they are so intertwined. There has been a certain amount of investigation of ways to enhance the weakened immune systems of ASD children. Certainly, removing foods that are toxic because of the child's hypersensitivity is necessary as a first step and providing essential nutrients to counteract the deficiencies comes next. We have already discussed in Chapter Seven the removal of heavy metal and other toxins which are well-known immune suppressors. We can use anti-fungal, anti-bacterial and anti-viral medications to treat the illnesses secondary to the immune impairment, but obviously something that could directly go to the cause of the problem and help the body's immune system would be extremely helpful.

Immunomodulators and Immune Boosters

Certain compounds seem to be beneficial in boosting the function of the immune system. Michael Goldberg MD, founder and director of NIDS (Neuro-Immune Dysfunction Syndromes), states that the mission of his organization is to facilitate the employment of immune-modulating therapies in the treatment of what he calls "acquired autism." He believes immune dysregulation or possibly viral-mediated states link all the multiple etiologies and various clinical manifestations of ASD. Dr. Goldberg is well known for his use of a combination of prescription medications for his patients including anti-virals, anti-fungals, and SSRI's. He also uses an older medication called Kutapressin, a porcine liver extract previously used as a medication for herpes zoster or shingles, known to inhibit human herpes viruses and reduce inflammation. This must be given by IM injection over an extended period of time and produces mixed results (as do many of our treatments) as reported by his clients in autism internet support groups. To my knowledge there is not yet a prescription drug category called immunomodulators and I know of no medication specifically used for that purpose other than Kutapressin and IVIG (discussed below).

Natural immunomodulators that I use in my practice are:

- Larch arabinogalactan, a naturally occurring polysaccharide extracted from the Larch tree and known to provide a number of immunological properties. I obtain this from Thorne as Arabinex and from NF Formulas in combination with Vit C as Buffered Vitamin C with Arabinogalactans. Larch is an almost tasteless water-soluble powder, easy for kids to take, and extremely effective in cutting down the number of infections.

- Moducare, from Thorne Research, is a "plant fat" extracted from the African potato (in the family of sterols and sterolins), and is considered an immune system modulator. Research studies have shown the sterols enhance NK and T-helper cell activity while dampening overactive antibody responses; clinically I have found it to be a very powerful immune enhancer. Its main drawback is that it must be taken on an empty stomach for maximal effectiveness.

- Inositol hexaphosphate (IP-6) has been documented to increase NK cell function and protect cells against damage from toxins. It is a phosphorus compound of plants particularly abundant in seeds, legumes and cereal grains. This is available from Enzymatic Therapy, Vitamin Research Products, JHS Natural Products, and Thorne Research.

- Dimethylglycine (DMG) has been shown in many studies to boost NK cells; it is non-toxic and naturally sweet.

- L-glutamine is the most prevalent amino acid in the bloodstream and is considered "conditionally essential." The gastrointestinal system is by far the greatest user of glutamine in the body; there are a large number of immune cells including fibroblasts, lymphocytes, and macrophages along the walls of the gut. The ability of glutamine to nourish these immune cells may account for its positive impact on immunity. Many ASD children with chronic gut problems test low on glutamine. I recommend 1000-4000 mg/day; it is non-toxic and very beneficial to gut function generally.

- Mushroom compounds contain proteoglycans and polysaccharides, including alpha and beta glucans. Studies have shown these preparations to be potent immune enhancers by increasing tumor necrosis factor alpha, stimulating macrophage phagocytic activity, improving NK cell number and activity, stimulating interleukins 1 and 2, B-lymphocyte stimulation, improvement of T-cell ratios, and gamma interferon stimulation. I use 10-15 drops in pear juice of Thorne's 7-mushroom compound Myco-Immune extract 2-3 times/day to bolster immune function in ASD children.

- Lauricidin, a component found in coconut and breast milk, has been researched by Dr. Jon Kabara, with studies showing effectiveness against certain viral groups. This nutrient comes in two forms: the Monolaurin capsule containing 300mg (obtained from Ecological Formulas), and Lauricidin (obtained from Med-Chem Labs), 8-oz jars of mini-pellets that are pure, highly concentrated and very helpful for prevention of herpes outbreaks. The bad taste of these pellets (long lingering and soapy) prevents me from administering them to some children who I am sure would benefit, but I can't find a way to get them down. The children who can take them usually benefit highly, particularly those children who get repeated herpes lesions on their lips or faces. A child must take 7 (large) Monolaurin capsules (which don't taste very good either) for the equivalent of one scoop of the mini-pellets, daunting enough whether the capsules are swallowed or dissolved in some medium which hopefully can hide the taste. I consider Lauricidin to be a safe and often effective natural antiviral, particularly against Herpes Simplex 1 & 2 and varicella.

Rosemary Waring, PhD is a well known expert on sulfur metabolic pathways at the University of Birmingham, UK, and parent researcher Susan Owens has studied with her on sulfation issues. In a recent response on our internet bio-medical group to parents' posts that Monolaurin had helped their children's bowel function, Ms. Owens reported that Dr. Waring's work on fatty acid effects on the gut has shown that lauric acid enhances an enzyme important for regulation of intestine function known to be low in ASD children (tyrosyl protein sulfotransferase). Dr. Waring's work has shown that the sulfur-transferase system is one of the body's major means of detoxification; many ASD children are deficient in sulfur.

- I am encouraging Dr. Kabara to continue his efforts to find a palatable form for such a valuable agent.

Other immune enhancers: **The best is fresh fruits and vegetables (which many of our children will not eat!).** Others are: whey protein (watch for casein), echinacea, elderberry extract, germanium, CoEnzyme Q10, garlic, N-acetyl cysteine (provides sulfur), astragalus root, licorice root, olive leaf extract, grapefruit seed extract, and A-lipoic acid (also provides sulfur), and many others not listed. Parents should educate themselves about any over-the-counter nutrients and heed warnings of dose and safety limitations.

Probiotics as Immunomodulators

There is mounting scientific evidence that probiotics may provide significant health benefits including modulation of the immune system. Probiotics are recognized to function in cell-mediated immunity (Th1) and humoral immunity (Th2) cells, directly interacting with the immune system to help immunological defenses such as down-regulating pro-inflammatory cytokines and up-regulating anti-inflammatory cytokines. Probiotics modulate localized endogenous flora (GALT–gut-associated lymphoid tissue), enhance secretory IgA production, and positively influence the gut immunological barrier.[16]

---

[16] Isolauri, E. Immunological aspects of probiotics and their clinical applications in pediatric patients. Gastroenterol Int 1998; 11:83-85

Oral probiotic supplementation may play a crucial role in severe inflammatory bowel conditions and usually without eliciting harmful inflammatory responses. Use of high potency and multi-spectrum probiotic formulations appear to provide clear safety as well as clinical efficacy in those with autism related gut disorders.

Klaire Labs' new Ther-Biotic™ line[16a] uses their proprietary InTactic™ technology to deliver far higher functional potency than other probiotic formulations, and these are the ones I use the most now for children who need a high level of intestinal support.

Nutrients

Certain nutrients known to be especially important to the immune system are the minerals zinc and selenium, the anti-oxidants A, C and E, and a balanced array of amino acids and fatty acids. (please see discussion in Chapter Six).

Glutathione, or GSH

Glutathione is a tri-peptide produced and stored in the liver that is made from the amino acids glycine, glutamic acid and cysteine. It protects the body against toxic agents such as heavy metals by acting as a powerful antioxidant that prevents formation of free radicals and inhibits cellular damage. The reduced form called L-glutathione is the most active kind and the one recommended for ASD children. It is expecially important during chelation, but some children have difficulty tolerating it, and some doctors advise omitting glutathione during the "on" days of chelation. IV glutathione is being used with great benefit by some practitioners. Since oral glutathione is not well absorbed, transdermal agents are being produced that may offer a more effective approach to providing this essential nutrient. It is important for the amino acid precursors to be taken in the diet or with supplementation to make sure enough glutathione can be produced to prevent oxidative stress caused by viral infections, environmental toxins including heavy metals, inflammation, and dietary deficiencies of GSH precursors and enzyme cofactors.

[16a]   Klaire Labs, www.Klaire.com, 866-216-6127

Sphingolin

Bovine myelin basic protein (bMBP) has been used to reduce autoimmunity to MBP in children with autism.[17] Sphingolin is a scientifically-designed supplement containing a specially-prepared source of bovine myelin sheath, a rich source of naturally-occurring Myelin Basic Protein. Ecological Formulas calls their compound an Organic Glandular, and writes, "The delicate enzymes are protected by lyophilization. Free of corn, soy, yeast, wheat, egg, and other common alleregens. Source is New Zealand bovine." This is considered a nutrient, not a prescription drug. Some children show improvement on Sphingolin, (more awareness, eye contact) some have a negative reaction, (hyperactivity) and most in my limited experience show little or no change attributable to the nutrient per parents' reports. However, I believe it is worth a try especially for those children who are low-functioning and/or show elevated autoantibodies to MBP. My suggestion is to start with a low dose (1/2 capsule/day for at least one week) and proceed slowly, building up the dose until some reaction is noted, good or bad. When benefit is seen, it is advised to stay at that level, and of course stop if an intolerance or negative reaction arises.

IVIG (INTRAVENOUS IMMUNE GLOBULIN [HUMAN])

Immunoglobulins are proteins produced by B-lymphocytes and are the major effector molecules of the humoral immune system. Generally, immunoglobulin molecules are antibodies that react with specific antigens. IVIG therapy is believed to act through inhibition of cytokines and the removal of autoantibodies, although medical literature also describes its antiviral effects. Panglobulin IVIG is an FDA approved drug for the treatment of primary immunodeficiencies made from human plasma collected from more than 16,000 volunteer donors at licensed donor centers in the U.S. This product contains primarily IgG, with a small amount of IgA, and traces of IgM. If tests show your child has immunoglobulin deficiency with recurrent infections, a total IgG deficiency, persistent seizures or some other indicated neurological indication, insurance compa-

---

[17] Singh V.K. et al., "Circulating autoantibodies to neuronal and glial filament proteins in autism." Pediatr Neurol. 1997 Jul;17(1): 88-90.

nies are bound under insurance rules to pay for this very expensive treatment. Autoimmune encephalopathy—which some researchers believe to be a form of autism—is not a reason for insurance companies to pay yet. Only laboratory documented immune disorders and intractable seizure disorders are covered by most insurance companies. There is no anti-measles remedy safe for children except for gamma globulin and Vitamin A (see p. 125).

ORAL HUMAN GAMMAGLOBULIN: See Appendix E

Pilot studies have recently been undertaken to check the effectiveness and safety of a new oral therapy for autoimmune disease. The studies use an encapsulated form of Intravenous Immunoglobulin (IVIG) for oral use, limited at the present time to investigational use. Children being accepted for these studies must show persistent gastrointestinal problems associated with autism. I learned of this from a parent in my practice. Her three year old child was in a study; she was over-joyed at the complete cessation of diarrhea present since birth in her son shortly after commencing the experimental drug. He also began sleeping through the night after starting the compound. Soon after the completion of the 12-week study, the child's diarrhea and abated autistic traits returned. His parents obtained more of the medicine and again saw positive results, and want to continue what they call "a miracle drug." Though IVIG is FDA approved, the oral form is still investigational, expensive, and will be paid for by insurance only with laboratory documentation of severe immune impairment. The compound must be obtained with a physician's prescription to a compounding pharmacy. I recommend parents institute an effective gut-healing program with appropriate dietary restrictions, testing and treating for IgG food (delayed) sensitivities and effective anti-pathogen strategies before resorting to this pooled human blood product. My hope is that oral immunoglobulin (OIG) will be used not only as a new treatment modality but also as a "reminder" to the body of what a normal immune system is, thereby helping to re-educate our children's immune systems. What we don't know is whether this can happen and if so, how long it might take. I recommend immune testing for myelin basic protein (MBP) antibodies and natural killer (NK) cytotoxicity as well as a viral screen to assess the status of the immune system before and again periodically throughout its use. Though promising, not all children I have given oral immunoglobulin have shown benefit, and it is not yet known how long it can or should be used or whether there may be any long term side effects that have not yet appeared from this new weapon in our ever-expanding arsenal against ASD.

ANTI-VIRAL PRESCRIPTION MEDICATIONS

For antiviral medications, I use acyclovir for the younger children and Valtrex, a form of acyclovir that is 6 times more biologically active, for kids over five or over 40 pounds as my first choice. For most children acyclovir is safe and effective against most but not all strains of HSV1, HSV2, and VZV, is ineffective against most cytomegalovirus strains, and has various levels of effectiveness against some strains of EBV and HHV6. In my experience and in reports of several other clinicians with very large autistic practices, acyclovir is estimated to be effective in about 30% of the children who take it. Another antiviral used when acyclovir or Valtrex becomes ineffective is Famvir, (famciclovir) which functions in a similar way to acyclovir. Rotating anti-virals sometimes seems to help maintain responsiveness to the drugs. "Safety" tests for blood count and chemistries are essential for any of these prescription medications since they may stress the liver. I usually perform these tests after the first month in an extended treatment course, and then every two or three months thereafter unless there is some indication clinically that something is not going well.

SUMMARY

The health of the immune system clearly plays a central role in the treatment of ASD. Immunity and autoimmunity are inseparable from the status of the gut, resistance to infections and other viral pathologies. Ultimately the treatment of ASD comes down to helping the children develop strong, self-regulating, infection-resisting and pathogen-suppressing immune systems. There are many natural substances and some prescription drugs that can be helpful in achieving this goal. I believe that in the final analysis, ASD cannot persist in a child with a healthy immune system.

PART THREE

Overview

NINE

OVERVIEW

With Teresa Binstock
Researcher in Developmental and Behavioral Neuroanatomy

A s I said at the outset, Children with Starving Brains (affection-
ately known to those of us who worked on this book as "CSB")
was written for parents willing to let their ASD child draw them into
an entirely new way of looking at healing, as well as for physicians
facing growing requests to treat children with ASD. I trust there are
still more than a few of you in both categories not only still reading at this point but growing increasingly drawn to the challenge of
understanding the nature and treatment of ASD.

Yes, the field is extraordinarily complex and still dominated by
questions and unknowns more than answers and understanding. Yet
an enormous amount of progress has been made by a relatively few
people—parents, physicians, research scientists and others—working in close partnership together. In fact, one of the great "gifts" created by the desire to heal so many children on the ASD spectrum has
been the remarkable ways in which the "community of interest" has
banded and worked together. That some children, even if it is still a
relatively small percentage of those treated, have actually been freed
of the diagnosis of autism or some other form of ASD is remarkable
and unthinkable when we all started on this journey only a few years
ago.

There are several reasons for the even limited success that has been achieved. The first is that understanding and treating autism involves virtually all of the medical and biological disciplines, since this disorder involves the entire human body systemically. In a sense then, research into autism has been going on for hundreds of years, indirectly—until the time, quite recently, when simultaneously technology was in full blossom and we finally realized that ASD is primarily a collection of biomedical rather than psychological illnesses.

A second reason is that there are a number of researchers who are particularly devoted and gifted at taking the systemic view, looking at the "big picture," willing to move away from the reductionistic tendencies of contemporary medicine and instead focusing on the interactions among the body's many complex subsystems. Many of these individuals are cited throughout CSB. At this juncture, I would like to honor one of these talented investigators—pioneers really—my colleague Teresa Binstock, who was so important in bringing CSB to whatever level of medical and biological authenticity we have achieved. Her unstinting devotion to detail and professional integrity has served this book well.

As a way of acknowledging her contributions and challenging her to let go of details for a moment, while at the same time having sympathy for the possibly overwhelmed reader, I have asked Teresa to help me summarize the biomedical approach to ASD in a few pages. I also asked her to speculate a little on the future directions of research and treatment of ASD, still all within a few pages. Her response appears below and in Appendix C. May it give the tired reader a moment of refreshment, knowing how much you have learned plowing through the material and how far we have all come together on this ASD journey in so short a time. What follows is a mix of Teresa and Jaquelyn.

Autism

Autism is a complex syndrome involving genetics, the digestive and immune systems, viral, fungal and other pathogen invasions, and an inability to detoxify poisons from heavy metals and pesticides. In recent years an appreciation of autism's biomedical aspects and their ramifications for treatment has become widespread. The new way autism is conceived has brought into clinical usefulness new approaches to diagnostics and treatment. As this paradigm shift continues—and as an increasing number of children outgrow their autism—parents, physicians, and researchers are developing a greater awareness of environmental factors that appear to be etiologically significant in many and perhaps most autism spectrum children. Environmental toxins such as heavy metals may be triggers for many ASD children. The broad-spectrum approach to the treatment of ASD uses biomedical profiling and a combination of treatment protocols to deal with underlying pathologies making up this complex disorder.

Uniqueness and Common Pathways in ASD Children

Autism from birth occurs in a relatively small percentage of ASD children. The medical histories of the majority of autistic children indicate a descent into autism after a period of relative normalcy. This "regressive" or "acquired" form of autism can be gradual or abrupt. For many children the sequence during the first 30 months unfolds as follows:

- **First stage:** vaccinations that include thimerosal's ethyl mercury, that can affect various tissues and contribute to a gradual weakening of detoxification and anti-pathogen immunities.

- **Second stage:** early intestinal pathology (e.g., colic related to food hypersensitivity; chronic diarrhea) and/or numerous episodes of otitis media.

- **Third stage:** continued effects of inadequate nutrition, weakened immunity, and impaired detoxification. Environmental toxins may begin to accumulate in a dangerous manner.

- **Fourth stage:** injection of live-viruses (vaccines) by which time the toddler has an acquired and/or genetic immunodeficiency, inadequate nutrition, and an increasing load of toxic metals.

Despite this common pattern, no single scenario accounts for "autism in general." Differences between ASD children remain important, not only in regard to the underlying biomedical pathologies but also in regard to the timing of the adverse reactions that precipitate regressions. In those children from 1991-2001 who received the thimerosal-laden HepB vaccination at birth, the first and second stages in the common pathways may have overlapped. We can surmise that the ethylmercury injection(s) and its gradual outflow into bile and intestinal tissue causing gut inflammation and immune system injury may have been the initial insult triggering the child into regression.

Although common themes can be observed when examining medical histories of hundreds of autistic children, specific patholo-gies prompting the descent into autistic regression vary from child to child, and clinical portraits of specific kids with ASD are often quite unique. Despite the complexity of ASD and the uniqueness of each ASD child, the strong message of this book is that the ASD child's persisting pathologies may be successfully investigated and treated through a broad-spectrum approach.

Cost Effectiveness and Treatment Efficacy

- **Costs:** Lab-test data can be expensive. The biomedical approach is not yet accepted by most insurance companies and the cost of a thorough set of medical tests is between $1,500 and $3,000—most or all of which may not be reimbursed. As we have emphasized, some sequencing of tests is medically sound and economically prudent. For more difficult cases that do not respond to the initial treatment protocols, obtaining a thorough set of lab-data collected *during a limited span of time* to get the full picture contributes to the likelihood of discovering the origin of a child's ASD pathologies and, therefore, to successful treatment.

- **Categories of Treatment Efficacy:** As this book goes to press, no clear statistics have been developed regarding the likelihood of success when parents undertake the broad-spectrum approach in treating their ASD child. However, from presentations at recent conferences, parents sharing via internet groups and physicians sharing data via professional listserves, four categories of treatment efficacy are clear:
  - Group-1: ASD children who outgrow the diagnosis completely
  - Group-2: ASD children who are helped a great deal but who retain an ASD diagnosis
  - Group-3: ASD children who are helped somewhat, but remain quite impaired.
  - Group-4: ASD children who are helped little or not at all.

When parents invest in the biomedical approach, there is no way of determining which group will characterize the progress of their child before lab-tests are undertaken and the various treatments attempted. However, even the group 3 level of success may be of great benefit to a particular family.

Consider the child, now eight, that inspired this book. Needless to say, her parents have followed the broad-spectrum approach. Chelsey's most dramatic improvement occurred after initiation of the GF/CF diet when she was five. Within weeks Chelsey became potty trained. Although she has made continued slow progress on many fronts since then, no other treatment protocol to date has precipitated such a dramatic short-term improvement, and several of her impairments remain, although abated. From her parents' perspective, however, it was extremely important that she finally became potty trained. How many diapers and pull-ups would still be needed each month if they had followed the advice of some professionals who belittle the value of the GF/CF diet?

What are the odds for parents who take the biomedical approach? Until biomedical treatment-efficacy results from thousands of ASD children are compiled, we can only rely on anecdotal information. Pooling our anecdotal impressions as grandparent, clinical physician, researcher, medical-data analyst, and participants in DAN! conferences and internet discussion groups, we conclude at this time that a small but growing number of autistic spectrum children actually outgrow autism and that many others improve significantly. Our impression has been re-enforced and enhanced by the recent successes of heavy metal chelation protocols.

Yet despite these positive indications, we do not want to give false hopes to parents of ASD children. Not all autistic children will improve taking the biomedically-based broad-spectrum approach. However, most will. We feel that the majority of parents who invest in this approach will celebrate their child entering into one of the three groups for which at least some significant improvement is experienced.

Thinking Ahead

The core of the ASD biomedical paradigm is that many of these children have one or more underlying, identifiable and treatable medical conditions. Comprehensive screening tests are necessary because apparently sub-clinical processes are not easily detected. Despite the variation from child to child, it is almost always beneficial to heal the gut, boost nutritional status, remove toxic metals, and—in some cases—address chronic and active infections. As this is being written, patterns in lab data and treatment-efficacy reports from an increasing number of autistic children suggest new biomedical and policy directions for the future.

- **New Directions in Diagnostics, Treatment, Research**
  The diagnostic protocols presented in this book are based upon the coordinated use of lab-tests as a significant part of a "screening" process. This approach is different from using lab-tests to confirm or rule out a pathology that exhibits well-defined symptoms. Quite the contrary, the underlying pathologies in many ASD children often do not produce obvious medical symptoms. Participation in the biomedical approach is based upon a shift away from the model "this must be genetic, so nothing can be done" to a model in which the underlying ASD pathologies are identified, their sources determined whenever possible and a sequential treatment protocol developed.

- **Back to the Future: New Directions in Policy**
  Several policy changes obviously merit consideration:

  a. Infants and toddlers who are sick or who were recently sick should not be vaccinated.

  b. Regulatory agencies should act in accordance with the reality that some neonates, infants, and toddlers have increased susceptibility.

  c. Regulatory agencies ought to shift from "risk management" to "risk avoidance" when determining "safe" levels of toxins in our foods, medicines, and environment.

  d. When researchers conduct autism research projects, they should include subgroup and susceptibility considerations both in the experimental design and in the use of statistics in the interpretation of findings.

We believe strongly that the epidemic of children with ASD demonstrates the folly of policies that consider injury to susceptible individuals an acceptable risk.

What Role Does the Physician Play?

When parents begin to realize that their child is not typical, individual beliefs about causes and treatments will shape the type of medical care they seek. Similarly, when the parents receive professional counsel from physicians, psychologists, and child-development specialists, those professionals' beliefs about ASD will shape the diagnostic strategies and treatment options made available to the child.

If a professional says, "nothing can be done," then parents may never learn if the biomedically-based broad-spectrum approach would have helped their child. But, *if parents are informed* and utilize doctors who are open to the biomedical approach (if they can find them), then the child will be given an opportunity to heal in ways that may well lead to behavioral and cognitive improvement.

TEN

STARVING BRAINS, STARVING HEARTS, WHAT DOES IT ALL MEAN?

By Jack Zimmerman, PhD

Messages

Why are there so many ASD and other special needs children now and what are we to make of the recent astounding growth in their ranks? Is there a message here for our culture beyond such obvious ones as cleaning up the environment of heavy metals, pesticides and other pollutants; improving the safety of vaccination and dental protocols; eating more wisely; and improving the health of our children's immune systems? Are there other levels of meaning in the ASD epidemic that we should be exploring? Is there a message all these children are trying to bring to us?

Have you found yourself asking questions like these?

Jaquelyn and I have been "living these questions" on our journey with Chelsey and the other special needs children who have come into our life during the past five years. It seems fitting that we end the book with a few of our own speculations about the meanings and messages these remarkable children are bringing into our lives.

We have come to believe that the special children are here in increasing numbers to change our fundamental cultural paradigm—to change the way we look at the world, practice medicine, educate our children, relate to each other, and, ultimately, the way we learn to become *more alive.*

The children with starving brains challenge our capacity to love—particularly in regard to the qualities of patience and perseverance, devotion beyond the usual parental call of duty and the capacity to think and act creatively "out of the box." Often, it is only after a profound challenge to our capacity to love, such as the rearing of an ASD child, that we come to realize how much more there is to discover about loving.

Jaquelyn and I have always seen our relationship as a path of awakening and the primary inspiration for our service to others, yet our love for this compelling, beautiful, mysterious creature added an entirely new dimension to our marriage. Chelsey upped the ante in the game of love, without ever asking us directly if we wanted to play!

When we looked around at other families struggling with their Chelseys, we saw that virtually everyone was living out their own unique version of the same experience. As we read and heard stories of families transformed by attempts to heal their ASD children, we began to see how the rapid growth in the ASD population had the potential to deepen and expand the ways we all love each other. It was not a huge step to see that the growing presence of all these special children was an opportunity for major personal and cultural transformation.

The children with starving brains are here to help us heal our starving hearts.

This realization began to dawn on us as we struggled to find effective biomedical treatment for Chelsey, while her parents searched for adequate schooling and tried to adjust to a new and sometimes overwhelming family life together. Our search for meaning in the epidemic of autism soon implicated the critical state of the environment, lack of sufficient vision and courage in the way we educate our children, limitations in the established allopathic approach of medicine and abounding unconsciousness in our understanding of family dynamics and intimate relationship.

Exploring such questions truly honors the "specialness" of these children because they embody these big issues in the most personal way possible. The special children have truly become "canaries in the mines of our culture;" they are compelling, not only because we come to love them so much for who they are individually, but also because they are here to catalyze the expanded awareness needed to change our culture—and sooner rather than later.

The vast and increasing numbers of ASD children are messengers reflecting critical unbalances in the ways we live our lives. In their silences and explosions of feeling, in the disruption of their biochemical makeup, in their obvious incompatibility with our established educational system and traditional medical paradigm, they are literally asking us to see how out of balance we have become, collectively and individually. They are a wake-up message, a desperate eleventh-hour call for us to realize the insanity of our priorities and the many dangers in our present courses of action.

In this final chapter of the book we will explore what these children are teaching us about family life and the future of medicine. Their message in regard to the way we educate our children and a few thoughts about the environmental implications of their growing presence appear in Appendix A.

Most important, we feel that *exploring these larger issues increases our capacity to heal the children.* Understanding why they are here in such numbers, on **both** the biomedical and cultural levels increases our ability to help them find a fulfilling life. We have come to see that, in short:

If we truly hear the whole message, we are more likely to heal the messenger.

We heard the message first through Chelsey so, before we explore issues, I want to tell you a little about these past five years with Jaquelyn, Chelsey and her mother, Elizabeth, as a way of inviting you to share the messages you have heard during the adventure of raising and healing your special child. To tell these stories is to honor the children, better understand who they really are and in this important way support their healing.

Jaquelyn, Chelsey and Elizabeth

I began to realize that Chelsey might play a major role in our lives when Jaquelyn became convinced that something was not quite right about her developmental progress. For several months we danced around Liz's assurances that her first two kids were slow to develop (true), so not to worry because Chelsey would finally catch up as they had. Meanwhile, Jaquelyn's agitation grew as she became convinced that Chelsey's behavior was way beyond a case of late blooming. Jaquelyn began to pore through written material on autism and visit the Internet every day. I saw a missionary fire in her eyes that I hadn't seen for quite a while. Our first challenge was to penetrate Liz's denial and bring the increasingly obvious reality about Chelsey into recognition by her parents. Those few months were extremely painful.

What followed was a burst of powerful maternal energy in Liz, along with fear, confusion and self-judgment, and an awakening of Jaquelyn's energy that was awesome to watch. Liz had always held a mysterious, primal place in Jaquelyn's heart, and Chelsey's plight added an entirely new dimension to their already profound connection. Much later on we realized that a part of this strong mother/daughter bond had to do with Liz's own touch of autistic behavior, particularly when she was a child. Chelsey fanned Jaquelyn's mother-love into a combined mother/grandmother/doctor's passion for making sure Chelsey got better and Liz would not be burdened by intense care-giving for the rest of her life. We were off and running: tests, evaluations by experts, behavior modification programs and a full plunge into the Internet.

By the time Chelsey was three-and-a-half, Jaquelyn was fully immersed in her healing, driven by curiosity and a growing attraction to this mysteriously compelling creature. Every ounce of her medical acumen became activated to make Chelsey better. I became an Internet widower. Our main private conversational theme shifted from the mystery of our own intimate relationship, our work with couples and other clients to the mystery of ASD and Chelsey's healing. I began to see the handwriting on the wall. As the saying goes, "If you can't lick 'em, you'd better join 'em!"

I began to fall in love with my step-granddaughter while following her around for two hours in Ojai's Libby Park several months before her fourth birthday. She made no eye contact with me at all while she wandered through the bushes and allowed me to push her on the swings. She said nothing to me, even though she had already developed the ability to use single word communication as a result of her behavioral modification training. At one point she stopped a moment under a tree and let me sit next to her for a minute or two. I was amazed at my reaction. I actually felt elated as if some extraordinary princess had given me hope that I might gain her favor.

My fate was sealed at the following Christmas family reunion.

I was stretched out (uncharacteristically) on the sofa in our small living room, dominated by a six-foot Christmas tree. Chelsey ran into the room, past the tree, swept by me on the sofa and disappeared back down the hall. This loop was repeated quite a few times before I realized that she was coming a little closer to the sofa on each successive pass around the room. I felt strangely stirred and put out a silent message that it was safe for her to come closer. Although she made no eye contact or other overt sign of recognition, *it became absolutely clear that Chelsey was relating to me, however indirectly, and, in fact, was subtly inviting me to pay attention to her.* I grabbed the opportunity, sending her a stronger silent message to approach the sofa more closely. When, on the next loop, she began to sing a line from a Christmas carol (perfectly in tune), she might as well have been a Siren or Circe herself. I was clearly no match for this goddess.

I moved a chair close to the sofa and sent her a silent message to sit in it a moment the next time around. It took four or five more passes through the living room before Chelsey accepted my invitation, sitting on the chair's edge for just two seconds at first. Several rounds later she was sitting in the chair (now pulled quite close to the sofa) for almost a minute. After a few more loops I was allowed to touch her arm. That hooked me completely. This little creature entered my inner world and took hold of some tender part previously hidden there. I became determined in that moment to find a way to relate to her as part of the healing process that had begun. I remember also having a feeling then (repeated often since) that some part of Chelsey knew perfectly well what was going on and was in a way "toying" with me. I kept such blasphemies to myself in those days.

By her fourth birthday Jaquelyn and Liz were deeply into the biomedical adventure that Chelsey inspired and, although they both were pleased that "I was taking a special interest in her," I felt on the fringe of the intense activity that had begun to dominate our life. Jaquelyn's photographic mind and amazing retentive capacity blew me away. Our dinners were filled with medical theories, lab test results, heart-breaking stories from the Internet and a growing rage that there was something very wrong about certain vaccinations.

There followed in fairly rapid sequence (considering she lived 360 miles away) a number of encounters with Chelsey that stoked my missionary fire. I would help to "regain" this princess and break the spell she was under in my own way through the relationship route while Jaquelyn was experimenting with secretin, nutritional supplements, transfer factors and the GF/CF diet. By that time Liz had engineered an expanded home schooling program with specially trained behavioral specialists and was already noticing how Chelsey had brought forth in her previously hidden organizational talents, not to mention patience and physical stamina.

A major break-though occurred one afternoon in the summer after Chelsey's fourth birthday when I urged Jaquelyn and Liz to leave her with me while they went out to have some time alone. (The two older kids, Andrea and Alisha, were with Jim, their father, visiting his parents.) . We lived in a little suburban house then whose back yard was almost completely filled with a small swimming pool. Chelsey had shown interest in the pool before, but after the ladies left us alone, she could hardly wait to put on her bathing suit. In fact, if she had had her way she would have gone in without being encumbered by something so civilized.

Water has always been my second home and swimming my favorite form of exercise, so I looked forward to being in the pool with my new friend. There's no way I could have anticipated what happened during the next four hours. After splashing about in the shallow end for a little while, Chelsey very deliberately made up a game. I was to stand waist deep in the water, while she jumped in and swam towards me. I was not to reach out to her or touch her in any way. All contact was to be left in her hands alone. After approaching within a few feet of me, she would turn around, dog paddle back to the steps and climb out. The sequence was repeated many times. The game challenged my restraint capability profoundly; I soon found it extremely difficult to keep my hands from reaching out as she came near. I managed to resist.

Then she added sound to our scenario. First, she shouted "AN-ARGY" as she jumped off the side of the pool. A few minutes later, in a more gentle voice, she said "Mabatu" and "Pabatu," alternately as she approached me in the water. I slowly moved further towards the deep end of the pool until only my shoulders were above water and let my hands float in front of me, all the while trying to figure out what she meant by these precisely repeated and obviously significant exclamations. "Anargy" was clearly a call to courage for the leap into the pool—a warrior's cry before the plunge. I finally concluded that Mabatu and Pabatu named figures of importance that somehow related to Chelsey's delight in being in the water. It was as if she had finally found her true home after a long and dry detour (living in Arizona!) of more than four years.

We had been playing this way for almost an hour when she reached out her arms spontaneously and embraced my shoulders after approaching me in the water. I felt a surge of excitement but resisted hugging her back. She repeated the gesture on several successive plunges, each time coming a little closer to me in the water. Finally, after several more passes, Chelsey embraced me with arms slightly outstretched and looked deeply into my eyes. It seemed like an eternity…that probably lasted three or four seconds. It was the first time I was privileged to look into what Liz came to call her "Big Browns." I saw a profound being in those eyes. I hadn't a shred of doubt of that. Then she said "Pabatu" and swam back to the shallow end of the pool.

I decided then that she was a dolphin child and immediately understood why some ASD children have been so drawn to make contact with these highly conscious allies of ours. I decided that Mabatu and Pabatu were the female and male names of dolphin gods and anargy was Chelsey's warrior's cry as she plunged into the water to greet them. I took the risk of asking Chelsey out loud whether my conjectures were correct. She didn't answer me directly, of course, but on the next plunge she made even longer eye contact. Then, abruptly, a few rounds later, she said, "Bath time." We filled the tub and Chelsey surrendered her slightly chilled body to the warm water for half an hour. We played with water toys while she made up songs in her clear, perfectly pitched voice and allowed me to soap her back and legs. After a while she said, "Pool" and we repeated the whole cycle.

I could hardly wait to tell Jaquelyn and Liz about my adventure. Naturally, they were delighted, although not quite sure what to make of my interpretation of what had happened. The next day, I tried to repeat the ceremony in the pool while they were about, but naturally Chelsey didn't cooperate. I wondered if I had embellished my experience of the day before. When they left the following day, Chelsey did not show any visible feelings, yet Liz told us on the phone that night that she had started sobbing uncontrollably as they drove off. It was the first time Chelsey had ever shown sadness separating from anyone. Although it broke Liz's heart to hear her cry, she was pleased to see such an outpouring of feeling.

That experience started Chelsey and me on a strong practice of water interaction that continues to this day. I am forever trying to figure out what pool or other body of water we can swim in next. Visits to Arizona or her visits to California are always planned around time in the water. When larger bodies are not available, long baths, sometimes two a day, have to do. Now, on occasion, Chelsey becomes part of the planning. She is completely unafraid and at home in the ocean, so our month-long times together on the Big Island of Hawaii are filled with delightful long afternoons in the surf, watching her develop her own dolphin-like movements under water and engaging in silent, playful interacting far more readily than on dry land. I used to play the water game of throwing her high into the air with the count of a "one, two, three…" literally for hours. Now she is too heavy for that, but Jaquelyn and I delight in trips to the "Hot Pool" in the southern part of the Big Island, where Chelsey moves gracefully beneath the surface in the warm sunlit mixture of hot vulcanic and ocean water, her hair moving in slow motion, a hint of a smile on her lips. We swim past each other underwater like two dolphins, close but not touching. Apart from the paucity of words, anyone watching us play would never guess she had any special needs at all.

Not long after our swimming relationship had begun, Liz and I took Chelsey to see a psychologist with extensive past experience doing movement work with ASD children.[1] After Beth observed Chelsey and Liz for more than an hour, I told her about our strong water connection, so Beth asked me to swim with Chelsey in their backyard pool. Watching us play together in the water, Beth immediately noticed the increase in Chelsey's relational capacity. When Jaquelyn and I returned a month later to receive her formal evaluation, Beth remarked how touched she had been watching us in the water. Jaquelyn took that moment to raise a question she had been incubating ever since our first extended time with Chelsey in Hawaii. "What do you think would serve Chelsey the most at this point in her life [she was then five], to live full time with Jack and me or continue on in Arizona with her family [now grown to six with the recent birth of Adam]?"

Beth hesitated only a moment. "I think the opportunity for Chelsey to spend that kind of time with you and Jack would be invaluable. She would get a lot of focused attention that would help her greatly at this age. With three other children in the family, Liz and Jim have their hands full. This is an important time in Chelsey's development. As she gets older, it will be more difficult for changes to be made." Jaquelyn gave me a look that would have awakened a statue. The following evening we went right to the edge.

"I have to go down the path with Chelsey all the way," Jaquelyn said. "There's something going on in all of this—even beyond her getting better, as important as that is to me. I don't pretend to understand the depth of my love for her, but I know I have to follow the call. I hope you can come with me, but if you can't, I still have to go."

"What do you mean, 'go,' " I said, suddenly feeling my mouth run dry.

"I don't know and I don't mean to sound threatening or dramatic. I just know that my love for Chelsey is an awakening of some-

---

[1] Dr. Beth Kalish-Weiss was a pioneer some thirty years ago in working with children in the autistic spectrum through individual and group movement therapy. She has published voluminously about her successful work, which was done quantitatively and with controls. Dr. Kalish-Weiss lives in Los Angeles where she now has a private practice for adults.

thing as strong as our relationship has been—and I have to follow it. I want her to get better more than anything else in the world and I want to do whatever I can to help that happen. The grandmother and doctor—and yes the mother in me—all hear the call strongly. I need for you to understand…I want you to come with me because I know you can be of great help in Chelsey's healing. I'm not sure I can do what needs to be done without you but, if I have to, I will."

The weeks that followed shook the foundations of our twenty-five years together. I knew, as did Jaquelyn, that I couldn't "go" along with her unless the healing journey with Chelsey was a profound reality for me as well. Otherwise, our relationship would veer out of balance, flounder and lose the remarkable synergy that had inspired every aspect of our life and work together.

By that time, I had already witnessed Jaquelyn's extraordinary emergence as "sleuth/physician" in her quest to find the right bio-medical treatment program for Chelsey. After the visits with Beth, it became clear that these talents would be well complemented by my way of relating to my granddaughter, entering her world and finding a common language—silent and even verbal—in which to express feelings. It was then that we began to see that together there was a possibility of using the power of our highly energetic relational "field" to help Chelsey emerge and heal. We saw that by working intimately together we might be able to create a conscious synergy between the biomedical treatments Chelsey was undergoing (with only limited success to that point) and the ongoing highly energized interactions we were having with her.

I had always been slightly uncomfortable with the singular focus on "getting Chelsey better." I wondered whose definition of `better' we had adopted. I wondered about this great goal of "normalcy" we were striving for. I found the temerity to ask Jaquelyn: "Why isn't Chelsey responding to the protocols you're using successfully with so many of the other kids in your practice?" Finally, I found the real questions that were stirring in me:

"What's the message in all this?"

And also, for the first time, I asked,

"By what authority do we have the right to try and 'fix' her?"

For a while Jaquelyn felt the second question was irrelevant and distracting. Obviously, Chelsey needed to get better because she was ill and otherwise wouldn't have an independent and creative life—one that would not be a perpetual burden on her parents. I saw the truth of that, of course, but still the question haunted me.

They haunted me right into realizing that I wanted to go down the path with Jaquelyn, not primarily because I didn't want to risk losing my life partner, but because *I saw that Chelsey was the next challenge in further deepening our relationship and our service to others, particularly in the realm of healing.* At the same time, I felt my life couldn't take Chelsey on full time because of all the many involvements that already filled it to overflowing. To take her on would mean giving up almost everything that I was doing, because I knew I would be the one primarily playing the interactive role in Chelsey's healing. Perhaps it was selfish; perhaps my resistance was appropriate. Looking back now, years later, I see that it was probably both. Liz and Jim were Chelsey's parents. I argued. She had entered their lives and it was their gift as well as burden to learn what they had to learn from this messenger of love. Yet, even though it appeared impossible, some part of me was tempted to say yes and release my entire life as I knew it—if only I could be sure I had something tangible to offer Chelsey.

Liz and I talked it all over. Giving up Chelsey for a while would greatly ease her over-filled parental life, but Liz agreed that she and Jim (and Andrea, Alisha—and now Adam too) had been given the gift of Chelsey's presence in their lives. They all needed to honor that, Liz felt. Our conversation that day launched a series of talks that continue regularly now, either face to face when that is possible or more usually on the phone, during which we discuss Chelsey as an awakener in our lives. Within a year Liz embraced that point of view completely. Now, even during the hard times dealing with the formidable parental challenges she faces (not only with Chelsey!) some part of Liz knows that it is all perfect and part of her adventure of awakening. I do know that if Chelsey had come to live with us full-time, Jaquelyn would never have been able to help as many families as she has and gather all the experience needed to write this book. Still, we have had the blessing to have Chelsey with us for four one-month "intensives" in Hawaii since she was four. May these times of healing continue!

Despite creating a GF/CF diet for Chelsey, implementing treatment programs and trying to find time for the other kids, Liz has been blessed with many personal realizations. By the end of Chelsey's third year, she began to recognize patterns in herself that were subtle versions of Chelsey ways of behaving. "Chelsey comes by her autism naturally," Liz told us one day with a mixture of chagrin and delight. "Being with her so intensely has led me to see those parts of myself that are just like her, only not so obvious. I often avoid direct eye contact and have some trouble expressing my deeper feelings to another person, even someone close to me. She does what I do but more so." It was at this moment that Jaquelyn and I solved a piece of the mystery of her indescribable connection with both Liz and Chelsey.

Besides personal revelations, Liz has reaped a nourishing harvest from raising Chelsey. The fruit includes deepening her practice of prayer, remembering wonderful dreams from which she derives guidance, learning how to search for an entirely new level of meaning in events and experiences, and the discovery of a variety of new strengths in herself that had never been tapped before. Shortly after Chelsey's seventh birthday, Liz told me on the phone one day, "I feel blessed to have Chelsey as my child. I was playing with her today when I suddenly realized that she's a very special being, a high being, probably higher than all of us. It's just hidden behind all those symptoms...I see her now." I put down the phone shortly after that with tears in my eyes. I had never felt such love and admiration for Liz!

The final commitment to the path of healing Chelsey took place in a "council" between Jaquelyn and me a few months after our visit with Beth Kalish-Weiss.[2] Chelsey felt quite with us in the way she had been literally many times during our councils together, though

---

[2]   In council a talking piece is passed among those present to indicate who is empowered to speak. Others in the group are not allowed to interrupt or interact until it is their turn. The basic intentions of council are to speak spontaneously and listen "from the heart." These intentions support authentic and honest communication, create a safe environment for risking greater intimacy and tend to open those in the council to a sense of presence not experienced in ordinary interactions. To our delight, Chelsey loved to be in council with Jaquelyn and me, often sitting on one of our laps for more than an hour at a time, She rarely spoke out loud, but on occasion held the talking piece with such concentration that it was not difficult to "hear" how she felt in the silence. For more information on the council process, go to the Center for Council Training website, www.counciltraining.org

she was many miles away sleeping in her bed in Phoenix. I picked up the talking piece and asked for guidance from our relationship (we call it our "Third"): "Do we have permission to attempt to change the basic course of Chelsey's life, to completely change her biomedical status and to 'bring her in' to the world of relationship?" We sat quietly for several minutes, listening for a response. It came in a few moments loud and surprisingly clear. Giving it an anthropomorphic voice, this is what we heard:

"You have permission to find ways to alter Chelsey's body and life so you can have a fuller relationship with her, as long as you are willing to transform your lives in an equally fundamental way."

That was so obviously right that neither of us had a moment's hesitation. Our "Yes" has never wavered over the years since then and Chelsey has held to her part of the bargain. She changes as we do, slowly, two-steps-forward-one step back, challenging us all the way.

Awareness of Subtle Relationships

Parts of our story are probably familiar to most of you. Many parents and grandparents we have spoken with over the years have stories to tell of deepening insights and awakenings inspired by their ASD child. Even before starting treatment, many parents begin to expand their old notions of what it means to relate. Our culture's primary focus on cognitive and verbal development tends to under-value and so under-nourish more subtle relationship skills. But having a child with ASD behavior—particularly in the more extreme portion of the spectrum—leaves us no choice but to learn how to relate without the support of words and familiar facial expressions. We begin to see that a lot of relating occurs beyond speech and in the silences between the few words that may be spoken. We learn to sense the nuances of expression that previously escaped our attention. Ways to "read the field" are found that almost certainly would never have been discovered were it not for facing the unique challenges of raising an ASD child.

We learn to observe in silence, watching patiently for a sign that our presence is being acknowledged. We begin to develop what might be called an *intuitive relational capacity* that expands on the familiar one often ascribed to mothers who "know" their children's needs from a subtle gesture or the tone of their cry. The ability to relate intuitively grows in raising a special needs child, because *it has to* in order to get through the day in one piece.

Soon, the pleasures of little gifts become an important part of our life. "We made eye contact during his bath today and I swear I saw the beginning of a smile when I showed him how to pour water from one cup into another." "I was singing a song to myself after a disastrous lunch, probably just to cheer myself up, and she stopped stimming for a moment and sat still. It was extraordinary." "It's almost as if I can sense what he's thinking inside that complicated brain of his. I'm learning to get his transmissions. I'm learning his silent language."

As educational and biomedical treatment begins—and hopefully language, eye contact and facial gestures become more developed (even if ever so slowly)—parents have the opportunity to "calibrate" their intuitive knowledge with more ordinary means of communication. This can be a rich period of exploration and learning for everyone involved. As we explore "language" in this way and enter our child's world more fully, he or she begins to enter ours. More truthfully, both adult and child enter an expanded *joint world of subtle communion* that is mysterious, compelling and at times profoundly satisfying. Soon we are launched on the journey of exploring that world together.

By the time parents and children have entered this phase of the journey, it is hard for anyone in the family to remember what life was like before autism spectrum disorder ("BASD") entered their lives. The BASD world seems two-dimensional in retrospect. On the other hand, the world after ASD ("AASD") is multidimensional, full of surprises and transformative almost on a daily basis. Priorities have shifted. What seemed important BASD now may feel quaint or distant. Life AASD usually feels more dramatic, passionate and directed by an intelligence beyond the familiar. When other children are involved, family dynamics may change dramatically.

The great amount of care required by the ASD child makes it difficult for siblings to receive what they and their parents may feel is their "fair share" of parental attention. Making this "all right" requires enormous patience, many dialogues with siblings, family meetings and special child care arrangements. Ultimately, the sibling issue also requires a major transformation in our notion of fairness, from one based primarily on each child getting "equal time" to one based on need. Reaching this level of understanding in a family with an ASD child is a major achievement and liberating for everyone involved.

The ASD child may be the source of other challenging "gifts" as well. Many parents speak of the uncanny ability of their special needs child to create exactly those demands that push everyone's creative capabilities to the limit. If Chelsey had responded in a significant way to the secretin protocol when she was four, or to anti-viral treatment at five, or chelation at six, or…Jaquelyn would probably never have written this book. Instead, Chelsey has continuously forced her grandmother/physician back to the drawing board to expand her medical horizons. Jaquelyn and I have been challenged continuously to work better together as a team, integrate our diverse perspectives about healing more creatively and generally become more conscious in all of our relationships. The gift-list is long and impressive—and continues growing as we write these words. Most of our "failures" have led to discovering new levels of perseverance, patience and creativity—and eventually to a clearer overview of the complex nature of ASD.

A Paradigm Change in Medicine

Perhaps the ASD children's most direct message is the necessity to change some of the ways many of us view medicine and the way we relate to physicians. Searching for ASD treatment protocols not only brings researchers and physicians to the edge of their knowledge about the human body but also questions some of our basic current allopathic values and practices. ASD is not the only arena in which these beliefs and practices are being challenged. Others include the mystery surrounding the growing epidemic of Alzheimer's Disease, the growing and inevitable ineffectiveness of antibiotics in the face of viral adaptability and diversity, the apparent growing weakening of the human immune system, the rapid rise of auto-immune illnesses, and the dilemmas surrounding whether and how to prolong the end of life through medical means—to mention just a few.

We suggest that the roots of the impending and inevitable transformation in allopathic medicine lie in the essential distinction between "healing" and "curing." The special children are virtually driving us to transform our contemporary obsession with *curing* and embrace the larger interactive process that deserves to be called *healing*. Our time with Chelsey forced us to make this distinction, not without the benefit of countless dialogues between Jaquelyn and me that were not always calm and objective.

In simple terms, I have come to see curing as a process in which one or more knowledgeable and (hopefully) compassionate individuals attempt to change the physiological and/or the psychological condition of another. The definitions of normal and healthy are set by the individuals applying the cure, again hopefully in dialogue with the one(s) requesting it—and all generally in the context of our existing cultural consensus of what it means to be healthy. In curing, the major change is to take place in the one being cured. In any event, unless something goes wrong in pursuing the cure, those "practicing the medicine" rarely go through a transformation as profound as that of the one being cured. Setting broken bones, hip replacement surgery, heart bypass surgery and many of the new laser surgeries for the eyes are examples of curings that are both remarkable and clearly beneficial.

Healing is a more reciprocal process in which the practitioner-healer(s) and patient are both transformed in a comparably profound, although possibly quite different way. Because it is fundamentally relational in nature, the exchange in the healing process is equally altering to both sides and usually has many more surprises in store for us than curing. It is not uncommon for physician and patient (including the patient's loved ones) to enter a situation thinking that curing is what is called for only to discover that they are drawn inexorably (and sometimes kicking and screaming) into the more demanding, multilevel experience of healing. No matter how physiological the "disease," healing always involves the human psyche as well as the body. Full healing is not possible unless the body/psyche is treated as an inseparable continuum. Examples of illnesses that call us into healing include asthma, fibromyalgia and many other auto-immune diseases, allergies, clinical depression—and ASD.

Chelsey has been quite clear that she will not be "cured." As Jaquelyn has indicated, her impairment is still at a level that spurs us on to try new treatments. She has not responded dramatically to secretin, antiviral treatments, multiple nutrient regimes, chelation protocols, etc., as many other children have in Jaquelyn's practice. Her bowel function did improve significantly (thankfully!) through the GF/CF diet; we believe that certain nutritional supplements have helped her (e.g. Vitamin B6 and DMG); and we are hopeful that current treatment of a probably long-standing yeast infestation (we were deceived by her beautiful stools!) will produce significant changes.

On the other hand, it is unquestionably clear that Chelsey is more responsive, more emotionally active, initiates more relationally and is increasingly capable in regard to such skills as reading, writing, arithmetic, swimming, trampolining, computer games, singing, and now even helping with household chores. Social speech remains her biggest challenge, though she loves being with other children now.

What is equally and undeniably clear is that Chelsey has changed the lives of many people directly and indirectly—her parents and siblings, of course, her grandparents, the many clients that Jaquelyn has worked with, those of us who have helped her with this book and (hopefully) the people who read it. The important point known by so many families with special needs children is that Chelsey is typical in this regard, perhaps more recalcitrant when it comes to "getting better," but typical nevertheless.

Chelsey has and still is delivering the message that curing will not do. "Nothing less than healing, thank you," is the message I get from Chelsey all the time. It is a message we have resisted at times of overwhelm and confusion but after five years have come to embrace, particularly in those moments when she spontaneously emerges into greater relationship with us. I believe that we have entered into a healing process with Chelsey that is mutually and profoundly transformative no less for all of us as for her. As readers of this book must surely now be convinced:

ASD is unbelievably complex—too complex to cure. It can only be healed and that is why these children are an imposing force for change in our medical culture.

What else are the ASD children teaching us about medicine?

- *A Systemic approach is essential.*

ASD involves almost every aspect of the child's non-skeletal physiology: the gut, the endocrine system, literally every aspect of the brain, the body as viral host, the immune system and so on. Treatment protocols need to be applied with systemic awareness, even if only a part of the system is being treated at a given time. That is exactly what led Jaquelyn to the broad spectrum approach that is described in this book. The reductionist drift of allopathic medicine over the past fifty years, fueled by established medicine's embrace of "specialists" and the explosion of technology needs a significant mid-course correction if ASD is to be eventually contained. Every physician/healer will have to develop her or his own way of working "broad spectrum" if we are to successfully heal the onslaught of ASD (as well as many other illnesses).

- *The patient (in this case, the parents) must take back responsibility for being a partner in the healing process.*

This is not a new challenge, of course. Many have spoken and written about it for years. But now it's time to walk our talk. Having an ASD child provides a powerful daily reminder to take that walk. Largely with the assistance of local support groups and a variety of closely bonded ASD Internet groups, parents have become a powerful force in the "Healing ASD Movement." Not only parents, but physicians, researchers and clinicians who have ASD children often participate at the frontier of this movement, which is another reason for its growing influence both medically and politically. As a result of the active role parents are playing, the projections of power and authority onto medical professionals that has so dominated contemporary medicine are diminishing and even disappearing in the healing of ASD children.

It is often parents who inform their pediatricians about the latest protocols and even begin their doctor's education in the mysteries of ASD. Moreover, parents are the primary clinicians in treating ASD. They are the ones trying to get the pills down, holding down squirming bodies for EEG's, injections or blood sampling, and getting up in the middle of the night to follow through with a chelation protocol. There are too many ASD children for physicians to treat without significant participation of parents, even when the doctors are willing to take on the enormously time-consuming challenges involved. The few who are have become swamped. As she has made clear, Jaquelyn wrote this book in part with the hope it would find its way to pediatricians and other physicians through the passionately involved parents of their ASD patients.

- *Strengthening the immune system is an inescapable component of healing.*

Prior to the increased incidence of autoimmune illnesses over the past twenty years, the primary thrust of establishment medicine has been to cure the symptoms of an illness and, occasionally, even remove its root cause *without any significant interruption of the patient's life style.* That has empowered our present medication mystique to the point that the general public expects that every disease will soon be curable through the taking of pills or other simple treatment. As a result, we consume a massive number of pills and live in the illusion that we are a healthy culture because of modern medicine's ability to generate the vast array of easily taken medications.

With the growing onslaught of autoimmune illnesses, this illusion is getting frayed around the edges. Having lost the ability to distinguish friend from foe, our bodies are turning on themselves to a greater and greater degree, crippling the functions of our digestive, hormonal and neurological systems as they kill off supposed enemies. The ASD children exemplify this situation to such a heart rendering degree that we can no longer avoid "getting the message" behind this exponential rise of autoimmune madness.

Humans have behaved as if there were little or no connection between their personal health and the "collective health" of the planet. We have polluted virtually every aspect of the environment and devoured natural resources voraciously, not understanding that we are literally part of this "Large Body." It seems clear to me that this disrespect for the Large Body is reflected in the epidemic of autoimmune illnesses.

The way we have objectified and "attacked" the environment is remarkably similar to an immune system that destroys its host body, no longer being able to differentiate friend from foe. Healing this fundamental autoimmune disease is the single most important challenge we face as a culture—physician and non-physician alike—during the next cycle. The disease of the Large Body will not be cured. It must be healed. The ultimate survival of both our personal bodies and the Large Body depends on our ability to better understand the combined mystery of our interdependent immune systems. Human medicine must direct a greater proportion of its resources towards strengthening and reeducating our immune systems, rather than continuing the present allopathic emphasis on destroying pathogens.

In the long run, the treatment of ASD will surely have to move in this direction. As indicated in the previous chapter, for example, there is strong evidence that the myelin sheath in the brains of some autistic children is being destroyed by the child's immune system. How can this insidious "mistake" be stopped? No more important question faces medicine than how to reprogram a malfunctioning immune system. Finding out how to do this will help us to understand exactly what compromises the immune systems of the children who were adversely affected by the normal vaccination sequence, and so continue to improve the safety of such procedures.

At best the present environmental disaster will be reversed slowly over a period of many years. A few generations of children cannot wait for this to happen. Might it be possible to find ways to test a child's immune system for efficacy *in utero* and nutritional remedies developed (much as can be done now with Down Syndrome), so that no child need be born with autism or with increased susceptibility to toxins?

Beyond ASD, there are more illnesses to work on than we have resources. Treating the many autoimmune illnesses may be more effectively accomplished by research into ways to help patients have stronger immune systems than putting so much effort into trying to contain the symptoms. In other words the allopathic model needs to be applied *consciously and selectively* under the new medical paradigm. It will be financially and medically more efficient to do so.

Final Words

I want to end on a personal note by adding a few witness comments about Jaquelyn. The quest to heal Chelsey has transformed my life partner into a combined medical sleuth *par excellence*, a human body systems analyst, a physician quite knowledgeable about the biochemistry of that body and, I must add, an alchemist working on the edge of the mystery of healing. Her love for Chelsey has been the primary force in forging all her talents together synergistically to help her become a member of the growing group who practice the "new medicine."

We need look no further than the writing of this book to see explicitly how a single ASD child inspired her grandmother/physician to be of service to many other children (not to mention how its writing has drawn me into a level of collaboration I never dreamed possible). And there are hundreds of professionals and lay people alike who have been inspired to serve others with similar devotion and success. We can only imagine what awakenings are now taking place in the lives of those just touched by one or more of the thousands of new ASD children that have appeared in recent years. As we each discover our unique path of healing with them, may we continue to nourish our hearts. That's our part of the bargain. That's the message we're being given. When we get it—really get it—then they will have done their job, our hearts will be more open and their brains will no longer need to be starving to get our attention.

Here it is, all much more briefly:

TO JAQUELYN

I am disappearing—white hot fire burning in a far away
    belly a lifetime below my heart—
Into this forever new moment of discovering what you call
    "Love's Body"

Disappearing—beaten by wind-chopped swells vanishing
    into union with the shore—
Into the image of your face, breast, smooth back-swell,
    thigh, sacred sea flower

Disappearance, I trust, leaves me transparent, so nothing
    comes between who you are
And what I see with these seventy year-old fading eyes of
    mine

I relish seeing my woman, fire-eyes blazing, riding a creature
    of Diana's
That surely knows the way and will not stop until she arrives
    home, done, finished

Through fresh ears, not numbed by years of listening to
    secular chatter,
I hear the hundreds of children you will touch celebrating:
    "Mommy, Daddy, we are free"

In this hoary heart, fired, shaped and tempered by our
    otherworldly blacksmith
I know they are preparing to shake off their curse of confused
    immunity

I am with you, slightly behind on your left, my hands
    reaching across our differences
To rub a back that aches with the consuming labor of your
    sixth love child

I am with you to learn how to serve a goddess sworn to devote her life
Completing a mission of redemption for her next embodiment as Chelsey

I have no choice for I am disappearing into loving both of you
—Or are you One? I am losing the patterns of my mind... and finding my heart

That loss and discovery will guide me to where you live in love's wildest imagination
And so inspired, we will do our part to bring the children home, clear and re-awakened

After the celebrations, we bower buddies are free to see what two Love's Bodies become
As they slowly vanish into boundary-less knowing of the Other

I am disappearing...
Take a good last look. Who will be saying "I love you" when next we meet?
And will you remind "me" who he used to be when at last we make the crossing?

J. Z.

REFLECTIONS ON EDUCATION AND THE ENVIRONMENT

by Jack Zimmerman, PhD

Education

One can learn a lot by deeply relating to just one child. My experience with Chelsey is a prime example. As I spent time with her during our extended "retreats" and at other times during the past several years, I began to fantasize about what it would take to create a school in which she would flourish. During this same period, I had the opportunity to speak with educators and health professionals who work with special needs students in both public and private school settings. The extent and depth of the work of the many talented people devoted to the education of special needs children was astounding to me. I barely scratched the surface of the enormous body of writings and research that has been accomplished in this field over the past seventy years—particularly in the last decade.

Before long, my mind was spinning with educational possibilities for all the Chelseys in the world. These ideas began to flesh themselves out, first into a basic "meta-curriculum" and then into a more detailed description of how such a community of children and adults might actually function. By a meta-curriculum I mean the (hopefully conscious) agreements and principles that shape both the curriculum and environment of a school.

The meta-curriculum of my ideal, fantasy school for Chelsey was based on five *foundation principles.*

- *Inclusiveness.*

Inclusive means that ASD students and neurologically typical (NT) students co-mingle to a great extent within an integrated school environment. Many of the arts, physical and social activities are shared by all the children, along with certain portions of the academic program. The ASD children receive special academic support, in very small groups (as do some of the NT children). As appropriate, older NT children are trained to tutor the ASD kids individually in academic skills.

- *Learning takes place in a relational environment or "field" that resembles that of a well-functioning clan.*

Whatever else a "school" must be for an ASD child, it must create an environment that stimulates safe and fulfilling relationships among adults and children. Whether it's called "floor time," "stimulating interaction" or just plain being with children, the inclusive school's curriculum should grow out of a fabric of trust and connectedness that resembles the extended clans in traditional peaceful cultures.[1] All three generations—children, parents and grandparents (as elders)—are fully present in the school and the educational program includes the exchange of life experiences, knowledge and wisdom among all the segments of the community *including the special children.*

---

[1] The Pre-Tahitian Hawaiian Culture is a good example of what I'm talking about. This clan-based culture flourished in the Islands before the more hierarchical and war-like Tahitian culture arrived. Clans were as large as 400-500, children were educated primarily by grandparents, aunts and uncles, as well as parents, and all the clans share a council-like practice called "ho'o pono pono."

- *Honoring the Undirected Mind.*

Effective learning (healing too!) requires fluidity in the academic structures (classes, curriculum content, schedules, etc.). Having room to breathe helps create a learning community in which spontaneous or "undirected" creative interactions—as well as academics—are encouraged.[2] To achieve such open and spacious interactions authentically requires a level of *acceptance* of all the children, ASD and NT alike, in all school activities (although, of course not necessarily of certain behaviors that the children may exhibit). Chelsey has taught us again and again that when we hold an agenda of changing her at all tightly, she moves away from our expectations by becoming less relational. She feels that we want her to be different than she is—and she reacts, sometimes strongly but usually subtly, by becoming less present. Of course, all children do this to some extent, at least until they learn to "play the game." It is just more noticeable with an ASD child.

We speak here, of course, of acceptance as an *active*, not passive, state of openheartedness that lies beyond patience and where the child has room to move. It is a truism of good teaching that to effectively support growth in children requires accepting them where they are in the learning process at that particular time. Real growth is from the inside out, encouraged first by acceptance of what is and *then* challenging the child to extend their capabilities, knowledge and talents. The simultaneous acceptance of the *being* of a child and challenging her or him to grow is not a paradox but rather the basic challenge of being a good teacher.

- *Curiosity replaces quantitative goals as the primary source of motivation.*

Having goals for each child's "improvement" are inevitable, but in a clan-like relational environment these goals are held compassionately without attachment to the outcome—and open to the possibility that student, teacher and even the goals themselves can evolve or even transform. What takes the place of the present

---

[2]   In his seminal book, "Letters to the Schools," Krishnamurti makes the strong statement that there is no true learning without leisure. By "leisure" he means an environment which encourages students and teachers to interact in a state of undirected mind.

philosophy of strongly held quantitative goals (grades, test scores, etc) is *passionate curiosity, a feeling of "what will the next moment of learning bring."* This level of curiosity brings with it at least a temporary suspension of fear-based judgment and the embracing of a "Yes/And" (rather than "Yes/But" or "No/But") way of relating.

- *Silence and Contemplation.*

Most schools are noisy places—and many children seem to both generate and thrive on a full menu of sound. Young people's music is often deafening, many sporting events are loud and urban schools are noisy places. It is debatable how well NT students handle all this input and what effects it has on their bodies and minds. What isn't debatable is that ASD children (particularly the autistic ones) are extremely sensitive to sudden and loud noises, even those that most children and adults find non-invasive. The fact that silence is becoming a rare commodity in our lives is a serious challenge for many special needs children and continuous awareness of their sensitivity to sound on everyone's part is important. Intervals of relative quiet and even silence are important for integration, reflection and release of the tensions that arise from relating. Quiet times are an essential manifestation of spaciousness. I have heard more than a few high school students yearn for the "good old days" (Primary School) when taking naps was part of the curriculum.

When adults join with the kids in undirected play and quiet time, the wordless dimension of their relationships is given an op-portunity to develop. This contemplative connection is essential in learning to listen deeply to children, entering their world and coming up with ideas for productive ways of engaging them. Strong nonverbal connections often feel spontaneous and touched by grace. Such moments are obviously important in creating a strong rela-tional field for the ASD children—and, of course for all children.

In brief then, the kind of school I wanted for Chelsey is

An educational community—a "clan"—for children, families and teachers that honors the undirected (as well as the academic) mind practices acceptance, incorporates time for contemplation and honors curiosity as a primary motivation for learning.

I knew immediately a few of the activities that had to be included in my fantasy school for Chelsey . Certainly there would be frequent **councils** of the ASD and NT kids all together. There would also be time for **movement and music.** Movement helps the ASD child to develop "I-ness"—that is, a sense of ego identity—by connecting rhythmic patterns with gross and fine motor movements. The dance therapist begins by watching the child move, either in silence or with musical accompaniment, and then imitating his or her movements. The "imitation dance" sets the relational field necessary to build trust and serves as the basis for subsequent movement dialogues that include call and response, spontaneous interaction and, ultimately a developing sense of "relational movement." A mixed group of special needs and NT children learning to move together would be an inspiring sight to behold.

Even in the early years when Chelsey's restlessness dominated her behavior, music always helped to focus her attention in a remarkable way. She would sit and listen to a favorite CD (endlessly over and over again!) all the while sitting quietly in a chair. At first she was still, except for a steady tapping of the CD case with her forefinger, the rhythm of her stimming bearing no relationship to the music's beat. As we explored and expanded her musical tastes (which now include a broad spectrum from popular Latino guitar, Bob Marley and Kenny Loggins to traditional Hawaiian music, Kitaro and Bach), she would intersperse the quiet, almost reverent, periods with dancing. She is quite clear—actually stubborn—about what she wants to hear at any given time and likes to dress for the occasion. Traditional Hawaiian music can precipitate a quick change into a sarong and the Latin guitar brings out a long skirt and blouse.

One of Jaquelyn's most joyous relational experiences with Chelsey involved teaching her all the words to "Silent Night" and "Joy to the World" when she was six. It took writing out all the words and hours of practice, but after I listened to their angelic duets, "there wasn't a dry eye in the house." Our musical experience with Chelsey is shared by other families gifted with an ASD child. Many of these children seem to possess considerable latent musical talent. (Chelsey has perfect pitch, a sweet voice with a natural vibrato and a "photogenic musical memory"—talents that are not rare among ASD children as we have discovered.)

Why does music have such a significant effect on these children? Observing Chelsey over the years suggests that the melodic, harmonic and rhythmic elements of music offer her a structure for the "uncoordinated" neurological activity going on in her brain. While she is listening and moving she is brought into better balance and self-awareness. It is as if the music provides a scaffolding that increases the coherence of her neurological activity. Surely, regular exposure to music and movement as part of school would strengthen coordination of auditory capability and both gross and fine motor skills with neurological development.

And, needless to say, Chelsey's school would have to have ready access to lots of **water.** A small natural looking pool would do. But if the school happened to be near a warm ocean that would be sublime!

Can a School Like This Really Be Created?

I have been describing a fantasy school, based on values and ideals, however desirable, that are obviously difficult to manifest in our current real-world situation. But perhaps continuing to try and make the present educational paradigm work is even more unreal. Within a few years a whole expanded generation of ASD children will become teenagers. The thousands of susceptible children who regressed into ASD in the late 1980's and early 1990's from viral and environmental triggers are about to become adolescent. Where and how will those among them who still need a lot of daily support live and continue their education?

I suggest that many of these ASD kids would thrive in cohesive communities—possibly even with their biological families—that are a mix of special needs and neurologically typical children and adults, communities much like my fantasy school for Chelsey. Our existing family and educational institutions will be strained to the breaking point by this surge of ASD children until they both are transformed in radical ways. Visionary Karl Konig, MD saw the potential of a community setting for special needs children many years ago when he started the Camp Hill Movement. There are now more than 90 Camp Hill Communities around the world, seven in the US alone.[3]

We are going to have to do something quite radical anyway with whatever portion of the now half-million autistic children and the untold millions of ADHD and ADD children who still may be impaired enough after biomedical treatment to need special attention. So why not set our intentions high, apply the wisdom gained from past experience (rather than the forms and familiar patterns of the past) and see what happens?

For these and one other reason I decided to share my vision of Chelsey's ideal school with my educator colleagues, realizing that many of them might feel I was being quite unrealistic. Fortunately I have come to anticipate even wild reactions from my colleagues with a certain amount of playful curiosity. The other reason I sought their council might be called the principle of "Marginal Group Innovation."

One of the most important catalysts for educational change has always been the inadequacy of the established approach to be effective with a *particular group of unusual students.* In other words, it's the marginal elements of the student population that often stimulate out-of-the-box educational thinking. Reading methods developed to work with dyslexic children have proven useful for helping "normal" children to learn to read more effectively.[4] To help certain atypical students learn arithmetic and deaf students geometry, visual and kinesthetic methods were developed that now have found use with students possessing normal cognitive and hearing capabilities.[5]

The population of special needs children, in general, and ASD children in particular, has reached a level that demands attention from the mainstream educational community. To support these students will require significant revision of a large portion of the standard curriculum, changes in the methods of training teachers and a substantial rethinking of the kind of school environments we tend to create. When I explored Chelsey's ideal school with my colleagues in the light of all these realities we all became quite clear—and ex-

---

[3] See "The Camp Hill Movement," Karl Konig, TWT Publications Ltd. 1993 (2nd edition).

[4] For example, the Gillingham reading method, developed more than seventy years ago in part at the Ethical Culture Schools in New York City, was inspired by the special needs of dyslexic students.

[5] I refer here to the now familiar "Cuisenaire Rods" for teaching arithmetic and Gattegno's invention of the "Geo-Board" for teaching geometry to deaf students.

cited—with the possibility that the ASD kids are creating a major opportunity to *transform the way we educate all children.* After going into greater detail than I have done here, the consensus seemed to be, "Why not make the kind of meta-curriculum you're suggesting the foundation for any school?"

Indeed! Why not?

One in five middle school classrooms in the Los Angeles Unified School District (LAUSD) is now devoted to special needs students—and this substantial percentage doesn't include many ASD children who cannot be served within the school system at all. Just the economics of this situation has created a crisis in the District. This situation is repeating itself in many parts of the country.

The present model of segregating special needs children within existing schools or sending them to special schools cannot handle the current explosion of this population. We have to face the challenge—actually the unusual opportunity—to educate all of our children within an inclusive school environment. The handwriting is on the wall. In fact, LAUSD's Division of Special Education recently published their long-awaited report, "Schools for All Children: A Strategic Plan for Achieving Measurable Results for All Students Including Those with Disabilities" and the District has set the goal to be 90% inclusive by 2005. In this plan, inclusion means mainstreaming ASD children whenever possible. The report sets 80% as the fraction of classes children with "disabilities" will share with their "normal" cohorts, supported by special classes that are geared to those children that learn in ways that are different than normal children. This decision is a bold and necessary step—and just the beginning of a long journey of educational transformation that may very well have tumultuous aspects.

This is not the place to explore these issues further. What is important for those of us on the *starving brains/starving hearts* journey is that many of our kids are going to be in the middle—not the fringes—of the mainstream educational scene in the future. Those of us who spend a lot of time with ASD kids inevitably will be drawn into the coming educational revolution.

Those who have "taught" special needs children are developing methodologies which will eventually be essential in rethinking the way we educate all our children. This transformation of education will be supported by embracing the principle of inclusion in schools, a principle we believe is and will be of great benefit to both the special and neurologically typical children.

The Environment

Miners in the coalfields of Pennsylvania and West Virginia often brought a canary down into the mines with them as a way to detect the presence of methane gas. As long as the canaries survived the miners were safe. When the birds stopped singing and began to die, the miners packed up their tools and headed for the surface in a hurry.

We believe that ASD children in general and autistic children in particular are the canaries in the "mines" of our culture, not only indirectly in regard to education and the need for more conscious family relationships, but also directly *in regard to our relationship with the environment.* Whatever the causes, their impaired immune systems cannot handle the toxins that other children and most adults are able to tolerate. They are letting us know already that the food we eat, the way in which we dispose of our industrial waste and some of the materials we have used in agriculture, dentistry and vaccines are not safe. But we are slow to get the message and continue to use many of these and related materials. It is time to pack up our tools, get to the "surface" (that is, wake up) and take care of these situations in a hurry!

It has been made quite clear that the presence of mercury in fish (Chapter 4), the excessive amounts of gluten in prepared foods as well as in breads and pasta, and the over-abundance of dairy products in our diets are intolerable to a large number of children (Chapter 5). The majority of us seem to be able to handle the unbalanced diets that are typical of children and adults today, but at what cost? Most of us may not show such dramatic symptoms as do the ASD children. But is it just a matter of time? If our immune systems become further compromised by stress, overuse of antibiotics and the cumulative effect of unbalanced diets, will more and more of our children "stop singing?"

The effluents of pesticides used since the beginning of the last century and long standing industrial waste disposal practices have already had a serious contaminating effect on our fresh water supplies and the oceans. Some think it is already at a critical level. The mercury in fish is just one direct result of these practices. We have only an educated guess of what effect the storage of nuclear wastes will have on our long-term health. Certain consumer products have altered the ozone layer, led to the dangers of the greenhouse effect, left a legacy of lead-poisoning and caused the destruction of much of the native rain forests that contain the vast majority of the earth's medicinal plant species.

We are making inroads in solving some of these problems, but has the pace and magnitude of the improvements been sufficient to stem the tide? Most environmentalists say, "No!" Others respond that people seem to be surviving, despite all the dire warnings. Besides, they say, economic factors must also be taken into consideration. But if the ASD children are seen as our advanced messengers of ill tidings, then perhaps we are already in a dangerous transition that will soon affect the health of a wider portion of the population. We feel this is the prudent hypothesis to pursue. There is a chance that if the frightening symptoms already exhibited by the ASD children are not treated *very* seriously, a greater portion of our population will become seriously ill as well.

We believe the link between environmental toxicity and the growing number of ASD children is sufficiently "causal" to embrace new dietary patterns and a radical rethinking of all of our policies concerning industrial waste disposal, agricultural practices, the preparation and use of vaccines, dental practices, and the manufacture of consumer products.

If we hear this message the children are bringing, we are more likely to heal the messengers. At the very least, we may be able to reduce the need for new messengers.

APPENDIX B

AUTISM, METALS, AND THE MERCURY IN VACCINES

Introduction by Teresa Binstock
Autism Researcher

In 1999, an FDA report revealed that ethylmercury was present in several vaccines mandated for infants and toddlers. That announcement caused several parents of autistic children to realize that injected ethylmercury may have caused their children's regression. That insight prompted extensive research and led to the writing of a medical paper called the "mercury/autism paper" published in a medical journal.[1]

Along the way, various individuals provided citations or other information including, but certainly not limited to, Woody McGinnis, MD, Boyd Haley, PhD, and Vas Aposhian, PhD. Thus far, this mercury/autism paper has led to a Congressional Hearing by the U.S. Government Reform Committee, to an international hearing hosted by the National Academy of Science's Institute for Medicine, and to the removal of ethylmercury from most vaccines.

---

[1] Bernard S., Enayati A., Redwood L., Roger H., Binstock T. Autism: A novel form of mercury poisoning. Med. Hypotheses. 2001 Apr;56(4): 462-71

An important question is why most children who were injected with ethylmercury did not become autistic? Medical literature describes individuals with increased susceptibility—whether from acquired and/or genetic reasons. Furthermore, medical history offers the lesson of acrodynia, also known as Pink Disease, a form of mercury poisoning from commercial powders used for diaper rash and teething. Acrodynia illustrates the significance of susceptibility. Approximately 1 in 400 exposed individuals developed symptoms of Pink Disease.[2]

Several CDC studies (Spring of 2000) found that early exposure to ethylmercury was indeed associated with autism-spectrum disorders including ADHD, tics, and autism. The CDC's internal documents—obtained by Freedom of Information Act filings—were more forthright than were early press releases describing those findings.[3]

During the final stages of writing the ethylmercury/autism paper, two versions were prepared for publication. One version focused upon comparing traits and physiological abnormalities common in autistic children and in victims of mercury poisoning. That version was submitted and published. An alternative version called attention to technical aspects and susceptibility was also prepared; that version is here published for the first time.

---

[2] Dally A. "The rise and fall of pink disease," Soc Hist Med. 1997 Aug; 10(2): 291-304
[3] "Thimerosal Linked to Autism in Confidential CDC Study." Mothering Magazine, March/April 2002

Autism:
Mercury Poisoning
by Thimerosal Injections

Sallie Bernard*[1], Albert Enayati[1],
Heidi Roger[1], Lyn Redwood[1], Teresa Binstock[2]

*sbernard@arcresearch.com—June 27, 2000
1. parent of autistic child
2. autism researcher (diagnosed with Asperger's Syndrome)

Abstract: Autism is a syndrome characterized by impairments in social relatedness, language and communication, a need for routine and sameness, abnormal movements, and sensory dysfunction. Mercury (Hg) is a toxic metal that can exist as a pure element or in a variety of inorganic and organic forms and can cause immune, sensory, neurological, motor, and behavioral dysfunctions similar to traits defining or associated with autism; the similarities extend to neuroanatomy, neurotransmitters, immunity, and epileptiform activity. Thimerosal, a preservative frequently added to childhood vaccines, has become a major source of Hg in human infants and toddlers. According to the EPA and the American Academy of Pediatricians, fully vaccinated children, within their first two years, receive a potentially neurotoxic quantity of Hg. A review of medical literature and U.S. government data suggests that

1. Many and perhaps most cases of idiopathic autism are induced by early exposure to Hg in thimerosal.

2. This type of autism represents a unique and heretofore unrecognized mercurial syndrome.

3. Certain genetic and non-genetic factors establish a predisposition whereby thimerosal's adverse effects occur only in some children.

4. Causal mechanisms include mercurial effects upon astrocytes, microtubules, neuronal function, and synaptogenesis and gastrointestinal function.

Introduction: Originally described by Kanner (1943;1), the incidence of autism and autism-spectrum disorders (ASD) has been steadily increasing, especially during the 1980s and again during 1990s (2,3). Since the 1930s, an ethylmercury compound (thimerosal; TMS) has been used as a preservative in certain mandatory vaccines (4), and increased ASD-rates during the last several decades may represent a heretofore unrecognized form of mercurialism. Recently, the FDA reported that the total amount of ethylmercury (eHg) injected into infants and toddlers during mandatory vaccinations is worthy of concern, and the CDC has recommended that TMS be removed from vaccines (5-6). In fact, the neurotoxicity of eHg compounds has long been known (7), and profound similarities between autism and mercury poisoning (HgP) suggest that many cases of autism and related neurobehavioral disorders may be manifestions of HgP caused by TMS injections during vaccinations.

This hypothesis is supported not only by traits comparisons but also by similarities in neuroanatomy, neurotransmitters, immune profiles, and epileptiform activity. Additional support derives from Hg's neurotoxic mechanisms and the timings of exposure to injected Hg. Furthermore, HgP literature provides basis for understanding why only some children develop CNS impairment from TMS. The fact that some children experience neurobehavioral improvements after chelation therapies (8) is consistent with a causal link between HgP and ASD.

Traits similarities: HgP literature describes traits consistent

1. with ASD's defining criteria, and
2. with virtually all ASD-associations such as sensory impairments, hand-flapping, and shifted immune profiles. For instance: juvenile monkeys prenatally exposed to mercury exhibit decreased social play, increased passive behavior, and impaired face recognition (9-11). Humans exposed to mercury vapor also perform poorly on face recognition tests and may present with a "mask face" (12). Emotional instability can occur in children and adults exposed to Hg. For instance, Iraqi children poisoned by methylmercury (mHg) had a tendency "to cry, laugh, or smile without obvious provocation" (13-14), a trait seen in ASD (15)).

HgP children show difficulties with speech (16-18). Even children exposed prenatally to "safe" levels of mHg performed less well on standardized language tests than did unexposed controls (19). Iraqi babies exposed prenatally either failed to develop language or presented with severe language deficits in childhood; many exhibited "exaggerated reaction" to sudden noise; and some had reduced hearing. Iraqi children who were postnatally poisoned from bread containing either methyl- or ethyl-mercury developed articulation problems, from slow, slurred word production to an inability to generate meaningful speech. Most had impaired hearing and a few became deaf (13-14,20). Acrodynia's symptoms include noise sensitivity and hearing problems (21).

Five additional examples:

1. The amygdala are increasingly implicated in autism in regard to gaze avoidance and dysregulations in sociality, emotions, appetite, anxiety, depression (22-24). Furthermore, via bidirectional pathways with the orbitofrontal cortex, amygdaloid dysfunction is linked with motor, cognitive, and other perseverative behaviors (25-27). Organic Hg migrates into amygdaloid nuclei of primates (28-29).

2. Similar cerebellar-changes occur in autism and HgP (30-31;32-34).

3. Elevated antibodies to myelin-basic protein (MBP) are associated with autism (35) and derive from CNS neurons (VK Singh, personal communication). HgP induces elevations of antibodies against MBP (36).

4. Hand-flapping is such an unusual trait that one author has suggested it can be an early diagnostic marker for ASD in some children (37). HgP can produce flapping motions (16,17)

5. Epileptiform activity occurs in many ASD children and is often subtle and hard to detect (38-39). HgP elevates extracellular glutamate, which inclines towards epilepiform activity, and can induce seizure activity with lower threshholds and reduced amplitude (40-43).

These examples illustrate that HgP/ASD similarities exist on numerous levels. Additional parallels are presented in Tables 1-3.

TABLE 1 HgP/ASD parallels for autism's diagnostic criteria

I. Social relatedness (45):

    ASD: 96, 105-108   HgP: 9-12,40,85,102

II. Communication impairments (45) including loss of speech, failure to develop speech, dysarthria, articulation problems, speech comprehension deficits, echolalia, pragmatic errors, lower verbal-IQ scores; deficits in abstract reasoning:

    ASD: 96,110-111   HgP: 16-21,33,40

III. Repetitive, perseverative, or stereotyped behaviors (45):

    ASD: 96,108,113-114,179   HgP: 115-117
    Amygdala/orbitofrontal substrates: 25-29,46,118

TABLE 2 ASD/HgP parallels for associated traits

Anxiety:

    ASD: 118   HgP: 40,119-120

Auditory impairments:

    ASD: 96,126-127   HgP: 18,20,33.

Clumsiness, mobility and postural impairments, toe walking, rocking, choreiform movements.

    ASD: 96,179,189   HgP: 12,18,20,21,76

Depression:

    ASD: 121-123   HgP: 119,124

OCD, schizoid traits, emotional lability:

    ASD: 15,96,121-123,125   HgP: 40,85,109,119,124

Touch aversion, excessive mouthing of objects, oral and tactile hypersensitivities, insensitivities to pain:

    ASD: 96,129-130.   HgP:14,17,20,90,109,128,132

Spatial orientation:

    ASD: 132,133.   HgP: 134

TABLE 3   An ASD/HgP miscellany

ASD/HgP parallels in neuroanatomy for amygdala, cerebellum, hippocampi:

    ASD: 22-24,30-31,137-139.
    HgP: 28,29,32,33,46,60,135,137-140.

ASD/HgP parallels in serotonin, dopamine, acetylcholine, glutamate:

    ASD: 141-144; 96,145-147; 148; 157-158.
    HgP: 147-152; 91,153-154; 47,155-156; 40, 159-160.

ASD/HgP parallels in sulfur, glutathione, purines, & mitochondria:

    ASD: 161-162; 80,161,164; 96,165; 140,167.
    HgP: 33,163; 33,78-79,159; 32-33; 168-169.

ASD/HgP parallels in allergy, autoimmunity, asthma; Th1/Th2 shifts, and NK cells:

    ASD: 81,167; 171; 172-173.
    HgP: 42,91,174; 82,84,175-176; 177.

Additional ASD/HgP parallels can be found in numerous areas including movement and motor funtion (178;40), cognition (179;40,180), behaviors (181-182;33,109), vision (96,183;13-14,20); rashes and dermatitis (170,184;108,185-186); autonomic disturbance (15,133;76,109); gastrointestinal atypicalities (78,187-188; 33,109,186).

Causal and temporal links between Hg-injections and autism: Organic mercury's effects upon microtubules, which participate in neuronal function and synaptogenesis, are increasingly described (cites below). Timings of infant and toddler thimerosal injections correspond to major critical periods of neuronal development (eg, Harlow et al, reviewed in 22; 44). Synaptogenesis during these post-natal months subserves eye-contact, smiling, early language, and other traits central to autism's diagnostic criteria (44-45). Injected eHg that enters the infant and toddler brain would interfere with critical periods for these developmental processes. Therefore, associations among vaccination timings, injected mercury, and autistic regressions are likely to have been both causal and temporal.

Ethylmercury toxicity is similar to that of mHg, and injected Hg is especially harmful (7, 46-48). When eHg's entry route is by injection delivering a vaccine, the amount of eHg that crosses the BBB (blood brain barrier) (49) or enters gastrointestinal tissues is likely to be increased via vaccination-induced elevations of cytokines such as interferon gamma, which expands permeability of tight-junction tissues (50-52).

Mechanisms of toxicity. Gradually, circulating organic-Hg compounds localize in brain areas implicated in autism (23,28-29,31). Within the CNS, organic Hg gradually converts to an inorganic form (Hg++) (28). Inorganic Hg is unable to cross the BBB, thus tends to remain in the CNS (central nervous system), and is more likely than organic Hg-compounds to induce autoimmune responses (53-54). CNS Hg has diverse mechanisms of neurotoxicity (36,55-57).

Ethyl-Hg has an affinity for –SH (sulfhydryl) molecules and is used as a vaccine preservative because of eHg's ability to inhibit cell function, leading to cellular stasis or death (58). Organic Hg–compounds primarily affect the CNS, are most toxic to a developing brain, and are more likely to enter postnatal brains because an infant's BBB is not fully developed (59-61) and because infants under 6 months are unable to excrete Hg, probably due to an inability to produce bile, the main excretion route for organic Hg (32,62). The longer Hg remains in the CNS, the greater the neurotoxic effects (63-64).

Hg++ and and eHg affect astrocytic and neuronal function (36,65-67) and interfere with microtubules (68-69), which participate in neuronal function and synaptogenesis (70-72). Furthermore, although most cells respond to mercurial injury by modulating levels of glutathione (GSH), metallothionein, hemoxygenase, and other stress proteins, neurons tend to be "markedly deficient in these responses" and thus are less able to remove Hg and more prone to Hg-induced injury (73-74).

Why only some children? Pink Disease (acrodynia) was caused by mercury in teething powders, ear ointments, and other topical remedies, occurred in approximately 1 in 500 to 1 in 1000 exposed children, and generated a range of symptoms with much inter-individual variation (29,75-76). Studies in humans and other species have identified genetic and non-genetic factors which, as co-factors, contribute to why only some children are affected by organic Hg compounds.

For instance, a child's response to injected eHg would be shaped by his or her GSH (glutathione) status (73-74), the presence of chronic or recent infections that alter GSH levels (77), gastrointestinal problems (78), hepatic function (79); and detoxification capabilities (80); and these variables occur in a background of the child's individual and familial genetics regarding autoimmunity (33,81-84).

Large inter-individual differences exist for Hg's adverse effects; and, as evidenced by acrodynia, these differences occur in children (76,85), especially those will asthma or other allergies (76). Genetic implications of autism's high concordance rate in monozygotic twins (86) may reflect a family's Hg-response genetics.

The various factors that influence detoxification and neurotoxicity of organic Hg interact in complex ways. Nonetheless, a dose response curve reveals that at low doses, only a small percentage of HgP victims develop adverse sequelae (79). As with mercury exposures that led to acrodynia, so too injected eHg's neurotoxic effects would occur only in some children; and the phenotypic range of these effects would be modified by other exposures (eg, RhoGam; 87) in susceptible individuals.

Discussion. Vaccines are a source of Hg; the amount injected into most infants and toddlers exceeds government safety limits (4,88); and since at least 1977, TMS has been recognized as potentially dangerous (42,89-90). In July of 1999, the CDC asked manufacturers to start removing TMS from vaccines and rescheduled the hepatitis B vaccine for 6 months of age instead of at birth (6). For infants and toddlers vaccinated during the 1990s, Hg-injection amounts are 12.5 micrograms at birth, 62.5 micrograms at 2 months, 50 at 4 months, 62.5 at 6 months, and a final 50 micrograms around 15 months. In relation to infant and toddler body weights, these Hg quantities are significant. The 2-month dose of Hg is at least 30 times higher than the recommended daily maximum exposure (88).

Present EPA "safe" limit for Hg ought to be lowered. Doses not thought to be associated with adverse effects have induced damage in humans (19); infants are especially vulnerable to Hg (91); and the EPA's recently published "safe" guideline is too high (47). Two points are noteworthy: *First*: Because vaccinations induce immune reactions that include extended cytokines pulses (eg, interferon gamma; 50), vaccinal mercury is more dangerous than injected-mercury; studies suggest this is because mercury compounds and interferon gamma increase permeability of tissues such as the blood-brain barrier and gastrointestinal tract (49,51-52). Thus, when a bolus dose of ethylmercury circulates during a vaccination response, more eHg is likely to enter the CNS. *Second*: The EPA's determination was based upon the amount of ingested mercury needed to induce adverse neurologic sequelae in 10% of exposed fetuses. But vaccinal eHg is not first filtered by the maternal liver or placenta, as was the HgP incident used in the EPA calculations.

Furthermore, a 10% rate of neurologic sequelae is clearly not acceptable. To induce a 1% rate of neurologic sequelae, the necessary Hg level would be even lower than the EPA's current estimate; and to achieve a .25% rate of neurologic sequelae—which approximates the rate of autism during the 1990s—an even lower level of organic mercury would be sufficient (92-95).

For these reasons and because of Hg's dose-response curve, the EPA's current guideline for mercury toxicity is artificially high and ought be lowered. In fact, substantial evidence suggests that there is no "safe" level for injected eHg in humans and, given susceptibility factors and the distribution of organic Hg's toxic effects (93-95), the amount of vaccinal-eHg already injected into infants and toddlers is likely to have caused neurologic damage in large subgroups of susceptible children.

Sex ratio: Autism is more prevalent among boys than girls, with the ratio generally recognized as approximately 4:1 (96). Mercury studies consistently report greater effects on males than females, except for kidney damage (47). At high doses, both sexes are affected equally; at low doses only males are affected. This is true of mice as well as humans (19,33,47,97-99).

Parallel increases for thimerosal & autism: Autism's initial description and subsequent epidemiological increase mirror the introduction and use of thimerosal as a vaccine preservative. In the late 1930s, Leo Kanner, an experienced child psychologist, first began to notice the type of child he would later label "autistic." His initial paper mentioned that this type of child had never been described previously: "Since 1938, there have come to our attention a number of children whose condition differs so markedly and uniquely from anything reported so far, that each case merits a detailed consideration of its fascinating peculiarities." (1) All these patients were born in the 1930s. TMS was introduced as a component of vaccine solutions in the 1930s (4).

The vaccination rate and total amount of injected eHg (via TMS) have steadily increased since the 1930s, with coverage-rates in 1999 as high as 90% for some vaccines (100). Relatedly, since the syndrome was first described (1), the incidence of autism and ASD has increased dramatically. Prior to 1970, studies described an average prevalence of 1 in 2000; for studies after 1970, the average rate had doubled to 1 in 1000 (2). In 1996, the NIH estimated the autism-incidence rate to be 1 in 500 (101); and, as documented by several states' departments of education, a large increase in preva-lence has been occurring since the mid-1990s (3). Thus, for several decades, these increased incidence-rates have paralleled the rising eHg-intake caused by vaccines containing eHg. In 1991, two vac-cines, HIB and Hepatitis B, both of which generally include TMS as a preservative, were added to the recommended vaccine schedule (4) and may account for the increasing prevalence of autism and related neurologic diagnoses, including anorexia (102). The likelihood of a causal relationship is augmented by the fact the eHg preferentially seeks the amygdala (46; 103).

Conclusion: Based upon extensive phenotype-parallels between autism and HgP, this review establishes the likelihood that vaccinal TMS is etiologically significant in ASD, even as HgP's latency period (20) served to mask the connection. Furthermore, prior HgP epidemics have generated unique phenotypes, none of which would be classified as autism; however, the injecting of eHg when vaccinating infants and toddlers has never been studied and would induce its own unique mercurialism—which our society is experiencing as an unprecedented increase in ASD and related disorders (3,104). Safe chelation therapies ought to be considered for children who have been injected with thimerosal as infants and toddlers.

REFERENCES

1. Kanner L. Autistic disturbances of affective contact. *The Nervous Child* 1942-1943;2: 217-250.
2. Gillberg C, Wing L. Autism: not an extremely rare disorder. *Acta Psychiatr Scand* 1999;99:399-406.
3. Yazbak F.E. Autism '99, a national emergency. Internet publication 1999. http://www.garynull.com/documents/autism_99.htm
4. Egan W.M. Thimerosal in vaccines. presentation to the FDA, September 14 1999.
5. CDC. Thimerosal in vaccines: a joint statement of the American Academy of Pediatrics and the Public Health Service. *MMWR* 1999;48.26:563-565.
6. CDC. Recommendations regarding the use of vaccines that contain thimerosal as a preservative. *MMWR* 1999;48.43.996-998.
7. Suzuki T, Takemoto T.I., Kashiwazaki H, Miyama T. Metabolic fate of ethylmercury salts in man and animal. Ch 12, p209-233 in: Mercury, Mercurials, and Mercaptans. Miller MW, Clarkson TW, editors; Charles C. Thomas, Springfield, 1973.
8. Redwood L. Chelation case-histories http://tlredwood.home.mindspring.com/case_studies.htm
9. Gunderson V.M., Grant K.S., Burbacher T.M., Fagan 3rd J.F., Mottet N.K. The effect of low-level prenatal methyl mercury exposure on visual recognition memory in infant crab-eating macaques. *Child Dev* 1986;57:1076-1083.
10. Gunderson V.M., Grant K.S., Burbacher T.M., Fagan 3rd J.F., Mottet N.K. Visual recognition memory deficits in methyl mercury exposed Macaca fascicularis infants. *Neurotoxicol Teratol* 1988;10:373-379.
11. Burbacher T.M., Sackett G.P., Mottet N.K. Methylmercury effects on the social behavior of Macaca fascicularis infants. *Neurotoxicol Teratol* 1990;12:65-71.

12. Vroom F.Q., Greer M. Mercury vapour intoxication. *Brain* 1972;95:305-318.

13. Amin-Zaki L, Elhassani S, Majeed M.A., Clarkson T.W., Doherty R.A., Greenwood M. Intra-uterine methylmercury poisoning in Iraq. *Pediatrics* 1974;54:587-595.

14. Amin-Zaki L, Majeed M.A., Elhassani S.B., Clarkson T.W., Greenwood M.R., Doherty R.A. Prenatal methylmercury poisoning. *Am J Dis Child* 1979;133:172-177.

15. Wing L, Attwood A. Syndromes of autism and atypical development. p3-19 in: Handbook of Autism and Pervasive Developmental Disorders; John Wiley & Sons, Inc., 1987.

16. Pierce P.E., Thompson J.F., Likosky W.H., Nickey L.N., Barthel W.F., Hinman A.R. Alkyl mercury poisoning in humans. *JAMA* 1972;220:1439-1442.

17. Snyder R.D. The involuntary movements of chronic mercury poisoning. *Arch Neurol* 1972;26:379-3381.

18. Kark RA, Poskanzer DC, Bullock JD, Boylen G. Mercury poisoning and its treatment with N-acetyl-D, L-penicillamine. *NEJM* 1971;285:10-16.

19. Grandjean P, Weihe P, White R.F., Debes F. Cognitive performance of children prenatally exposed to "safe" levels of methylmercury. *Environ Res* 1998;77:165-172.

20. Amin-Zaki L, Majeed M.A., Clarkson T.W., Greenwood M.R. Methylmercury poisoning in Iraqi children: clinical observations over two years. *Br Med J* 1978; 1(6113):1613-616.

21. Farnesworth D. Pink Disease Survey Results. Pink Disease Support Group Site, 1997 http://www.users.bigpond.com/difarnsworth

22. Baron-Cohen S, Ring H.A., Bullmore E.T., Wheelwright S, Ashwin C, Williams S.C. The amygdala theory of autism. *Neurosci Biobehav Rev* 2000;24:355-64.

23. Bachevalier J. Medial temporal lobe structures: a review of clinical and experimental findings. *Neuropsychologia* 1994;32:627-648.

24. Waterhouse L, Fein D, Modahl C. Neurofunctional mechanisms in autism. *Psychol Rev* 1996;103:457-89.

25. Rolls E.T. Memory systems in the brain. *Ann Rev Psychol* 2000;51:599-630.

26. Bechara A, Damasio H, Damasio A.R. Emotion, decision making and the orbitofrontal cortex. *Cereb Cortex* 2000;10:295-307.

27. Breiter H.C., Rauch S.L., Kwong et al. Functional magnetic imaging of symptom provocation in obsessive-compulsive disorder. *Arch Gen Psychiatry* 1996;53:595-606 1996.

28. Vahter M, Mottet N.K., Friberg L, Lind B, Shen D.D., Burbacher T. Speciation of mercury in the primate blood and brain following long-term exposure to methyl mercury. *Toxicol Appl Pharmacol* 1994;124:221-229.

29. Warfvinge K, Hua J, Logdberg B. Mercury distribution in cortical areas and fiber systems of the neonatal and maternal cerebrum after exposure of pregnant squirrel monkeys to mercury vapor. *Environ Res* 1994;67:196-208.

30. Bauman M., Kemper T.L. Histoanatomic observations of the brain in early infantile autism. Neurol 1985;35:866-874.

31. Courchesne E. Brainstem, cerebellar and limbic neuroanatomical abnormalities in autism. *Curr Opin Neurobiol* 1997; 7:269-78.

32. Koos B.J., Longo L.D. Mercury toxicity in the pregnant woman, fetus, and newborn infant. *Am J Obstet Gynecol* 1976;126:390-406.

33. Clarkson T.W. Mercury: major issues in environmental health. *Environ Health Perspect* 1992;100:31-8.

34. Faro L.R.F., Nascimento J.L.M., Alfonso M, Duran R. Acute administration of methylmercury changes In vivo dopamine release from rat striatum. *Bull Environ Contam Toxicol* 1998;60:632-638.

35. Singh V.K., Warren R.P., Odell J, Warren W et al. Antibodies to myelin basic protein in children with autistic behavior. *Brain Behav Immun* 1993;7:97-103.

36. El-Fawal H.A., Waterman S.J., DeFeo A., Shamy M.Y. Neuroimmunotoxicology: humoral assessment of neurotoxicity and autoimmune mechanisms. *Environ Health Perspect* 1999;107:sl5:767-775.

37. Brasic J.R. Movements in autistic disorder. *Med Hypoth* 1999;53:48-9.

38. Lewine J.D., Andrews R., Chez M., Patil A.A. et al. Magnetoencephalographic patterns of epileptiform activity in children with regressive autism spectrum disorders. *Pediatrics* 1999;104:405-18.

39. Rapin I. Autistic regression and disintegrative disorder: how important the role of epilepsy? *Semin Pediatr Neurol* 1995;2:278-85.

40. O'Carroll R.E., Masterton G., Dougnall N., Ebmeier K.P. The neuropsychiatric sequelae of mercury poisoning: The Mad Hatter's disease revisited. *Br J Psychiatry* 1995;167:95-98 1995.

41. Scheyer R.D. Involvement of Glutamate in Human Epileptic Activities. *Prog Brain Res* 1998;116:359-69.

42. Rohyans J., Walson P.D., Wood G.A., MacDonald W.A. Mercury toxicity following merthiolate ear irrigations. *J Pediatr* 1984;104:311-313.

43. Szasz A, Barna B, Szupera Z, De Visscher G et al. Chronic low-dose maternal exposure to methylmercury enhances epileptogenicity in developing rats. *Int J Dev Neurosci* 1999;17:733-742.

44. Greenspan S., Greenspan N.T. First Feelings: milestones in the emotional development of your baby and child. Penguin Books, 1985.

45. Diagnostic and Statistical Manual of Mental Disorders, Fourth Edition, Washington D.C., American Psychiatric Association, 1994.

46. Magos L., Brown A.W., Sparrow S., Bailey E., Snowden R.T., Skipp W.R. The comparative toxicology of ethyl- and methylmercury. *Arch Toxicol* 1985;57:260-267.

47. Environmental Protection Agency (EPA); Hassett-Sipple B., Swartout J., Schoeny R., et al. Health Effects of Mercury and Mercury Compounds. Mercury Study Report to Congress, v5, December 1997.

48. Santucci B, Cannistraci C, Cristaudo A, Camera E, Picardo M. Thimerosal positivities: the role of SH groups and divalent ions. *Contact Dermatitis* 1998;39:123-6.

49. Kuwabara T, Yuasa T, Hidaka K, Igarashi H, Kaneko K, Miyatake T. [The observation of blood-brain barrier of organic mercury poisoned rat: a Gd-DTPA enhanced magnetic resonance study]. [Article in Japanese] *No To Shinkei* 1989;41:681-5.

50. Pabst H.F., Boothe P.M., Carson M.M. Kinetics of immunologic responses after primary MMR vaccination. *Vaccine* 1997;15:10-4 1997.

51. Madara J.L., Stafford J. Interferon-gamma directly affects barrier function of cultured intestinal epithelial monolayers. *J Clin Inv* 1989;83:724-7 1989.

52. Huynh H.K., Dorovini-Zis K. Effects of interferon-gamma on primary cultures of human brain microvessel endothelial cells. *Am J Pathol* 1993;142:1265-78.

53. Pedersen M.B, Hansen J.C., Mulvad G, Pedersen H.S., Gregersen M, Danscher G. Mercury accumulations in brains from populations exposed to high and low dietary levels of methyl mercury. Concentration, chemical form and distribution of mercury in brain samples from autopsies. *Int J Circumpolar Health* 1999;58:96-107.

54. Hultman P, Hansson-Georgiadis H. Methyl mercury-induced autoimmunity in mice. *Toxicol Appl Pharmacol* 1999;154:203-211.

55. Dave V, Mullaney K.J., Goderie S, Kimelberg H.K., Aschner M. Astrocytes as mediators of methylmercury neurotoxicity: effects on D-aspartate and serotonin uptake. *Dev Neurosci* 1994;16:222-231.

56. Fujiyama J, Hirayama K, Yasutake A. Mechanism of methylmercury efflux from cultured astrocytes. *Biochem Pharmacol* 1994;47:1525-1530.

57. Philbert M.A., Billingsley M.L., Reuhl K.R. Mechanisms of injury in the central nervous system. *Toxicologic Pathol* 2000;28:43-53.

58. FDA Panel Report: Mercury Containing Drug Products for Topical Antimicrobial Over-the-Counter Human Use; Establishment of a Monograph. Federal Register, January 5 1982 ;47:436-442.

59. Grandjean P, Budtz-Jorgensen E, White R.F., Jorgensen P.J. et al. Methylmercury exposure biomarkers as indicators of neurotoxicity in children aged 7 years. *Am J Epidemiol* 1999;150:301-305.

60. Davis L.E., Kornfeld M, Mooney H.S., Fiedler K.J. et al. Methylmercury poisoning: long term clinical, radiological, toxicological, and pathological studies of an affected family. *Ann Neurol* 1994;35:680-688.

61. Wild G.C., Benzel E.C., Essentials of Neurochemistry, Jones and Bartlett Publishers, Inc., 1994.

62. Clarkson,T.W. Molecular and ionic mimicry of toxic metals. *Annu Rev Pharmacol Toxicol* 1993;32:545-571.

63. Bakir F, Damluji S.F., Amin-Zaki L, Murtadha M et al. Methylmercury poisoning in Iraq. *Science* 1973;181:230-241.

64. Aschner M, Aschner J.L. Mercury Neurotoxicity: mechanisms of blood-brain barrier transport. *Neurosci Behav Rev* 1990;14:169-176.

65. Charleston J.S., Body R.L., Bolender R.P., Mottet N.K., Vahter M.E., Burbacher T.M. Changes in the number of astrocytes and microglia in the thalamus of the monkey Macaca fascicularis following long-term subclinical methlymercury exposure. *Neurotoxicol* 1996;17:127-38.

66. Huszti Z, Madarasz E, Schlett K, Joo F, Szabo A, Deli M. Mercury-stimulated histamine uptake and binding in cultured astroglial and cerebral endothelial cells. *J Neurosci Res* 1997;48:71-81.

67. Kramer K.K., Zoelle J.T., Klaassen C.D. Induction of metallothionein mRNA and protein in primary murine neuron cultures. *Toxicol Appl Pharmacol* 1996;141:1-7.

68. Miura K, Koide N, Himeno S, Nakagawa I, Imura N. The involvement of microtubular disruption in methylmercury-induced apoptosis in neuronal and nonneuronal cell lines. *Toxicol Appl Pharmacol* 1999;160:279-88.

69. Trombetta L.K., Kromidas L. A scanning electron-microscopic study of the effects of methlymercury on the neuronal cytoskeleton. *Toxicol Lett* 1992;60:329-41.

70. Roos J, Kelly R.B. Preassembly and transport of nerve terminals: a new concept of axonal transport. *Nat Neurosci* 2000;3:415-417.

71. Sanchez C, Diaz-Nido J, Avila J. Phosphorylation of microtubule-associated protein 2 (MAP2) and its relevance for the regulation of the neuronal cytoskeleton function. *Prog Neurobiol* 2000;61:133-68.

72. van den Pol A.N., Spencer D.D. Differential neurite outgrowth on astrocyte substrates: interspecies facilitation in green fluourescent protein-transfected rat and human neurons. *Neurosci* 2000;95:603-16.

73. Aschner M, Mullaney KJ, Wagoner D, Lash L.H., Kimelberg H.K. Intracellular glutathione (GSH) levels modulate mercuric chloride (MC)- and methylmercuric chloride (MgHgCl)-induced amino acid release from neonatal rat primary astrocyte cultures. *Brain Res* 1994;664:133-40.

74. Sarafian T.A., Bredesen D.E., Verity M.A. Cellular resistance to methylmercury. *Neurotoxicol* 1996;17:27-36.

75. Cheek D.B. Acrodynia. In: Brennemann's Practice of Pediatrics, Chapter 17D, as reprinted on Pink Disease website, http://www.users.bigpond.com/difarnsworth/pcheek42.htm

76. Warkany J, Hubbard D.H. Acrodynia and mercury. *J Ped* 1953;42:365-386.

77. Aukrust P, Svardal A.M., Muller F, Lunden B, Berge R.K., Froland S.S. Decreased levels of total and reduced glutathione in CD4+ lymphocytes in common variable immunodeficiency are associated with activation of the tumor necrosis factor system: possible immunopathogenic role of oxidative stress. *Blood* 1995;86:1383-1391.

78. Horvath K, Papadimitriou J.C., Rabsztyn A, Drachenberg C et al. Gastrointestinal abnormalities in children with autistic disorder. *J Ped* 1999;135:559-563.

79. Klaassen C.D., editor. Casaret & Doull's Toxicology: the Basic Science of Poisons. 5th ed; McGraw-Hill, 1996.

80. Edelson S.B., Cantor D.S. Autism: xenobiotic influences. *Toxicol Ind Health* 1998;14:553-563.

81. Comi A.M., Zimmerman A.W., Frye V.H., Law P.A. et al. Familial clustering of autoimmune disorders and evaluation of medical risk factors in autism. *J Child Neurol* 1999;14:388-394.

82. Johansson U, Hansson-Georgiadis H, Hultman P. The genotype determines the B cell response in mercury-treated mice. *Int Arch Allergy Immunol* 1998;116:295-305.

83. Hultman P, Nielsen J.B. The effect of toxicokinetics on murine mercury-induced autoimmunity. *Environ Res* 1998;77:141-148.

84. Bagenstose L.M., Salgame P, Monestier M. Murine mercury-induced autoimmunity: a model of chemically related autoimmunity in humans. *Immunol Res* 1999;20:67-78.

85. Clarkson, T.W. The toxicology of mercury. *Crit Rev Clin Lab Sci* 1997;34:369-403.

86. Bailey A, Phillips W, Rutter M. Autism: Towards an integration of clinical, genetic, neuropsychological, and neurobiological perspectives. *J Child Psychol Psychiatry* 1996;37:89-126.

87. Luka R.E., Oppenheimer J.J., Miller N, Rossi J, Bielory L. Delayed hypersensitivity to thimerosal in RhO(D) immunoglobulin. *J Allergy Clin Immunol* 1997;100:138-9.

88. Halsey N.A. Limiting infant exposure to thimerosal in vaccines and other sources of mercury. *JAMA* 1999;282:1763-6.

89. Fagan D.G., Pritchard J.S., Clarkson T.W., Greenwood M.R. Organ mercury levels in infants with omphaloceles treated with organic mercurial antiseptic. *Arch Dis Child* 1977;52:962-964.

90. Matheson D.S., Clarkson T.W., Gelfand E.W. Mercury toxicity (acrodynia) induced by long-term injection of gammaglobulin. *J Ped* 980;97:153-155.
91. Gosselin R.E., Smith R.P., Hodge H.C. Clinical toxicology of commercial products, section III, Therapeutic index (ed 5). Baltimore, Williams & Wilkins, 1984: pp262-271.
92. Gilbert S.G., Grant-Webster K.S. Neurobehavioral effects of developmental methylmercury exposure. *Environ Health Perspect* 1995;103;s6:135-42.
93. Hattis D, Banati P, Goble R. Distributions of individual susceptibility among humans for toxic effects. How much protection does the traditional tenfold factor provide for what fraction of which kinds of chemicals and effects? *Ann N Y Acad Sci* 1999;895: 286-316.
94. Hattis D. The challenge of mechanism-based modeling in risk assessment for neurobehavioral end points. *Environ Health Perspect* 1996;104:s2:381-90.
95. Hattis D, Glowa J, Tilson H, Ulbrich B. Risk assessment for neurobehavioral toxicity: SGOMSEC joint report. *Environ Health Perspect* 1996;104:s2:217-26.
96. Gillberg C, Coleman M. The Biology of the Autistic Syndromes; 2nd ed, Mac Keith Press, 1992.
97. Rossi A.D., Ahlbom E, Ogren SO, Nicotera P, Ceccatelli S. Prenatal exposure to methylmercury alters locomotor activity of male but not female rats. *Exp Brain Res* 1997;117:428-436.
98. Sager P.R., Aschner M, Rodier P.M. Persistent differential alteration in developing cerebellar cortex of male and female mice after methylmercury exposure. *Brain Res Dev Brain Res* 1984;12:1-11.
99. McKeown-Eyssen G.E, Ruedy J, Neims A. Methyl mercury exposure in northern Quebec: II. Neurologic findings in children. *Am J Epidemiol* 1983;118:470-479.
100. CDC press release. Record Immunization Rate, 80% of Kids Getting Vaccinated. Associated Press, September 23, 1999.
101. Bristol M, Cohen D, Costello E, Denckla M et al. State of the science in autism: report to the National Institutes of Health. *J Aut Dev Disorders* 1996;26:121-157.
102. Florentine M.J., Sanfilippo DJ 2d. Elemental mercury poisoning. Clin Pharm 1991;10:213-21.
103. Szczech J. Phosphatase and esterase activity in the amygdaloid body of rats after ethylmercury p-toluenesulfonyl poisoning. (Polish) *Neuropathol Pol* 1980;18:71-81.
104. Kelleher K.K., McInerny T.K., Gardner W.P., Childs G.E., Wasserman R.C. Increasing identification of psychosocial problems: 1979-1996. *Pediatrics* 2000;105:1313-1321.
105. Capps L, Kehres J, Sigman M. Conversational abilities among children with autism and children with developmental delays. *Autism* 1998;2:325-44.
106. Tonge B.J., Brereton A.V., Gray K.M., Einfeld S.L. Behavioural and emotional disturbance in high-functioning autism and Asperger's syndrome. *Autism* 1999;3:117-130.
107. Klin A, Sparrow S.S., de Bildt A, Cicchetti D.V., Cohen D.J., Volkmar F.R. A normed study of face recognition in autism and related disorders. *J Aut Dev Disorders* 1999;29: 499-508.
108. Rapin I, Katzman R. Neurobiology of autism. *Ann Neurol* 1998;43:7-14 1998.
109. Fagala G.E.,Wigg C.L. Psychiatric manifestions of mercury poisoning. *J Am Acad Child Adolesc Psychiatry* 1992;31:306-311.
110. Bailey A, Luthert P, Dean A, Harding B et al. A clinicopathological study of autism. *Brain* 1998;121:889-905.

111. Dawson G. Brief report: neuropsychology of autism: a report on the state of the science. *J Aut Dev Disorders* 1996;26:179-184.
112. Adrien J.L., Martineau J, Barthelemy C, Bruneau N, Garreau B, Sauvage D. Disorders of regulation of cognitive activity in autistic children. *J Aut Dev Disord* 1995;25: 249-63.
113. Howlin P, Asgharian A. The diagnosis of autism and Asperger syndrome: findings from a survey of 770 families. *Dev Med Child Neurol* 1999;41:834-9.
114. Turner M. Annotation: repetitive behaviour in autism: a review of psychological research. *J Child Psychol Psychiatry* 1999;40:839-49.
115. Elsner J. Testing strategies in behavioral teratology. III. Microanalysis of behavior. *Neurobehav Toxicol Teratol* 1986;8:573-84.
116. Cuomo V. Evidence that exposure to methyl mercury during gestation induces behavioral and neurochemical changes in offspring of rats. *Neurotoxicol Teratol* 1990;12: 23-28.
117. White R.F., Feldman R.G., Moss M.B., Proctor S.P. Magnetic resonance imaging (MRI), neurobehavioral testing, and toxic encephalopathy: two cases. *Environ Res* 1993;61:117-23.
118. Muris P, Steerneman P, Merckelbach H, Holdrinet I, Meesters C. Comorbid anxiety symptoms in children with pervasive developmental disorders. *J Anxiety Disord*1998;12:387-393.
119. Haut M.W., Morrow L.A., Pool D, Callahan T.S., Haut J.S., Franzen MD Neurobehavioral effects of acute exposure to inorganic mercury vapor. *Appl Neuropsychol* 1999;6:193-200.
120. Uzzell B.P., Oler J. Chronic low-level mercury exposure and neuropsychological functioning. *J Clin Exp Neuropsychol* 1986;8:581-93.
121. Clarke D, Baxter M, Perry D, Prasher V. The diagnosis of affective and psychotic disorders in adults with autism: seven case reports. *Autism* 1999;3:149-164.
122. DeLong G.R. Autism: new data suggest a new hypothesis. *Neurology* 1999;52:911-916.
123. Piven J, Palmer P. Psychiatric disorder and the broad autism phenotype: evidence from a family study of multiple-incidence autism families. *Am J Psychiatry* 1999;156: 557-563.
124. Hua M.S., Huang C.C., Yang Y.J. Chronic elemental mercury intoxication: neuropsychological follow up case study. *Brain Inj* 1996;10:377-84.
125. Howlin P. Outcome in adult life for more able individuals with autism or Asperger syndrome *Autism* 2000;4:63-84.
126. Rosenhall U, Johansson E, Gillberg C. Oculomotor findings in autistic children. *J Laryngol Otol* 1988;102:435-439.
127. Vostanis P, Smith B, Corbett J, Sungum-Paliwal R et al. Parental concerns of early development in children with autism and related disorders. *Autism* 1998;2:229-242.
128. Joselow M.M., Louria D.B., Browder A.A. Mercurialism: environmental and occupational aspects. *Ann Int Med* 1972;76:119-130.
129. Williams D. Autism - An Inside-Out Approach. 1996, Jessica Kingsley Publishers Ltd, London.
130. Baranek G. Autism during infancy: a retrospective video analysis of sensory-motor and social behaviors at 9-12 months of age. *J Aut Dev Disorders* 1999;29:213-224.

131. Tokuomi H, Uchino M, Imamura S, Yamanaga H, Nakanishi R, Ideta T. Minamata disease (organic mercury poisoning): neuroradiologic and electrophysiologic studies. *Neurology* 1982;32:1369-1375.

132. Grandin T. Brief report: response to National Institutes of health report. *J Aut Dev Disord* 1996;26:185-187.

133. Ornitz E.M. Neurophysiologic studies of infantile autism. p148-65 in: Handbook of Autism and Pervasive Developmental Disorders. John Wiley & Sons, Inc., 1987.

134. Dales L.D. The neurotoxicity of alkyl mercury compounds. *Am J Med* 1972;53:219-232.

135. Anuradha B, Rajeswari M, Varalakshmi P. Degree of peroxidative status in neuronal tissues by different routes of inorganic mercury administration. *Drug Chem Toxicol* 1998;21:47-55.

136. Abell F, Krams M, Ashburner J, Passingham R et al. The neuroanatomy of autism: a voxel-based whole brain analysis of structural scans. *NeuroReport* 1999;10:1647-1651.

137. Hoon A.H., Riess A.L. The mesial-temporal lobe and autism: case report and review. *Dev Med Child Neurol* 1992;34:252-265.

138. Otsuka H, Harada M, Mori K, Hisaoka S, Nishitani H. Brain metabolites in the hippocampus-amygdala region and cerebellum in autism: an 1H-MR spectroscopy study. *Neuroradiol* 1999;41:517-9.

139. Kates W.R., Mostofsky S.H., Zimmerman A.W., Mazzocco M.M. et al. Neuroanatomical and neurocognitive differences in a pair of monozygous twins discordant for strictly defined autism. *Ann Neurol* 1998;43:782-791.

140. Larkfors L, Oskarsson A, Sundberg J, Ebendal T. Methylmercury induced alterations in the nerve growth factor level in the developing brain. *Brain Res Dev Brain Res* 1991;62:287-91.

141. Chugani D.C., Muzik O, Behen M, Rothermel R et al. Developmental changes in brain serotonin synthesis capacity in autistic and nonautistic children. *Ann Neurol* 1999;45:287-95.

142. Leboyer M, Philippe A, Bouvard M, Guilloud-Bataille M. Whole blood serotonin and plasma beta-endorphin in autistic probands and their first-degree relatives. *Biol Psychiatry* 1999;45:158-63.

143. Cook E.H. Autism: review of neurochemical investigation. *Synapse* 1990;6:292-308.

144. McDougle C.J., Holmes J.P., Bronson M.R., Anderson G.M. et al. Risperidone treatment of children and adolescents with pervasive developmental disorders: a prospective open-label study. *J Am Acad Child Adolesc Psychiatry* 1997;36:685-693.

145. Ernst M, Zametkin A.J., Matochik J.A., Pascualvaca D, Cohen R.M. Low medial prefrontal dopaminergic activity in autistic children. *Lancet* 1997;350:638.

146. Gillberg C, Svennerholm L. CSF monoamines in autistic syndromes and other pervasive develomental disorders of early childhood. *Br J Psychiatry* 1987;151:89-94.

147. Rimland B, Baker S.M. Brief report: alternative approaches to the development of effective treatments for autism. *J Aut Dev Disord* 1996;26:237-241.

148. Perry E, Lee M, Court J, Perry R. Cholinergic activities in autism: nicotinic and muscarinic receptor abnormalities in the cerebral cortex. Presentation to Cure Autism Now Foundation, 2000.

149. O'Kusky J.R., Boyes B.E., McGeer E.G. Methylmercury-induced movement and postural disorders in developing rat: regional analysis of brain catecholamines and indoleamines. *Brain Res* 1988;439:138-146.

150. Thrower E.C., Duclohier H, Lea E.J., Molle G, Dawson A.P. The inositol 1,4,5-trisphosphate-gated Ca2+ channel: effect of the protein thiol reagent thimerosal in channel activity. *Biochem J* 1996;318:61-66.

151. Sayers L.G., Brown G.R., Michell R.H., Michelangeli F. The effects of thimerosal on calcium uptake and inositol 1,4,5-triosphate-induced calcium release in cerebellar microsomes. *Biochem J* 1993;289:883-887.

152. Atchison W.D., Joshi U, Thornburg J.E. Irreversible suppression of calcium entry into nerve terminals by methylmercury. *J Pharmacol Exp Ther* 1986;238:618-624.

153. Bartolome J, Whitmore W.L., Seidler F.J., Slotkin T.A. Exposure to methylmercury in utero: effects on biochemical development of catecholamine neurotransmitter systems. *Life Sci* 1984;35:657-670.

154. McKay S.J., Reynolds J.N., Racz W.J. Effects of mercury compounds on the spontaneous and potassium-evoked release of [3H]dopamine from mouse striatal slices. *Can J Physiol Pharmacol* 1986;64:1507-1514.

155. Hrdina P.D., Peters D.A., Singhal R.L. Effects of chronic exposure to cadmium, lead and mercury of brain biogenic amines in the rat. *Res Comm Chem Pathol Pharmacol* 1976;5:483-493.

156. Kung M.P., Kostyniak P.J., Olson J.R., Sansone F.M. et al. Cell specific enzyme markers as indicators of neurotoxicity: effects of acute exposure to methylmercury. *Neurotoxicol* 1989;###:41-52

157. Carlsson M.L. Hypothesis: is infantile autism a hypoglutamatergic disorder? Relevance of glutamate-serotonin interactions for pharmacotherapy. *J Neural Trans* 1998;###:525-535.

158. Moreno-Fuenmayor H, Borjas L, Arrieta A, Valera V, Socorro-Candanoza L. Plasma excitatory amino acids in autism. (Spanish) *Invest Clin* 1996;7:113-128.

159. Volterra A, Trotti D, Cassutti P, Tromba C et al. High sensitivity of glutamate uptake to extracellular free arachidonic acid levels in rat cortical synaptosomes and astrocytes. *J Neurochem* 1992;9:600-6.

160. Aschner M, Yao C.P., Allen J.W., Tan K.H. Methylmercury alters glutamate transport in astrocytes. *Neurochem Int* 2000;37:199-206.

161. O'Reilly B.A., Waring R. Enzyme and sulfur oxidation deficiencies in autistic children with known food/chemical intolerances. *J Orthomol Med* 1993;4:198-200.

162. Alberti A, Pirrone P, Elia M, Waring RH, Romano C. Sulphation deficit in "low-functioning" autistic children: a pilot study. *Biol Psychiatry* 1999;46:420-424.

163. Markovich D, Knight D. Renal Na-Si Cotransporter NaSi-1 is inhibited by heavy metals. *Am J Renal Physiol* 1998;274:283-289.

164. Golse B, Debray-Ritzen P, Durosay P, Puget K, Michelson A.M. Alterations in two enzymes: superoxide dismutase and glutathione peroxidase in developmental infantile psychosis. *Revue Neurologic* (Paris) 1978;134:699-705.

165. Fuchs J, Packer L, Zimmer G. Lipoic Acid in Health and Disease. Marcel Dekker, Inc., 1997.

166. Page T, Coleman M. Purine metabolism abnormalities in a hyperuricosuric subclass of autism. *Biochim Biophys Acta* 2000;1500:291-296

167. Lombard J. Autism: a mitochondrial disorder? *Med Hypoth* 1998;50:497-500.

168. Atchison W.D., Hare M.F. Mechanisms of methylmercury-induced neurotoxicity. *FASEB J* 1994;8:622-629.

169. Rajanna B, Hobson M. Influence of mercury on uptake of [3H]dopamine and [3H]norepinephrine by rat brain synaptosomes. *Toxicol Let* 1985;27:7-14.

170. Whiteley P, Rogers J, Shattock P. Clinical features associated with autism: observations of symptoms outside the diagnostic boundaries of autistic spectrum disorders. *Autism* 1998;2:415-422.

171. Gupta S, Aggarwal S, Rashanravan B, Lee T. Th1- and Th2-like cytokines in CD4+ and CD8+ T cells in autism. *J Neuroimmunol* 1998;85:106-109.

172. Plioplys A.V., Greaves A., Kazemi K., Silverman E. Lymphocyte function in autism and Rett Syndrome. *Neuropsychobiol* 1994;29:12-6.

173. Warren R.P., Margaretten N.C., Foster A. Reduced natural killer cell activity in autism. *J Am Acad Child Adolesc Psychiatry* 1987;26:333-335.

174. Nielsen J.B., Hultman P. Experimental Studies on genetically determined susceptibility to mercury-induced autoimmune response. *Ren Fail* 1999;21:343-348.

175. Peterson J.D., Herzenberg L.A., Vasquez K, Waltenbaugh C. Glutathione levels in antigen-presenting cells modulate Th1 versus Th2 response patterns. *Proc Nat Acad Sci USA* 1998;95:3071-6.

176. Hu H, Moller G, Abedi-Valugerdi M. Mechanism of mercury-induced autoimmunity: both T helper 1- and T helper 2-type responses are involved. *Immunol* 1999;96: 348-357.

177. Ilback N.G. Effects of methyl mercury exposure on spleen and blood natural-killer (NK) cell-activity in the mouse. *Toxicol* 1991;67:117-124.

178. Kugler B. The differentiation between autism and Asperger syndrome. Autism 1998;2:11-32.

179. Filipek P, Accardo P, Baranek G, Cook E et al. The screening and diagnosis of autistic spectrum disorders. *J Aut Dev Disord* 1999;29:439-484.

180. Myers G.J., Davidson P.W. Prenatal methylmercury exposure and children: neurologic, developmental, and behavior research. *Environ Health Perspect* 1998;106;s3: 841-847.

181. Richdale A.L. Sleep problems in autism: prevalence, cause, and intervention. *Dev Med Child Neurol* 1999;41:60-6.

182. Gedye A. Anatomy of self-injurious, stereotypic, and aggressive movements: evidence for involuntary explanation. *J Clin Psychol* 1992;48:766-778.

183. O'Neill M, Jones R.S. Sensory-perceptual abnormalities in autism: a case for more research? *J Aut Dev Disord* 1997;27:283-293.

184. O'Neill J.L. Through the Eyes of Aliens. Jessica Kingsley Publishers Ltd., 1999.

185. Pfab R, Muckter H, Roider G, Zilker T. Clinical course of severe poisoning with thiomersal. *Clin Toxicol* 1996;34:453-460.

186. Florentine M.J., Sanfilippo II D.J. Grand Rounds: elemental mercury poisoning. *Clin Pharm* 1991;10:213-221.

187. D'Eufemia P, Celli M, Finocchiaro R, Pacifico L. Abnormal intestinal permeability in children with autism. *Acta Paediatr* 1996:85:1076-1079.

188. Shattock P, Savery D, Autism as a Metabolic Disorder, Autism Research Unit, University of Sunderland, Sunderland, UK, 1997.

189. Kugler B. The differentiation between autism and Asperger syndrome. *Autism* 1998;2:11-32

190. Teitelbaum P, Teitelbaum O, Nye J, Fryman J et al. Movement analysis in infancy may be useful for early diagnosis of autism. *Proc Nat Acad Sci USA* 1998; 95:13982-13987.

APPENDIX C

NEW DIRECTIONS IN AUTISM

A Miscellany

Teresa Binstock
Researcher in Developmental and Behavioral Neuroanatomy

Summary

Autism has long been interpreted by means of "models." For decades, many professionals accepted Bettelheim's notion of "refrigerator mothers" whose emotional withdrawals caused autism. Similarly, perhaps prompted by the identification of fragile X syndrome's primary genetic-locus,[1] autism became considered as "necessarily genetic" in origin and thus was erroneously understood as a syndrome for which little could be done.

However, in recent years an appreciation of autism's biomedical aspects and their ramifications for treatment has become widespread. Pioneers Rimland, Stubbs, Warren, Fudenberg, and others[2-5] have changed the way autism is conceived and have brought into clinical usefulness a biomedical approach to diagnostics and treatment.

As this paradigm shift continues—and as an increasing number of children outgrow their autism—parents, physicians, and researchers are developing a greater appreciation for environmental factors that appear to be etiologically significant in many and perhaps most

ASDs. Still, some environmental factors or their effects persist as underlying pathologies that are identifiable and treatable.

Susceptibility: Acquired and/or Genetic

An individual's level of *susceptibility* contributes to the likelihood of whether or not environmental factors will induce adverse effects. Increased susceptibility can be *acquired and/or genetic*, and—in a given individual—the acquired component of increased susceptibility can vary across time. In regard to environmental factors that contribute to the development of an autism-spectrum disorder, an infant, toddler, or neonate may have been more susceptible at certain times, for instance, while sick or recuperating. During such times, the course of otherwise routine infections may have been different. The effects of toxic metals—whether injected or ingested—may have been exacerbated. In various combinations, these factors may have induced a pathway towards autistic regression

Dale Hattis has written extensively about the fact that in a large population, some individuals are more susceptible to developing adverse reactions to a given environmental factor.[6] Patricia Martin and Duff Wilson have documented that hazardous waste can be relabeled as fertilizer, used on farmland, and ingested by eating food.[7] Bernard et al, Mark Blaxill, and others have established that large numbers of children are likely to have been injured by vaccinal ethylmercury.[8-9] The fact that toxic metals are pouring forth from numerous autism-spectrum children being treated with physician-supervised chelation supports this hypothesis.[10]

Various regulatory agencies have allowed low-dose exposures to be deemed "safe" and have ignored scientific literature about effects upon individuals with increased susceptibility. Yet when millions of individuals experience a cumulative series of "low dose" exposures, adverse effects are likely to develop with infants, toddlers, and the elderly being at increased risk.

Some individuals have a genetic basis for impaired immunity. Extreme cases of immune dysfunction have long been described in medical literature,[11] but polymerase chain reaction (PCR) has enabled genetic studies to reveal *subtle immune weaknesses*, which are associated with chronic low-level infections, intestinal pathologies, and excessive inflammation.

An autism example is instructive. A series of immune studies of autistic children documented associations between autism and (a) null alleles of the gene for complement protein C4b, and (b) weak alleles for immune genes whose protein product participates in recognizing pathogens.[12-13] At least one of those immune genes (DRB*0401) is associated with chronic infections from the Epstein Barr virus (EBV) and with a subgroup of persons with rheumatoid arthritis.[14] Then, in 2000, Caruso et al described a group of children with atypical EBV and autism-spectrum traits.[15] These studies are by three research groups and demonstrate that a "minor" immune-predisposition can be associated with atypical viral presence, with arthritis, and with autism-spectrum traits.

At this time (2003), the percentage of autistic spectrum children having an etiologically significant chronic-active infection is not known. However, lab-data from these children— although anecdotal—suggest the existence of subgroups wherein one or more pathogens is etiologically significant. This information justifies using immune-related lab-tests as part of the diagnostic protocol, especially since some of these children make significant improvements when an antiviral medication is prescribed.[16]

Some neonates, infants, or toddlers can acquire increased susceptibility. Medical literature documents that an infection can lead to a lowering of glutathione (GSH), which participates in detoxification, interacts with metallothioneins, and supports many crucial aspects of immunity.[17-18] A link between GSH and autistic regression may derive from the fact that transient or chronic intestinal problems can impair an infant's or toddler's nutritional status, thereby minimizing the levels of amino-acids required for the production of GSH.[19-21]

A practical ramification of increased susceptibility is that an infant or toddler who is sick should not be vaccinated. Well-baby, well-infant, and well-toddler vaccinations are far preferable. As I said in my recent letter to William Egan, M.D. (FDA; CBER), Neal Halsey, M.D. (Director, Institute for Vaccine Safety), and others.[22]

> "…the policy change [from not vaccinating sick children]
> to allowing, even encouraging the vaccinating of sick kids
> was a HUGE contributing-factor to the autism epidemic.

The act of vaccinating a sick child, tens of thousands of sick kids, would mean that some would have had increased susceptibility to adverse effects from vaccines—whether from ethylmercury or from live viruses.[9,23] Three categories of increased risk are crucial:

1. Kids with a mild genetic-susceptibility (e.g., weak GST allele; e.g., a DRB*0401 allele; a pro-inflammatory IL-1ra allele).

2. Kids with an acquired susceptibility (e.g., chronic gastro during infancy; e.g., low glutathione, low lysine).

3. Kids with both an acquired and a genetic susceptibility would be at even higher increased risk."

We should consider the possibility that the current epidemic of ASD may well derive from the facts (i) that exposure to toxins is increasing, (ii) that many items sold as "food" are non-nutritious, (iii) that factors such as these combine in ways which impair resistance to infections and inhibit detoxification of low-dose toxins, and (iv) that so-called "safe" levels are likely to adversely effect neonates, infants, and toddlers with increased susceptibility.

Autism's "genetic component:" At conferences and in the popular media, statements like "autism has a genetic component" are often repeated. What do such statements mean? For understanding autism's genetic component" two situations are important: (a) when considering large numbers of autistic children, and (b) when evaluating a specific autistic child.

For large numbers of autistic children, the statement "autism has a genetic component" is somewhat true. Researchers have found a number of soft associations between autism and various genes and chromosomal loci. Of course, none of the identified chromosomal regions is specific to autism, even though they have a degree of importance. Furthermore, many people stating that "autism has a genetic component" then mention twin-concordance studies but fail to mention placentation effects or pathologies that may have occurred in utero and affected each twin.

More accurate would be the statement: Autism is statistically associated with several genes and with several chromosome regions. Twin studies suggest some genetic loading, but factors like placentation, maternal and infant infections, and toxin exposures need to be considered. Most important, a specific child's autism-spectrum disorder need not have a "genetic component."

Acquired vulnerability during colic or chronic diarrhea of infancy: As cited elsewhere in this book, glutathione (GSH) is important in immunity and detoxification. A pathology that impairs digestion or absorption can result in low GSH.[19-20] Thus an infant or toddler with chronic colic or with prolonged diarrhea of infancy[24-26] is likely to have low GSH and so have a sustained period of increased susceptibility.

Colic has various etiologic subgroups and is often difficult to treat, but colic subgroups with food hypersensitivity are increasingly observed.[27-30] Infants with colic due to food-hypersensitivity may have impaired digestion and/or absorption and thus may have low GSH. Because these conditions are typical of many autistic children, let us consider some recent findings about colic:

- "Cow's milk allergy affects approximately 2% of infants under 2 years of age... The clinical spectrum ranges from immediate-type reactions, (indicated by urticaria and angioedema) to intermediate and late-onset reactions, (including atopic dermatitis, infantile colic, gastro-oesophageal reflux, oesophagitis, infantile proctocolitis, food-associated enterocolitis and constipation)." [31]

- "Dietary protein enterocolitis generally presents in the first year of life with diarrhea, emesis, and irritability. When there is a delay in diagnosis, persistent exposure to the offending dietary antigen leads to increasing enteric inflammation manifesting as bloody diarrhea, anemia, dehydration, and failure to sustain normal patterns of weight gain and growth... The offending antigen is usually cow's milk protein or soy protein... European studies have emphasized the alterations in enteric permeability noted in both enteropathy and enterocolitis." [32]

- "About 20 % of infants fed with breast-milk substitutes suffer from Gastro Esophageal Reflux (GER) and 1/3 of them also show Cow's Milk Allergy (CMA) symptoms." [33]

- "Development of cow's milk allergy in breast-fed infants" can occur because the mother continues to ingest milk while breast feeding[34].

- "Of the exclusively breast-fed infants, 2.1% had CMA..." [35]

- "An exclusively breast-fed-8-week-old boy presented with irritability and non-bilious projectile vomiting... A more detailed history revealed that the patient also had episodes of colicky pain and bloody stools. An infectious colitis was subsequently excluded and rectal biopsy supported the diagnosis of allergic proctocolitis... The infant responded well to the withdrawal of cow's milk and dairy products from the maternal diet..." [36]

- "Since the turn of the century, CM (cow's milk) formulas have become progressively more common as breast milk substitutes when mother's milk is unavailable, and CM allergy (CMA) has thus gradually become a more common disorder." [37]

Because suboptimal nutritional status can impair glutathione-related immunity and detoxification, the interplay of colic, chronic diarrhea, and vaccinations merits further consideration—especially for vaccines containing toxic metals or live viruses.

Concepts for Near-Future Research

A. *HSV: seizures, language, LKS.* Herpes simplex virus (HSV) is associated with language impairment and seizures.[38-39] Landau Kleffner syndrome (LKS) is defined as late-onset language-loss, often accompanied by seizures,[40] Is there an LKS subgroup in which HSV is the etiologic agent? In clinical settings, should acyclovir or Valtrex be prescribed soon after first symptoms of LKS appear in a young child?

B. *CMV: seizures, colitis, BBB-inflammation.* Cytomegalovirus (CMV) in autism has been described[41] and may be like the "tip of an iceberg" because CMV can be present in humans who have no titers against CMV.[42] The fact that CMV can dwell within intestinal tissue and is associated with colitis[43-44] suggests that a subgroup of autism-spectrum children's gastrointestinal problems may have CMV as an etiologic agent. Furthermore, CMV is associated with a subgroup of children with seizures,[45] and CMV within peripheral blood mononuclear cells can interact with the blood-brain barrier (BBB) and thereby induce inflammation and possibly trait-related hypoperfusion.[16] PCR-based lab-evaluations for viral presence and viral load in peripheral-blood mononuclear cells (42,46) seem a logical next step for identifying autism-spectrum subgroups wherein CMV is subclinical but etiologically significant.

C. *GSH: immunity, detoxification, metallothioneins.* Glutathione (GSH) illustrates how susceptibility can be increased for acquired and/or genetic reasons. Glutathione is formed from three amino-acids and enters cells via glutathione transferases[47-48] (GSTs). Allison Plant, an autism parent and medical researcher, recently summarized the many roles of glutathione:

> "Adequate levels of glutathione are needed for many aspects of immune response including: lymphocyte reactions, T-cell proliferation, T and B cell differentiation, cytotoxic T-cell activity, and natural killer cell activity (a familiar sounding list!). In the absence of adequate glutathione to offset oxidative stress, a vicious cycle is perpetuated that reduces immunity and allows opportunistic infections (like yeast and parasites) to proliferate and this in turn increases TNF alpha and other inflammatory cytokines and this increases oxidative stress which further depletes glutathione and the downward spiral follows. Low glutathione impairs

immune system function which leads to frequent infection; poor infection response leads inflammatory response and oxidative stress, which in turn lowers glutathione."[49]

Westphal and colleagues have documented that sensitivity to thimerosal (which is 49.6% ethylmercury by weight) is associated with a weak allele of a GST gene. Conversely, a subsequent study has shown that thimerosal itself impairs GST function.[9,52-53] An infant or toddler with low GSH and/or with a weak GST allele would be at increased risk for developing reactions to vaccinal ethylmercury. A child injected with thimerosal would have impaired immunity due to reduced effectiveness of processes dependent upon GSTs. Two other GSH findings appear significant to autism.

First, atypical GSH function is associated with colitis.[19-20] Thus, some children with colitis or living in a family with colitis may have impaired GSH function and thus would be at increased risk for chronic infections and would be likelier to have problems in detoxifying toxic metals.

Second, Bill Walsh has found that more than 95% of autistic children in his clinic have atypical Cu/Zn ratios.[54] In interpreting these data, Dr. Walsh speculates that these children are likely to have a genetic defect in metallothionein (MT) genes or in upstream or downstream genes that affect MT function. However, there is an interplay between GSH and MT. Thus some children's altered Cu/Zn ratios may derive from inappropriate GSH, whether acquired via intestinal pathology or via a genetic subtlety such as a weak GST allele.

D. *Better screening.* Guidelines for vaccination exemptions list categories of children for whom vaccinations might be harmful. The existence of such guidelines indicates a realization that vaccinations can have adverse effects. Some parents, researchers, and physicians are using medical records and medical literature as a basis for creating better screening of newborn and infant candidates for vaccination. Since PCR studies have become widespread and since hundreds of autism-parents have purchased in-depth lab-data for their ASD child, a data base exists whereby new categories ought be added to newborn and infant screening.

For instance, an allele for excessive inflammation (IL-1ra) might intensify post-vaccinal inflammation,[55] a weak GST allele might preclude proper detoxification of adjuvants[42]; and an infant with colic or diarrhea—or a toddler with chronic diarrhea, colitis, or constipation—would be likelier to have low GSH and thus likelier to be at risk from various environmental exposures, both infectious and toxic.

E. *Sulfation*: Rosemary Waring has documented impaired sulfation in a large subgroup of autistic children.[56] These findings have prompted ongoing research by Susan Owens, whose current projects also include analysis of amino-acid profiles.[57] A child with atypical sulfation—for whatever reasons—would be likelier to have weakened immunity and less than optimal detoxification.

F. *Subgroups & statistics*. Increasingly, autism-spectrum disorders are seen as syndromes wherein various etiologies are present. As Dr. McCandless and a growing number of physicians are appreciating, in some children, a pathology that is etiologically significant to the child's autism-spectrum traits is identifiable and treatable. In many cases, the child's traits improve. However, a pitfall awaits researchers.

The existence of subgroups has ramifications of experimental design. If only 30% of autism-spectrum children respond favorably to acyclovir, and among the 30%, there is a range of improvement, then researchers wanting to verify ayclcovir efficacy will need an appropriate experimental design. Similarly, a treatment that works in 5% of children may not be seen as "statistically significant"— unless the researchers make clear how they selected the autistic children for whom the treatment-protocol was utilized. Without digressing into the complexities of statistics, the following precaution is offered:

Subgroup and susceptibility considerations should be included when designing autism-research projects and when using statistics for interpreting findings.

Conclusion

Tragically, the United States and other nations are experiencing an epidemic of autism-spectrum disorders. In many and perhaps a majority of cases, environmental factors are implicated. Fortunately, positive developments abound. Wakefield et al's description of an autistic variant of ileal-lymphoid hyperplasia has been confirmed. Jyonouchi's cytokines-findings and related treatments are linking immune irregularities and clinical diagnostics. Clinical physicians describe subgroups responsive to antivirals. And as Dr. McCandless has so elegantly delineated, an increasing number of autism-spectrum children improve in response to gut healing, nutritional support, and chelation.

REFERENCES

1. Lubs H et al. XLMR genes: update 1998. Am J Med Genet. 1999 Apr 2;83(4):237-47.
2. Rimland B. Infantile Autism; The Syndrome and Its Implications for a Neural Theory of Behavior. Prentice Hall, 1964.
3. Stubbs EG, Crawford ML. Depressed lymphocyte responsiveness in autistic children. J Autism Child Schizophr. 1977 Mar;7(1):49-55.
4. Warren RP et al. Immune abnormalities in patients with autism. J Autism Dev Disord. 1986 Jun;16(2):189-97.
5. Fudenberg HH. Dialysable lymphocyte extract (DLyE) in infantile onset autism: a pilot study. Biotherapy. 1996;9(1-3):143-7.
6. Hattis D et al. Human interindividual variability in parameters related to health risks. Risk Anal. 1999 Aug;19(4):711-26. (see also: Ann N Y Acad Sci. 1999;895:286-316.)
7. Wilson D. Fateful Harvest: The True Story of a Small Town, a Global Industry, and a Toxic Secret. HarperCollins, 2001.
8. Blaxill MF. Rising Incidence of Autism: Association with Thimerosal. Institute of Medicine hearing: Thimerosal-Containing Vaccines and Neurodevelopmental Outcomes. Cambridge, MA; July 16, 2001. http://www.iom.edu.

9. Bernard S et al. Autism: a novel form of mercury poisoning. Med Hypotheses. 2001 Apr;56(4):462-71.

10. Holmes A, Cave S, El-Dahr JM. Open trial of chelation with meso-2-3-dimercapto succinic acid (DMSA) and lipoic acid (LA) in children with autism. IMFAR conference, San Diego, CA, USA; 2002.

11. Rosen FS. Primary immunodeficiency. Pediatr Clin North Am. 1974; 21(3):533-49.

12. Warren RP et al. Increased frequency of the null allele at the complement C4b locus in autism. Clin Exp Immunol. 1991 Mar;83(3):438-40.

13. Warren RP et al. Strong association of the third hypervariable region of HLA-DR beta 1 with autism. J Neuroimmunol. 1996 Jul;67(2):97-102.

14. Takeda T et al. Lytic Epstein-Barr virus infection in the synovial tissue of patients with rheumatoid arthritis. Arthritis Rheum. 2000 Jun;43(6):1218-25 (see also: Arthritis Rheum 2001 Sep;44(9):2038-45; Arthritis Res. 2000;2(2):154-64).

15. Caruso JM et al. Persistent preceding focal neurologic deficits in children with chronic Epstein-Barr virus encephalitis. J Child Neurol. 2000 Dec;15(12):791-6.

16. Binstock T. Intra-monocyte pathogens delineate autism subgroups. Med Hypotheses. 2001 Apr;56(4):523-31.

17. Ciriolo MR et al. Loss of GSH, oxidative stress, and decrease of intracellular pH as sequential steps in viral infection. J Biol Chem. 1997 Jan 31;272(5):2700-8.

18. Sato M et al. Induction of metallothionein synthesis by glutathione depletion after trans- and cis-stilbene oxide administration in rats. Chem Biol Interact 1995 Oct 20;98(1):15-25.

19. Koch TR et al. Induction of enlarged intestinal lymphoid aggregates during acute glutathione depletion in a murine model. Dig Dis Sci. 2000 Nov;45(11):2115-21.

20. Iantomasi T et al. Glutathione transport system in human small intestine epithelial cells. Biochim Biophys Acta. 1997 Dec 4;1330(2):274-83.

21. Wahab PJ et al. Glutathione S-transferases in small intestinal mucosa of patients with coeliac disease. Jpn J Cancer Res. 2001 Mar;92(3):279-84.

22. February 25, 2002. Full email can be retrieved from autism@maelstrom.stjohns.edu.

23. Kawashima H et al. Detection and sequencing of measles virus from peripheral mononuclear cells from patients with inflammatory bowel disease and autism. Dig Dis Sci. 2000 Apr;45(4):723-9.

24. Estep DC, Kulczycki A Jr. Colic in breast-milk-fed infants: treatment by temporary substitution of neocate infant formula. Acta Paediatr 2000 Jul;89(7):795-802.

25. Estep DC, Kulczycki A Jr. Treatment of infant colic with amino acid-based infant formula: a preliminary study. Acta Paediatr 2000 Jan;89(1):22-7. Comment in: Acta Paediatr 2000 Jan;89(1):1-2.

26. Lo CW, Walker WA. Chronic protracted diarrhea of infancy: a nutritional disease. Pediatrics 1983 Dec;72(6):786-800.

27. Garrison MM, Christakis DA. A systematic review of treatments for infant colic. Pediatrics 2000 Jul;106(1 Pt 2):184-90.

28. Hill DJ, Hosking CS. Infantile colic and food hypersensitivity. J Pediatr Gastroenterol Nutr 2000;30 Suppl:S67-76.

29. Lindberg T. Infantile colic and small intestinal function: a nutritional problem? Acta Paediatr Suppl 1999 Aug;88(430):58-60.

30. Barr RG. Colic and crying syndromes in infants. Pediatrics1998 Nov;102(5 Suppl E): 1282-6.

31. Heine RG et al. Cow's milk allergy in infancy. Curr Opin Allergy Clin Immunol 2002 Jun;2(3):217-25.

32: Lake AM. Dietary protein enterocolitis. Curr Allergy Rep 2001 Jan;1(1):76-9.

33. Garzi A et al. An extensively hydrolysed cow's milk formula improves clinical symptoms of gastroesophageal reflux and reduces the gastric emptying time in infants. Allergol Immunopathol (Madr) 2002 30(1):36-41.

34. Jarvinen KM, Suomalainen H. Development of cow's milk allergy in breast-fed infants. Clin Exp Allergy 2001 Jul;31(7):978-87.

35. Saarinen KM et al. Breast-feeding and the development of cows' milk protein allergy. Adv Exp Med Biol 2000;478:121-30.

36. Patenaude Y et al. Cow's-milk-induced allergic colitis in an exclusively breast-fed infant: diagnosed with ultrasound. Pediatr Radiol 2000 Jun;30(6):379-82.

37. Cantani A. Feeding high-risk infants with family history of allergy. Eur Rev Med Pharmacol Sci 1999 3(3):143-6.

38. Greer MK et al. A case study of the cognitive and behavioral deficits of temporal lobe damage in herpes simplex encephalitis. J Autism Dev Disord. 1989;19(2):317-26.

39. Cornford ME, McCormick GF. Adult-onset temporal lobe epilepsy associated with smoldering herpes simplex 2 infection. Neurology. 1997 Feb;48(2):425-30.

40. da Silva EA et al. Landau-Kleffner syndrome: metabolic abnormalities in temporal lobe are a common feature. J Child Neurol. 1997 Nov;12(8):489-95.

41. Stubbs EG et al. Autism and congenital cytomegalovirus. J Autism Dev Disord. 1984 Jun;14(2):183-9.

42. Larsson S et al. Cytomegalovirus DNA can be detected in peripheral blood mononuclear cells from all seropositive and most seronegative healthy blood donors over time. Transfusion. 1998 Mar;38(3):271-8.

43. Wakefield AJ et al. Detection of herpesvirus DNA in the large intestine of patients with ulcerative colitis and Crohn's disease using the nested polymerase chain reaction. J Med Virol. 1992 Nov;38(3):183-90.

44. Klauber E et al. Cytomegalovirus colitis in the immunocompetent host: an overview. Scand J Infect Dis. 1998;30(6):559-64.

45. Darin N et al. Clinical, serological and PCR evidence of cytomegalovirus infection in the central nervous system in infancy and childhood. Neuropediatrics 1994;25(6):316-22.

46. Reddehase MJ et al. The conditions of primary infection define the load of latent viral genome in organs and the risk of recurrent cytomegalovirus disease. J Exp Med. 1994 Jan 1;179(1):185-93

47. Lu SC. Regulation of hepatic glutathione synthesis. Semin Liver Dis. 1998;18(4):331-43.

48. Whalen R, Boyer TD. Human glutathione S-transferases. Semin Liver Dis. 1998;18(4):345-58.

49. Plant A. Glutathione functions. Personal communication; March, 2002.

50. Jakobsson I, Lindberg T. A prospective study of cow's milk protein intolerance in Swedish infants. Acta Paediatr Scand 1979 Nov;68(6):853-9.

51. Lindberg T. Infantile colic and small intestinal function: a nutritional problem? Acta Paediatr Suppl 1999 Aug;88(430):58-60.

52. Westphal GA et al. Homozygous gene deletions of the glutathione S-transferases M1 and T1 are associated with thimerosal sensitization. Int Arch Occup Environ Health. 2000 Aug;73(6):384-8.
53. Muller M et al. Inhibition of the human erythrocytic glutathione-S-transferase T1 (GST T1) by thimerosal. Int J Hyg Environ Health. 2001 Jul;203(5-6):479-81.
54. http://www.hriptc.org/MetalMetabolism_and_Autism.htm
55. Witkin SS et al. Influence of interleukin-1 receptor antagonist gene polymorphism on disease. Clin Infect Dis 2002 Jan 15;34(2):204-9.
56. Alberti A et al. Sulphation deficit in "low-functioning" autistic children: a pilot study. Biol Psychiatry. 1999 Aug 1;46(3):420-4.
57. Susan Owens <lwo@iadfw.net>

APPENDIX D

RECENT TREATMENT DEVELOPMENTS

1) TRANSDERMAL ALLITHIAMINE (TTFD)
2) ORAL IMMUNOGLOBULIN
3) INJECTABLE CONCENTRATED METHYL-B12
4) METHYLATION SCIENCE AND THE
   "THERAPEUTIC QUINTET"

1) TRANSDERMAL ALLITHIAMINE (TTFD)

Recent research has shown that a chemical closely related to allithiamine is useful in treating autistic children.[1-2] Garlic contains naturally occurring allithiamine, a disulfide derivative of thiamine (Vitamin B1), and thiamine tetrahydrofurfuryl disulfide (TTFD) is its "synthetic counterpart." Derrick Lonsdale, M.D. and colleagues have described beneficial effects in 8 of 10 ASD children.

Lonsdale et al suggest three possible sulfur-related mechanisms to account for TTFD's beneficial effects in autism. First, TTFD may improve energy metabolism in the CNS. Second, TTFD functions as a chelating (more properly, extracting) agent; several metals—with arsenic the most common—were documented at increased levels in urinary excretions. Third, 3 of the 10 children had indications of "intracellular thiamine deficiency," which the TTFD may have alleviated.[2]

Derrick Lonsdale's view is that it is TTFD's disulfide bond that is broken at the cell membrane. The thiamine molecule, consisting of a pyridinium ring and a thiazolium ring joined by a methylene bridge, passes through the membrane and the thiazolium ring closes. TTFD does not require the transport system needed for water-soluble thiamine that is rate limiting for the usual method of getting thiamine into the cell. Thus, a large concentration of thiamine is built up inside the cell where it is capable of stimulating thiamine-dependent activity. This includes the formation of thiamine triphosphate which is essential as a phosphate donor in synthesizing ATP and is important for mitochondrial energy synthesis. The tetrahydrofurfuryl moiety stays outside the cell and becomes a mercaptan. It is probably this that binds the SH-reactive metals and is the "business end" of the molecule. Though it is clear that TTFD is "chelating" SH-reactive metals, we still do not know about redistribution of the mercury: mercaptan complex into brain tissue with this agent any more than is the case with the other commonly used "chelators." Dr. Lonsdale hopes this essential study may be conducted by Dr. Boyd Haley at the University of Kentucky.[3]

Dr. Lonsdale's study group utilized TTFD rectal suppositories. Subsequently transdermal TTFD was conceived by Lauren Underwood, PhD, Developmental Neurobiologist, working with Tyrus Smith, Pharm D. at Coastal Compounding in GA. This transdermal form was tested and approved by Dr. Lonsdale, and has proven to be more effective than oral or rectal use per clinical benefits. Notable excretion of metals appear on urine testing, especially arsenic, cadmium, nickel, lead, and mercury. I now advise caretakers with amalgams to use rubber gloves or the back of a spoon to apply the cream to avoid the possibility of dental mercury being redistributed to other body areas.

In a short-term (12-week) informal clinical trial with transdermal TTFD as part of a treatment protocol for autistic children, I found that arsenic and cadmium tended to come out first in most urine tests[4] and after a while mercury greater than in trace amounts started being excreted by some patients, similar to the pattern described by Lonsdale et al. One child who had excreted very little mercury with a DMSA challenge test and had received no other chelating agents since the challenge, was noted to excrete mercury in the elevated range on the 1st urine test two weeks after starting the TTFD, with a noticeable beneficial clinical response. However, I found no predictable sequence to the metals excreted by any individual autistic child, which is similar to what I have noticed in my use of other chelation agents such as DMSA, DMSA with ALA, and DMPS. (Note: My personal opinion is that the oral form of TTFD will help those with thiamine deficiency but probably will not extract metals as well as the transdermal.)

In this recent 12-week use of transdermal TTFD with 12 of my ASD patients (1/2 cc was applied twice daily, or total of 100mg/day), metal-excretion levels were checked with urinary samples (taken two hours following application) after 2, 4, and 8 weeks. Samples were taken on days when no other chelating agents were being used. No side effects attributable to the TTFD were noted except a garlicky "skunky" odor and rarely a slight irritation at the site of application, which may have developed in children highly allergic to soy in the TTFD carrier. Dr. Lonsdale had noted that irritation of the rectal mucosa had been a problem with some of the children in his study using rectal suppositories, with the transdermal being rarely irritating to most of the children using it.

I did find that two of the three children using the allithiamine on the same days that they used the DMSA (3 day-week-end) seemed more hyperactive and "stimmy." I suggested to the parents that it may be better for TTFD and DMSA not be given simultaneously, and one parent then stopped the DMSA. One child on DMPS did not have any negative effect, another on MTP[5] had no negative effect, and the other six children received no other chelation agent other than TTFD. As an adjunct, I (routinely) try to elevate each child's level of reduced glutathione (GSH) and often use amino-acid precursor compounds, oral GSH, and transdermal GSH along with the transdermal TTFD. In conjunction with other therapies unique to each child, the TTFD and GSH treatments have resulted in good clinical results with most of the children I am treating with this combination[6]. One of the children was highly intolerant of GSH in any form, but still excreted respectable levels of toxic metals per urinary tests, so I cannot say adjunctive GSH is essential for chelation purposes. Nevertheless, I believe GSH is generally beneficial for all those who can tolerate it.

As the autism community has eagerly embraced this new weapon in our armamentarium to help our children, there were some recent reports of a few children having pale stools and/or constipation when starting to use TTFD. A few using the oral allithiamine also have noted this. (This actually is not an uncommon finding in ASD children aside from the use of TTFD). Dr. Lonsdale told me he had not experienced this in his studies (nor did I in my small group) and suggested I check with Dr. Jon Pangborn. Dr. Pangborn informed me that TTFD has cysteine oxidase activity, and can cause cysteine to be broken down into the sulfite rather than the taurine branch of metabolism. Since biliary function needs taurocholic acid for bile formation, he informed me that in his opinion giving taurine along with the TTFD would probably take care of this problem.[7]

Over 60% of our ASD children are found to be low in taurine on testing. If cysteine is insufficient, also often found through testing, there would be even more taurine insufficiency and adequate supplementation would be even more important. Taurine functions as a neuromodulator and is known to be a very important amino acid for thinning bile and preventing gallstones. It has also been shown to help decrease epileptic seizures in some children at doses between 400 and 1200 mg per day, and can be given up to 2000 mg or more per day (in divided doses) without toxicity, starting low and building up. Vitamin B6 along with magnesium is known to be necessary for taurine to be metabolized from methionine to cysteine to taurine.

Since all of my patients were using optimal levels of vitamins and minerals as needed per testing, this may have been why I did not see the problem of pale stools and constipation in my group. Diligent use of Vitamin C seems to help constipation, and needs to be administered preferably three or four times a day but at least twice daily, since it stays in the blood stream for a very short time after administration. (Most of our children need at least 750-1000mg a day and some of them need and benefit from much more, especially during any chelating process). I am now advising parents to make sure B6, magnesium, Vit C, and taurine are well in place before starting TTFD. As Dr. Lonsdale has said, "We have to remember that no nutrient works alone—if you push the metabolism through the use of TTFD at the mitochondrial level, you may well uncover vitamin deficiencies that have remained latent previously. In over some 30 years of almost continuous use of TTFD, I have never seen any major toxicity. It has a very powerful vector force in stimulating aerobic metabolism and these kids are notoriously bad eaters so their vitamin deficiencies can easily become overt if metabolic processes accelerate."[8] This certainly must be something to consider when our children have a strong response to any new treatment. Dr. Lonsdale emphasized that his study was a PILOT study and this all needs a lot more research in a clinical setting.

SUMMARY

The use of transdermal TTFD is new, and more controlled studies will be needed before we understand all the dynamics of this process. I believe the agent is benign and beneficial and a welcome addition to our treatment armamentarium, particularly for those children susceptible to the "gut-bug" overgrowth we struggle with so often with the use of DMSA and ALA (less so with DMPS in my experience). I do not consider any chelation process a "first-line" treatment, but believe it needs to be preceded and then accompanied by work on healing the gut and the administration of necessary nutrients based on proper testing. I advise good gut health measures such as probiotics, judicious use of enzymes, and dietary restrictions to be in place before and while doing chelation.

According to parental reports, it appears that those children who can tolerate the glutathione especially benefit from the combination of GSH with TTFD. Almost all the patients in my study group, as well as many of my other patients, show rare evidence of negative side effects so far except for the unpleasant odor of the cream and the occasional pale stools and constipation that some children experienced before we learned that co-administration of taurine along with the TTFD was important. (Note: TTFD now available as Authia from Ecological Formulas.)

REFERENCES

1. Lonsdale D. Summary of TTFD clinical results. Research Conference sponsored by Autism Research Institute, San Diego CA, October 24, 2002.
2. Lonsdale D, Shamberger RJ, Audhya T. Treatment of autism spectrum children with thiamine tetrahydrofurfuryl disulfide: A pilot study. Neuroendocrinology Lett 2002;23(4):303-8.
3. Personal correspondence, 11-16-02.
4. Urinary toxic-metals test (Doctor's Data)
5. MTP refers to a nutritional amino-acid supplement (metallothionein promoter) designed by William Walsh, Ph.D., and colleagues associated with Pfeiffer Treatment Center in Naperville, Illinois.
6. Documented weekly parental reports for 10-12 weeks
7. Personal correspondence, 1-02-03
8. Personal correspondence, 12-11-02

2) ORAL IMMUNOGLOBULIN

IVIG (Intravenous Gamma Globulin) prepared from volunteer donor plasma is an FDA approved agent for use in immunodeficient conditions. Multiple steps are employed to help assure virus elimination, including screening all donors for prior viral exposure and tests for presence of current viruses. However, as with all plasma-derived products, the potential to transmit infectious agents cannot be totally eliminated. Though it has never been reported, this agent theoretically may carry a risk of the Creutzfeldt-Jakob disease (CJD). I highly recommend that any parents desiring to have their doctor use this medicine study the literature on pooled human blood products and that the physician require signed informed consent forms from both parents prior to its use just as they are expected to do with the usual intravenous form of administration.

Investigational trials to check the effectiveness and safety of an oral form of IVIG for children with severe juvenile rheumatoid arthritis have been underway with promising early reports. I became interested in this compound when one of my young patients in a pilot study conducted in Arizona (no published results yet) showed significantly reduced gastrointestinal symptoms and autistic symptoms in general. The primary criterion of acceptance of patients into this study, besides their autistic diagnosis, was persistent diarrhea or constipation.

I asked a compounding pharmacy to make up oral immunoglobulin from IVIG in 200 mg capsules and treated a group of 12 autistic children in my private practice in an informal "intensive healing" program with 400mg nightly for a period of 6 weeks, followed by 200mg nightly for another six weeks. I stress that this was an informal "study" since the group remained on their existing protocols of targeted nutrients, including transdermal glutathione (GSH), transdermal allithiamine (TTPD), and continuation for 5 of them on their ongoing chelation programs (DMSA or DMPS) and metallothionein promotion (MTP) for 1 child. My focus for this informal program was for long-term (relatively older) patients where diarrhea had mostly been adequately treated, with my primary motivation being to see whether cognition and relatedness would be affected by this treatment. The children ranged from 5-11, with the average age between 6-1/2 and 7. One child's mother wanted to experiment with alternative and varying doses of the immunoglobulin and dropped out of the group after 4 weeks. (She reported continued benefits with her use of varying doses). Another child started an intensive anti-bacterial gut-healing program around the time the group started, and I do not include him in the results as I cannot say whether the substantial benefit shown was from the gut treatment, the oral immunoglobulin or a combination of the two.

In summary, 6 of the 10 children remaining made impressive gains in language and cognition as indicated by weekly progress reports, 2 children made impressive gains at first but then behaviorally regressed, and 2 did not seem to show any effect positive or negative. Almost all of the parents intend to continue the oral immunoglobulin treatment as long as they are seeing benefits. Clearly, much research needs to be done to elucidate issues brought up in the use of oral immunoglobulin versus the knowledge we already have from studies on the use of the intravenous form. The strong connection between the immune system and the gut and the disorders in both of these systems in most ASD children make this a very important area of investigation.

ADDITIONAL COMMENTS

Why may oral immunoglobulin help some autistic children? (speculations by Teresa Binstock based upon medical literature)

BACKGROUND

Human oral and intestinal tissues secrete immunoglobulins.[1-2] Oral immunoglobulin therapy has been described in humans.[3-5] Ellen Bolte's hypothesis[6] about Clostridium tetani in autism prompted a clinical trial of 11 autistic children, 8 of 10 of whom showed improvement in response to oral Vancomycin[7]. A subsequent study has documented unusual Clostridia colonizations in autistic children compared to controls[8]. Furthermore, numerous autistic children, with much interindividual variation, have been shown via culture and microscopy to have atypical colonizations by pathologic bacteria, fungi, and/or parasites.[9]

Finegold and colleagues have evaluated fecal flora in controls and in autistic children who had regressed.[8] The researchers' summary justifies concern for what are called "gut bugs" in autism. "*The number of clostridial species found in the stools of children with autism was greater than in the stools of control children... In gastric and duodenal specimens, the most striking finding was total absence of non-spore-forming anaerobes and microaerophilic bacteria from control children and significant numbers of such bacteria from children with autism.*"

Torrente et al view their recent findings as consistent with and as an elaboration of earlier findings by Horvath et al.[10,11] Torrente et al describe a number of findings, of which the most significant was complement protein C1q co-localizing with excessive IgG, thus writing "*...the most striking finding was the deposition of IgG on the basolateral enterocyte membrane and the subepithelial basement membrane in 23/25 of the autistic children...largely co-localised on the epithelium with complement C1q...*" The researchers concluded that the findings are "*suggestive of an autoimmune lesion.*"

The data from Sander, Feingold, Torrente, and their various colleagues[7-8,10] suggest that oral immunoglobulin (OIG) therapy might be helpful for autistic children with adverse colonizations and/or with other gastrointestinal symptoms that might reflect a chronic, intestinal autoimmune lesion. Oral immunoglobulin use in children has been reviewed.[3] For instance, increased intestinal permeability occurs in a high percentage of autistic children[12] and OIG has reduced intestinal permeability in pediatric patients with Crohn's disease.[4] Furthermore, neutralizing anti-pathogen antibodies are present in commercial immunoglobulin preparations and were apparently effective for rotavirus diarrhea, prompting the researchers to comment "*Children who received immunoglobulin had significantly faster clinical improvement of clinical condition and stool pattern than control children.*" They conclude that "*Oral administration of immunoglobulin is associated with a faster recovery from acute gastroenteritis and should be given to children hospitalized with this illness.*"[5]

POSSIBLE MECHANISMS

Now, let us return to the question of why oral immunoglobulin generated improvement in autism-related traits in 6 of 10 children in this relatively short (12 week) informal study. Described earlier, discussions in the Finegold et al and Torrente et al papers are instructive.

Finegold et al contemplate "how the bacteria in the gut effect the damage that results in... autism..." and suggests that bacterial toxins, autoantibodies that cross-react with neuronal tissue, and other toxic metabolites related to bacteria all could affect neuronal development or function.[8]

Torrente et al offer several possible interpretations of the relationship between the intestinal autoimmunity and autistic traits, including—for example—impaired detoxification of "neuroactive substances originating from the flora" as well as subtle genetic abnormalities that might affect both gut and brain.[10]

Clearly, nearly all the children treated with Vancomycin demonstrated improvement in traits related to the diagnosis of autism.[7] That Vancomycin killed Clostridia and thus reduced the level of toxins remains a major possibility. A similar action may have been part of oral immunoglobulin's effectiveness.

In addition, another mechanism may have been affecting the children's improvements.

Commercial immunoglobulin preparations are known to reduce Ig-mediated autoimmunity.[13] Torrente et al have described a number of immune pathologies in the guts of autistic children.[10] While reducing atypical Clostridia and their toxin,[7-8] the oral immunoglobulin may also have induced a diminishing of the children's Ig-related intestinal autoimmunity. If so, how did that improvement translate into cognitive and behavioral gains during treatment?

The answer may lie within anterior insular cortex (aIC), which is a primary destination area for neurons that innervate mucosal tissues and which is also crucial to language and other higher cognitive functions. Binstock has hypothesized that the cognitive improvements attendant with various gut-healing protocols in autism may derive from a reduction of pathological neuronal impulses into the aIC.[13, 14]

In the presently described group, such improved gut-related neuronal signaling might derive from a reduction in pathologic bacteria and their toxins, from a diminishing in local inflammation, and from a lessening of C1q- and Ig-related autoimmune activity within intestinal tissue. In other words, oral immunoglobulin-related improvements in these several domains may have been altering intestinal tissue in a healthful direction, thereby causing an improvement of neuronal signals to and thus within the anterior insular cortex.[14] Furthermore, the relationship between (a) intestinal-tissue changes in autistic children, and (b) atypical neuronal signals from intestinal tissue to the aIC may be a primary cause of or major contributing factor to impaired traits in many and perhaps most autistic children.

This speculation about possible reasons why oral immunoglobulin helped 6 of 10 children is tentative—yet it is rooted in medical literature linking gut innervation to various higher mental functions via the anterior insular cortex. If intestinal tissue in an autistic child is chronically sending inappropriate signals to the aIC, the autistic's brain is experiencing "static" in two most crucial nuclei. We hope that the newer imaging techniques will be able to examine the aIC in regard to its function during gut healing and traits improvements.

REFERENCES

1. Marcotte H, Lavoie MC. Oral microbial ecology and the role of salivary immunoglobulin A. Microbiol Mol Biol Rev 1998;62(1):71-109.
2. Brown WR. Relationships between immunoglobulins and the intestinal epithelium. Gastroenterology 1978;75(1):129-38.
3. Dattani SJ, Connelly JF. Oral immunoglobulins for gastroenteritis. Ann Pharmacother 1996;30(11):1323-4.
4. Tjellstrom B et al. Oral immunoglobulin treatment in Crohn's disease. Acta Paediatr 1997;86(2):221-3.
5. Guarino A et al. Oral immunoglobulins for treatment of acute rotaviral gastroenteritis. Pediatrics 1994;93(1):12-6.
6. Bolte ER. Autism and Clostridium tetani. Med Hypotheses 1998;51(2):133-44.
7. Sandler RH, Finegold SM, Bolte ER et al. Short-term benefit from oral vancomycin treatment of regressive-onset autism. J Child Neurol 2000;15(7):429-35.
8. Finegold SM, Molitoris D, Song Y, Liu C, Vaisanen ML, Bolte E et al. Gastrointestinal microflora studies in late-onset autism. Clin Infect Dis 2002;35(Suppl 1): S6-S16.
9. Binstock T. Perusal of more than 200 medical records of autism-spectrum children (Autism Research Institute Project, Spring of 2001). One fecal-culture panel is the CDSA (Comprehensive Digestive Stool Analysis) offered by the Great Smokies Diagnostic Lab. A similar panel is offered by Meta-Metrix Lab. The "comprehensive parasitology" option of the CDSA (or similar assays by other labs) is useful because a small percentage of autistic children have documented parasite colonization of the intestines. Doctor McCandless' clinical files indicate similar bacterial, fungal, and/or parasitic colonizations in many autistic children.

10. Torrente F, Ashwood P, Day R, Machado N, Furlano RI et al. Small intestinal enter-opathy with epithelial IgG and complement deposition in children with regressive autism. Mol Psychiatry 2002;7(4):375-82, 334.
11. Horvath K et al. Gastrointestinal abnormalities in children with autistic disorder. J Pediatr 1999 Nov;135(5):559-63.
12. D'Eufemia P et al. Abnormal intestinal permeability in children with autism. Acta Paediatr. 1996;85(9):1076-9.
13. Larroche C et al. Mechanisms of intravenous immunoglobulin action in the treat-ment of autoimmune disorders. BioDrugs 2002;16(1):47-55
14. Binstock T. Anterior insular cortex: linking intestinal pathology and brain function in autism-spectrum subgroups. Med Hypotheses 2001;57(6):714-7.

3) INJECTABLE CONCENTRATED METHYLCOBALAMIN (M-B12)

We have become more interested in the importance of vitamin B12 in our ASD patients as the body requires B12 in many critical and complex metabolic functions such as the folate-methionine cycle and the making of myelin sheath. This interest was heightened by the numbers of children with anemia, positive myelin basic protein (MBP) antibodies in their immune test reports, and by the often el-evated marker (methylmalonate (MMA) for functional vitamin B12 deficiency in the urinary organic acid test.

B12 is the largest vitamin known and not easily absorbed. It re-quires intrinsic factor in the stomach in order for it to be absorbed in the end of the small intestine. This very sophisticated and complex biochemical pathway requires about 30 enzyme-mediated steps for synthesis.[1] Deficiencies can be caused by low intestinal B12 intake, which has been noted in strict vegans and infants born to strict veg-an mothers, since B12 must be derived from animal sources. Those low in hydrochloric acid in the stomach are deficient in intrinsic factor, which is necessary for absorption, and the dysbiosis common in our ASD children often produces impaired absorption.[2] Many of our young patients have been shown to have difficulties in excreting heavy metals and it is probable that the transport of vitamin B12 to the brain can be especially disturbed by inorganic mercury.[3,4].

Methylcobalamin, an active coenzyme form of B12, is an im-portant cofactor in the enzyme methionine synthase, which is essential for recycling homocysteine and the formation of methyl donors involved in heart function, sleep, blood cell formation, and nerve function. I had been using oral methylcobalamin in my treatment protocol but became inspired by the reports of Dr. James Neubrander, a colleague in Edison, NJ, who started giving injections of concentrated vitamin B12 in the form of pure methylcobalamin. His clinical experience showed the methyl form of cobalamin was the most effective.[5] Vitamin B12 is only present in the brain and central nervous system as methylcobalamin, transporting vitally important methyl groups to proteins in the myelin sheath surrounding nerves.

The concentrated form (25,000 mcg/cc) of pure methylcobalamin for injection requires a very small amount: from 1000mcg (0.04cc) for very small children, up to 4000 (0.16cc) or more for larger kids. I learned from Dr. Neubrander that this can be given with ultra short needles in 30 gauge 3/10th cc ultra-fine BD-insulin syringes named "short." (Be sure not to use the–½cc "short"–the needles are much larger). Parents can easily be taught to give the injections and many small children do not even wake up when it is administered. Pre-filled syringes must be ordered by a physician from a compounding pharmacy. I stress that only pure concentrated methylobalamin (not Vitamin B12 or cyanocobalamin) should be used, as some of the other forms contain aluminum in their carrier. OTC (ELA-Max) or prescribed anesthetic cream may be used at the injection site for very sensitive children, though that is rarely needed.

Frequency of dosing varies based upon response, and doses have been assessed to be most beneficial in Dr. Neubrander's large clinical practice at 65mcg/kg every 3 days. Initially I started giving the injections once or twice weekly but some parents reported loss of gains between injections. I then started giving 1250mcg daily, which I found that some children need for sustained benefit, but saw more hyperness with daily dosing in some children. Now I usually start with 75mcg/kg twice a week; for those children who show a very positive response which fades after 1 or 2 days, I order more frequent injections for several months before again trying the twice-weekly routine to see if that maintains them between injections.

The most frequent positive response to methylcobalamin injections is in the area of cognition and language, with most DAN! clinicians seeing benefit in 75% of cases ranging from mild to dramatic. One of my patients, a child adopted from another country, has consistently shown immediate positive response but has needed daily injections for 9 months so far. (We believe he was subjected to many and excessive vaccinations before and during his adoptive process at age two.) He responds with increased and meaningful speech within hours of his injection (not unusual) and still relapses if not given daily injections. All children do not respond, and up to 15% may respond with hyperactivity and increased "stimming," sometimes accompanying much greater language increase. Parents must decide in these cases whether the gains outweigh side effects; we work to reach a happy medium.

Other clinicians may prefer different formulations and different schedules, and as we all learn more our medical community may come up with more standardized protocols. Methylcobalamin therapy needs research, as do many other areas of ASD treatment, but since B12 is non-toxic and shows benefit to most of the children, using it seems reasonable, since impaired methylcobalamin metabolism may be present in a particular child without the obvious anemia or increased MMA in urine. There is no easy way to measure a child for need of methylcobalamin in the brain other than spinal fluid tests, which none of us want to routinely do; clinical trial and observation is the most reliable and efficient way to proceed at the present time. I and many DAN! doctors are not willing to wait for definitive studies that could take years before using this very safe and exciting new treatment for our patients, and that includes our own children and grandchildren.

Adequate B1, B6 and other B vitamins and now folinic acid (preferable to folic acid) are known to be essential for proper B12 utilization as well as adequate calcium and vitamins C and E. Adequate levels of essential fatty acids, particularly the Omega-3's, are also known to be important for proper brain function including myelination. Our children should be taking these substances regularly in any event for general health and to aid detoxification, particular as most are on deficient or restricted diets. Occasionally, a particular child may have difficulty handling folates, which should be started at low doses and gradually increased as tolerated.

REFERENCES

1. Cell Mol Life Sci 2000 Dec;57(13-14):1880-1893, Biosynthesis of cobalamin (vitamin B12): a bacterial conundrum. Raux E, Schubert HL, Warren MJ. School of Biological Sciences, Queen Mary and Westfield College, London, UK

2. Ann Intern Med 1977 Nov;87(5):546-551. Production of vitamin B12 analogues in patients with small-bowel bacterial overgrowth. Brandt LJ, Bernstein LH, Wagle A

3. Arch Microbiol 1982 Mar;131(2):176-7. Involvement of mercury methylation in microbial mercury detoxication. Pan-Hou HS, Imura N.

4. Life Sci 1990;47(2):167-73. A relationship between vitamin B12, folic acid, ascorbic acid, and mercury uptake and methylation. Zorn NE, Smith JT.

5. Scientific Advanced Practitioners' Meeting, DAN! Conference, October 2002

4) METHYLATION SCIENCE AND THE "THERAPEUTIC QUINTET" IN ASD

We have known for a long time that Vitamin B12, folate, and thiamine are important players in the body's metabolic cycles. Since every cell in the body expresses the folate/methionine cycle, defects in transmethylation can affect vital biochemical reactions at many places in intermediary metabolism. Methylcobalamin is a key factor in the transference of methyl groups (transmethylation) of folate to methionine. Vitamin B12 in its coenzyme form as methylcobalamin together with folinic acid (after it's conversion to 5-methylTHF) participates in methionine synthesis and affects the metabolism of sulfur-containing substances. Recent studies are making it even more evident that sulfhydryl (SH) reactive metals such as mercury, lead, arsenic and cadmium appear to be "triggers" for multiple disease symptoms in ASD and other diseases.

Evidence of transmethylation defects in autism disorders is accruing thanks to highly qualified and devoted researchers helping us to understand the basic science supporting clinical evidence that certain treatments help our ASD children. At the 2003 Fall DAN! conference in Portland, OR, we heard Richard Deth, PhD from Northeastern University describe his and cohorts' research showing the effects of thimerosal on methionine synthase and emphasized the devastating role this neurotoxin can have in disordered methylation in our afflicted children. This invaluable research has now

(2004) been published in the Journal of Molecular Psychiatry.[1] Dr. Deth's studies show how methylation events play a critical role in the ability of growth factors to promote normal development and how neuro-developmental toxins, such as thimerosal, interrupt growth factor signaling and exert adverse effects on methylation. Dr. Deth's findings outline a novel growth factor signaling pathway that regulates methionine synthase activity and thereby modulates methylation reactions including DNA methylation, essential for normal development.

Also at the same 2003 Fall DAN! conference, S. Jill James, PhD (from Arkansas University Dept. of Pediatrics) presented research in cultured neurons and astrocytes showing that thimerosal can deplete glutathione, the major intracellular antioxidant, resulting in oxidative stress and neuronal cell death. Pretreatment of the cells with glutathione precursors protected the cells from thimerosal cytotoxicity by increasing intracellular levels of glutathione. If our children are genetically limited in their methylation and antioxidant capacity, oxidative insults such as thimerosal would be less well tolerated and may explain the unusual sensitivity in ASD.[2]

Dr. James discussed the implications for symptoms of autism with decreased glutathione antioxidant potential, demonstrating REDUCED CELLULAR METHYLATION CAPACITY in her autistic study group. Disordered methylation leads to reduced DNA methylation, and she found as Dr. Deth that methyltransferase inhibition reduces ability to detoxify heavy metals and other environmental toxicants which leads to NEUROTOXICITY. The cellular consequences of oxidative stress include:

1. Altered structure and function in proteins due to oxidation of sylfhydryl groups

2. Decreased liver glutathione synthesis, leading to reduced transport of cysteine to the brain

3. Degeneration of gut epithelium and increased permeability

4. Increased T helper-2 and altered T cell subsets that could promote AUTOIMMUNITY

5. Reduced total antioxidant capacity due to active (reduced) Vitamin C and E dependence on glutathione

6. Glutathione antioxidant potential lower in males than females, with implications for sex ratio in autism

In discussing intervention strategies for ASD children, Dr. James listed zinc, choline, Vitamin B6, selenium, creatine, N-acetyl cysteine, and antioxidants Vit E, C, and a-lipoic acid as important nutrients to support methylation and antioxidant capacity. This is further support of what many of us have discovered as helpful in our children's nutrient protocols.

Dr. James also presented for the first time the results of a small clinical trial in 20 children with autism. She found that the metabolites of the transsulfuration pathway were severely abnormal in these children and were consistent with decreased methylation capacity and decreased antioxidant capacity. A targeted nutritional intervention trial with folinic acid and TMG (trimethylglycine, or Betaine) in this group was described.

Folinic acid (5-formylTHF) enters the folate pathway in a reduced form which is more easily assimilated into folate metabolism than the synthetic folic acid. TMG provides a folate-independent pathway for methionine regeneration via the betaine-homocysteine methyltransferase that occurs primarily in the liver. Supplements of folinic acid, 800mcg and betaine 1000mg were both given twice daily for three weeks. Dr. James' tests showed a highly significant increase in plasma methionine, cysteine, and glutathione levels suggesting that these nutrients had a strong positive impact on antioxidant capacity for these autistic children. Eight of the children continued the nutrient program for 3-4 months longer, with the addition of injected methylcobalamin to the regimen. Metabolites in the transsulfation ratio pathway were no different from control children with the combined intervention.

The evidence shown by Dr. James' nutrient intervention studies of increase in methylation and glutathione antioxidant capacity has inspired the DAN! community of practitioners to start adding these nutrients to our treatment protocols if they were not already being used. What I originally called the "Therapeutic Trio" (the 1st 3) has now evolved into the "Therapeutic Quintet:"

- Transdermal Allithiamine (TTFD), 50mg twice daily
- Transdermal glutathione (GSH), 125 mg twice daily

- Concentrated injected methylcobalamin (MB-12), 75mcg 2X wk

- Folinic Acid, 800mcg twice daily

- Trimethylglycine (TMG), 500-1000mg twice daily

[Note: Dimethylglycine (DMG) provides a similar methylation enhancing function as TMG and is better tolerated by some; it has long been noted that DMG is an instigator of speech in some children. Some do better with TMG, some do better with DMG, some do well with either, or neither. (I give DMG 125mg per age year in sub-lingual tablets all at once in the morning). Clinical trial and observation tell us which treatments work best for a particular child, as there are as yet few laboratory tests that will show specific deficiencies clearly enough to guide us in this complex healing.]

As a bio-medical autism community, DAN! is blessed by the enthusiastic efforts of talented researchers like Dr. Deth and Dr. James who explore and help us explain the scientific rationale for our ever-increasing repertoire of effective treatments for ASD. May our therapeutic "orchestra" continue to improve and expand!

REFERENCES

1. Waly, M, Olteanu, H, Banerjee, R, Choi, S-W, Mason, JB, Parker, BS, Sukumar, S, Shim, S, Sharma, A, Benzecry, JM, Power-Charnitsky, V-A, and Deth, RC, *"Activation of methionine synthase by insulin-like growth factor-1 and dopamine: a target for neurodevelopmental toxins and thimerosal"*, Molecular Psychiatry (2004) 1-13.
2. James, Jill, Professor, Dept. Pediatrics, Arkansas Children's Hospital Research Institute, Presentation at 2003 DAN! Conference: *Impaired transulfuration and oxidative stress in autistic children: Improvement with targeted nutritional intervention*

A CALL TO PEDIATRICIANS AND FAMILY DOCTORS

From Jaquelyn McCandless, MD

C HILDREN with STARVING BRAINS is the book I desperately searched for and could not find in 1996 when I first learned of my grandchild's autism. The books I found consisted mainly of behavioral approaches by educators/psychologists or psychiatric texts that I knew were outdated. *Biological Treatments for Autism and PDD* by William Shaw, PhD was greatly appreciated when it was published in early 1998 and helped open me to new ideas and approaches; internet autism-lists became a goldmine of useful information and directions to explore. As time went on my appetite was enormously whetted by responses I began seeing to dietary and nutrient treatments and to improvement in subsets of autistic/ASD children to secretin, anti-fungal and anti-viral treatments, immune enhancing agents, and most recently to oral chelation protocols that reduce the accumulated loads of heavy metals in these children. I attribute the discovery and success of many of these helpful approaches to dedicated and persevering parents and to a few doctors and researchers (mostly parents of autistic children themselves) who refused to accept that they could do nothing to help these children recover. I have been repeatedly humbled by what I have learned from the knowledgeable parents of these children. I urge all of you as physicians to let them be our partners in this endeavor. They have the intense motivation and willingness to learn about new therapies that may help their beloved children. Should we do less?

There are organizations to help. For example, the DAN! (Defeat Autism Now!) group co-founded by Bernard Rimland, PhD, Sidney M. Baker, MD, and Jon B. Pangborn, PhD offers a useful compendium of tests and procedures that is the result of a consensus of DAN! doctors. However, I must admit I knew so little when I first started my search that this list was daunting. My questions were basic: How and where to start? Which child needed what tests, and how could those tests be interpreted? I yearned for a clinician's logical explanation and guide through the maze of possible evaluative procedures and treatments for this complex disorder.

As a grandmother and psychiatrist, my passion to find answers made me impatient with psychiatry and behavioral medicine's head-in-the-sand attitude that autism is definitely genetic and thus incurable and untreatable except for early educational intervention and the use of behavior controlling drugs. In the early days of my autism practice I had painful experiences with physicians who refused to collaborate when parents who were their patients consulted me to explore medical reasons for their child's problems. Not only did my colleagues refuse to consider ordering tests for immune function, viral, heavy metal or metabolic studies but several even implied or outspokenly told the parents that my pursuit of these treatments was "alternative," "unsubstantiated," "non-scientific," or worse. Many medical doctors still advise parents not to bother with special diets or vitamins and minerals, even with a child whose diet is self-restricted to a very few non-nutritious foods. One doctor insisted that if there was no evidence of mercury in the blood test then there was no point in pursuing the heavy metal issue further, not aware or interested in the fact that the presence of mercury, except for a very recent heavy exposure, will not show up on regular blood tests.

To no avail I pointed out in those early days that many of the doctors and researchers who pursue these "new" approaches are parents or grandparents of children with autism and would not be trying these methods on their own kin if they thought they weren't safe and effective. Indeed, many of us have changed our specialties and our lives to concentrate on treating these incredibly complex and interesting children. Deeply entrenched paradigms do not change easily, but in the last few years it has become painfully evident that we are facing a full-fledged epidemic of autism. This fact has dimmed all but the most die-hard proponents of the genetics-only theory. Few authorities deny there is a genetic predisposition in play, but something has to be triggering this genetic element to manifest such large numbers of affected children now. In any event they should be offered whatever treatments can be helpful regardless of the etiology.

I have asked parents who seek my assistance to get my book to you, and their primary doctor, if they find it helpful. I know you want to help them, but you may not be aware of the many new tools that are being added to our armamentarium of tests and treatments. Laboratories rising to the challenge of this epidemic are devising new and better tests to help us target the best treatments. We can identify food sensitivities (not allergies) to help remove offending gut-inflammation-producing foods and begin healing the ubiquitous intestinal problems our patients endure. Better immune-function tests help us identify offending viruses and immune deficiencies that many of our children have so we can develop better ways to help them. We have learned ways to discover the effects of mercury poisoning by what it does to the mineral balances even though no test will directly show diagnostic mercury levels in blood, urine, hair or feces without the administration of a chelating agent to bind it and remove it. Prescription medications such as anti-fungals, anti-bacterials, anti-virals, SSRI's and other drugs are often necessary, and progress must be monitored with tests that show us the body is maintaining balance throughout treatment.

We have a long way to go and it is our obligation to listen, learn and help parents make the best treatment choices for their child. Those of us who have been at this for some time now have learned the hard way which tests and treatment sequences are ineffective and which beneficial; certainly none of us can know them all. Sharing information can help those just starting to explore this area to avoid making the same mistakes we did. I have tried to share what I have learned in my own practice and from other generous clinicians in my book, *"Children with Starving Brains: A Medical Treatment Guide for Autism Spectrum Disorder,"* published by Bramble Books, Spring

2002, 2nd Edition, January 2003. I also urge you to obtain the new DAN! consensus report, *Biomedical Assessment Options for Children with Autism and Related Problems* published by the Autism Research Institute, 4882 Adams Avenue, San Diego CA 92116. Their DAN! Protocol on Mercury Detoxification describes how to oversee the extremely safe and effective process of oral chelation to remove heavy metals from the bodies of these children, which I detail in my book. Chapters Three and Seven in my book go into detail about the mercury and heavy metal problem and describe how I and other clinicians diagnose and treat this condition.

We must forge a new medical paradigm for autism out of ne-cessity. Our currently afflicted children cannot wait for the inter-minable process required for peer-reviewed studies before getting treatment, as long as it is safe. All the evidence points to better outcomes the sooner we get started. As clinicians on the firing line we all need to contribute and share our special experiences so as to add to the enlarging pool of information that will benefit everyone in this important healing endeavor. There is a dire shortage of doc-tors available for the myriads of children needing this help now. I urge you to do everything you can possibly do to add the new bio-medicine of autism to your healing armamentarium. I also encour-age you to attend DAN! conferences which are now being held each spring in the eastern part of the country and in San Diego or other west coast locations each fall; these meetings include both beginning and advanced special seminars for practitioners. Please be willing to add your name to the list of DAN! doctors. If you do, you will have ample opportunity to help as many of these children as you can pos-sibly fit into your practice.

INVITATION

Come, take my hand
So I can find you in the eye of the whirlwind
Calling medicine back to its spirit home
And welcoming the lost tribe of children
Our little adept among them
As you keep reminding me, we need to work from
    another level
Which means creating an entire heartscape, nothing less
Chelsey is waiting—I see the message in her big browns
"Only full surrender satisfies my mission."

Take my hand—again
As at our birth when you led me out
Of a flat world into the delights and shadows of Eros
Now, our toes curled around the edges of the past
We hesitate, seeking a still greater revelation of Love
Are we too heavy with treasured wounds and attachments
    to fly
Or is it fear of the demons at the doorway to ecstasy?
No matter, our courage will soon rise to the new occasion
Since it always starts with, "Gramma—Grampa will you
    dance with me?"

And so leaps of faith and healing are merging movements
Connecting you and Chelsey inside the Mystery
That we touch as well when our trust is great enough
To fall more wildly into Love's uncharted forests
And then to guide us into the clearing of our hearts
We can create similar shamanic celebrations
To re-awaken our unrelenting messenger
And so embrace her healing with enough persistent passion
To wholly feed that starving brain

This enlightening of our aim to cure
Will see through the harvest of impaired immunities
Into the innate wholeness of each ancient soul
So too our little Buddha, our Christ Child, asks for recog-
     nition
I heard the call again the night I phoned to celebrate her
     tenth
She said, "Hi, Grampa" in that soft and rounded voice
That opens my heart and wild eyes to smiling
She waits for us to leap and doesn't need fixing
As much as being met half way with laughter

"Here, take my hand"
Excites the biggest grin of all
Since she's been longing for our commitment
To meet in Rumi's field together
That consummation meets her challenge
To claim our fullest lives while still embodied
"But words don't matter," she says, "The joke's on you
"You jumped a long time ago and have been falling forever
"There's nothing else to do."

Jack Zimmerman
February, 2004

INDEX

EPILOGUE

From Jack and Jaquelyn: We leave you with a few personal reflections and an invitation to a vision of healing.

Before life catapulted us into autism, we regularly practiced meditation, visualization and energetic approaches to healing in council circles. In the early days of our ASD journey Jaquelyn felt that the children were so ill that they needed biomedical treatment first in order to be receptive to the effects of these more subtle healing techniques. Jack felt that all treatments offered a chance for parents, siblings, grandparents and even healthcare providers to relate more consciously and creatively to these children. Before long our teacher Chelsey made it clear in her inimitable way that such debates over emphasis were swamps on the journey to the promised land of her emergence. Finally, we surrendered to the obvious reality that biomedical and relational healing approaches were equally essential and inseparable. It was no surprise to hear that recent research has suggested that intensive, consciously structured interaction with ASD children affects their brain chemistry and, in particular, stimulates dendritic growth.

We have come to see that biomedicine does not stop at the boundaries of emotion, thought or the mysteries of the human spirit. Studies of the efficacy of different approaches to healing are confirming the traditional wisdom that "love heals"—that it matters, for example, not only what we do with an ASD child but also what happens to us as we do it. What are we learning about ourselves and relationship as we try to get the supplements down? What uncharted qualities of Spirit do we touch trying to maintain our energy one more hour, one more day, one more lifetime as healers and guardians of our young teachers? Many of us have come to see that becoming more conscious and creative in the ways we relate to our special children makes a difference in their healing. The ripple effect from this expanding awareness into all of our relationships can be significant. Chelsey has helped us to see that her healing is a seamless process of medically informed, courageous relating that affects every part of her life as well as ours.

The complexity of healing just one autistic child is as mysterious as the entire Universe, while the onslaught of the worldwide ASD epidemic is overwhelming to anyone who takes a deep look. Despite the progress made in current biomedical and educational/relational treatment programs, the harsh realities suggest that we need to find a differently empowered level of healing if we are to overcome the astounding inertia in our present political/medical/pharmaceutical complex. We need to expand our capability to utilize the power of loving relationship in more conscious and creative ways. From what we have learned from Chelsey and many other children, we believe an expanded level of healing can be created by concentrated imaging of a future in which all ASD children live a fulfilling relational life. Our unifying statement is: "We want all our children to be able to taste the full spectrum of relationship—intimacy, friendship, loyalty, devotion and eroticism, as well as disappointment, confusion, loss and grief." The visualization of such relationships has to be done uniquely and co-creatively for each child at a level so magnetic that the future story is literally drawn into manifestation—and we have to "know" the child so well that a narrative unfolds authentically as if they were full participants.

Relieving Chelsey of her dysfunctional gut, confused immune system and distraught neurological environment while educationally mainstreaming her and helping her to communicate affectively has for us now come under the over-arching, powerful image of her ability to relate to at least one contemporary outside of her family in profoundly loving, unbounded ways. We have become fully engaged in an exploration of how a truly conscious loving relationship can create an energetic "field" in which both participants experience greater wholeness throughout their mind/body continuum.

We invite you to join in this experiment to consciously create a relationally healing future for your child. The love which parents and others in this growing community of healers brings into our children's lives is what makes such a real "future healing story" possible. We need to support each other in carrying out an expanded visionary experiment. We need to deepen our understanding of how to work together—possibly using various forms of visualization, meditation and council—to use the enormous power of shared intention to create a unified healing field for all of us. We need the synergy of the clan and a variety of healing practices to help each family reach the inspired level of intentional imagination required.

We invite you to envision a community of your own design that is safe enough for your child to risk the delights and dangers of loving deeply. Families may want to create ways to come together periodically to share their visions and empower them collectively. Hopefully these gatherings and practices will become a coherent force that will heal our children and create the cultural revolution their growing presence demands.

March 2004